IMAGES
of America

THE HASH KNIFE AROUND HOLBROOK

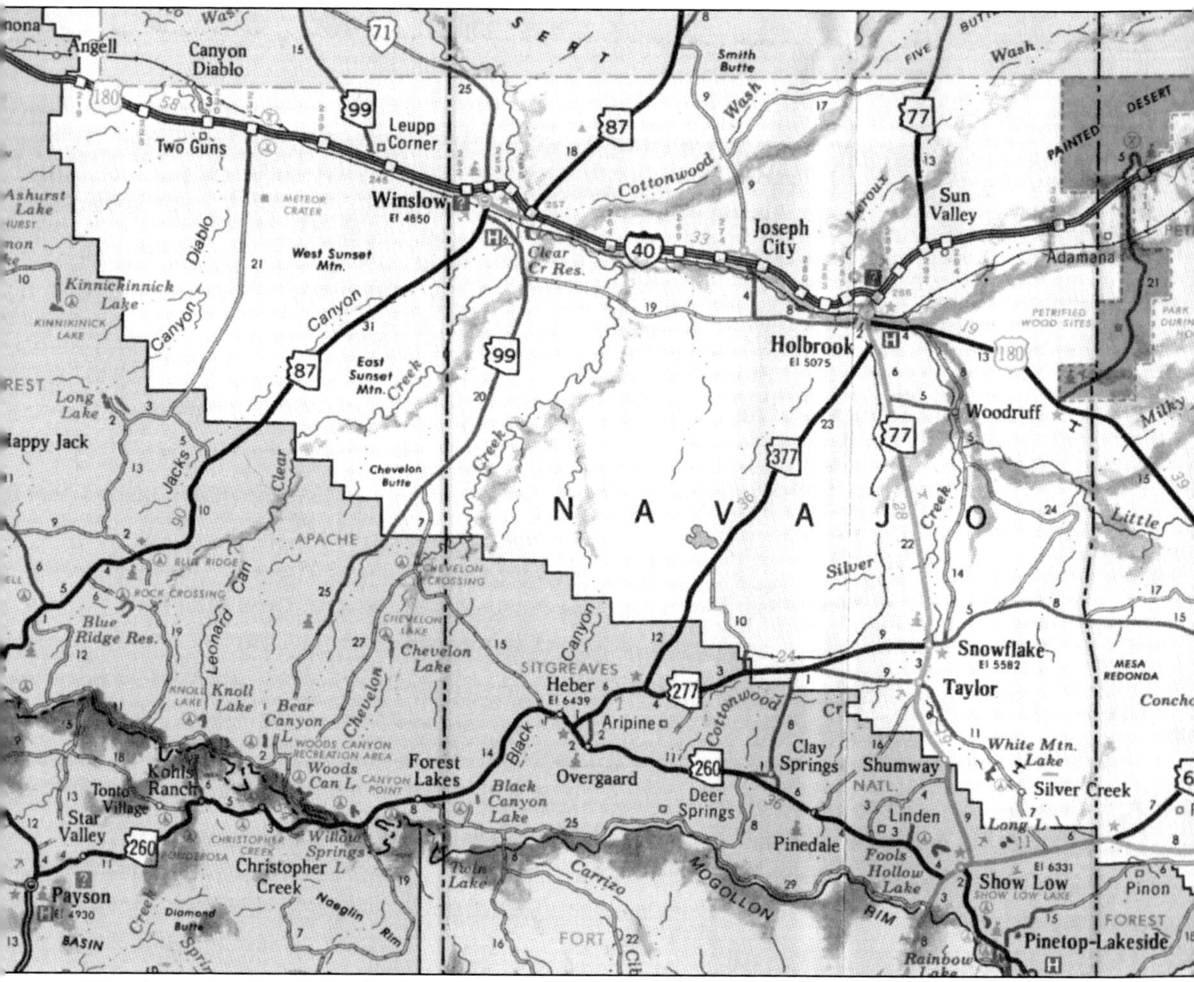

The Aztec Land and Cattle Company was comprised of some 2 million acres at its peak. The range included headquarters in and near Holbrook and Joseph City, and spanned as far south as Payson. Hash Knife cowboys traveled by horseback between the four headquarters, eight official line camps, and a number of other more primitive camps as part of their daily duties. (Jan MacKell Collins.)

On the Cover: Although the Hash Knife is best known in Arizona, the brand had its beginnings in Texas. John Nicholas Simpson moved to Weatherford, Texas, from Tennessee in 1866, operating a dry goods store before turning to ranching. He relocated to Taylor County in 1872. His first brand, the "Long S," was soon replaced by that of a hash knife: a common cooking tool whose brand was difficult to alter. At least a few Hash Knife cowboys, such as these men pictured in Taylor County in 1880, later moved with the brand as operations expanded to Montana and finally Arizona. (Abilene Photograph Collection, Hardin-Simmons University, Abilene Texas.)

IMAGES
of America

The Hash Knife Around Holbrook

Jan MacKell Collins

ARCADIA
PUBLISHING

ISBN 978-1-4671-3093-6

Published by Arcadia Publishing
Charleston, South Carolina

Printed in the United States of America

Library of Congress Control Number: 2013940974

For all general information, please contact Arcadia Publishing:
Telephone 843-853-2070
Fax 843-853-0044
E-mail sales@arcadiapublishing.com
For customer service and orders:
Toll-Free 1-888-313-2665

Visit us on the Internet at www.arcadiapublishing.com

For Papa, DeDaddy, and Dad

Contents

ACKNOWLEDGMENTS

Writing about your own family can be a little scary. It is one thing to write history and hope you have your facts straight. It is quite another to write history about your relatives and hope you are not banned from all future family functions.

That being said, I am extremely grateful to my relatives who contributed their advice, criticism, knowledge, and photographs to the writing of this book. They include my dad; my cousins Suzanne Peterson, David Moritz, Kris and Graham Wontney, and Joe Ramos; my other mom, Barbara Espino; and my amazingly patient husband, Corey.

None of us would have such a good grasp of our family history without the diligent recording of it by our ancestors. I am particularly grateful to Cora Taylor Forbes Wallace, Frances Wallace Hennessey, and Evelyn Mae Hennessey Smith for carefully saving everything for my family to enjoy. Aunt Betty, Uncle Charlie and Aunt Marian, Aunt Berba, Aunt Dude, Amy Wallace, and many others also played an integral part in preserving our family history. I also thank my mother, Eleanor, for making sure I listened to all the stories. Thanks to them, most of the images in this book are being provided by myself and my family unless otherwise noted.

I also wish to thank Jolynn Fox at the Navajo County Historical Society in Holbrook; Lita Slaggle at the Baylor County Free Library in Seymour, Texas; Grace McNellis of the Vandervert Ranch in Oregon; and Chioko Hammel of the Carter County Museum in Ekalaka, Montana, for their help and for sharing their materials for this project. My dad and I are also indebted to Ed Delph and Larry Boeschling for allowing us a tour of the beautiful OW Ranch as it stands today.

Dozens of books and articles out there give the writer's best perspective on the history of the Hash Knife. Without these histories, the truth and legend behind the brand might have been forgotten. I am very appreciative of those authors who have set a precedent and offered their own interpretations of the outfit's history.

Introduction

The Hash Knife brand—fashioned after a common cooking tool popular among camp cooks and ranch wives—has been a staple of cattle history for roughly 140 years. Established by John Nicholas Simpson in Texas, the brand has served ranches in Montana, Arizona, and beyond. Companies who owned the brand—namely the Continental Land and Cattle Company, the Aztec Land and Cattle Company, and Babbitt Brothers—functioned as some of the largest and most profitable organizations of their time. Between 1878 and 1901, five large-range ranches were established using the Hash Knife brand.

Through the years, the brand has taken on a romance of its own. The admiration seems equally shared by those who worked for the Hash Knife, those who know of someone who did, or those who wish they had done so themselves. The picture or even a memory of cowboys roping cattle on the dusty prairies or gathering around the chuck wagon evokes a sentimental love for the cowboy way of life. Forget that working on the range was hard and often dangerous. To those men who did it, working cattle was worth the risk and gave them some of the best memories of their lives.

In fact, the Hash Knife seems to have grown into its own symbol of cowboy life. During the last century, the name has come to identify any cowboy, ranch, or company associated with the brand, and there were plenty of them. The men of the Hash Knife ranged from studious businessmen from New York, to hard-working cow punchers, to rustlers and outlaws. The rustlers and outlaws are of particular interest to history buffs, since they add a bit of color to the story.

It is true that by the 1880s, the Hash Knife's association with the notorious Millett brothers in Texas, plus a shootout in Montana, had somewhat tainted the brand's good name. When the Aztec Land and Cattle Company was formed to bring the Hash Knife to Arizona in 1884, the owners likely hoped the outfit would shed itself of its unsavory reputation. Some of the hands had been with the brand since the beginning. Many of them were good, hardworking men. A few others were not.

The Aztec, as it was often referred to, acquired 2 million acres between Holbrook and Flagstaff. The cattle had hardly settled in before stories began circulating about rowdy cattle thieves, drunks, and robbers terrorizing Holbrook. Their well-publicized exploits eventually inspired authors Zane Grey, W.C. Tuttle, Clarence W. Durham, and others to expand on the boys' daring adventures and write fictional novels about them. The Hash Knife soon became, and remained, a fascinating entanglement of fact, fiction, and folklore.

By the time Burton C. "Cap" Mossman was hired as superintendent in 1898, rustlers and outlaws did seem to be rampant around the Hash Knife. Mossman set to work cleaning house, firing half the crew within a month. He was assisted by foreman Benjamin Franklin "Frank" Wallace, with whom he had worked in Texas and hired soon after joining the Hash Knife. Wallace in turn hired cowboy George W. Hennessey, and the three men became lifelong friends.

By 1899, there were some 30 hands working for the brand. There is no denying that a few questionable characters may have still been in the group, but by then the good guys far outweighed the bad guys. "The Hash Knife had the name of being a hard drinking, hard fighting outfit," Hennessey later remembered, "but I never worked with a better bunch of men."

Good or bad, the cowboys of the Hash Knife worked hard. The Aztec had suffered through a particularly hard winter in 1898 and was now combating feed shortages and a four-year drought. After 17 years of owning the Hash Knife brand, the Aztec sold out to Babbitt Brothers of Flagstaff. It took about a year to settle matters and ship out the cattle, after which Cap Mossman resigned. Wallace and Hennessey followed suit within a few years.

Babbitt Brothers carried on the brand, but many considered the sale the end of an era. Improved railroads, automobiles, telephones, and other newfangled inventions were slowly changing the way of life across the West. The four Aztec headquarters between Holbrook and Joseph City, as well as eight line camps out on the range, slowly fell into disuse and all but disappeared. Some of the cowboys stuck around and worked for other outfits while others rode off into the sunset, never to be heard from again. But none of them forgot about the Hash Knife brand.

For Wallace and Hennessey, working for the Hash Knife evolved into quite the family affair both during their time with the Aztec and after. Upon leaving the company, Hennessey, Wallace, Wallace's son Emmet, and fellow cowboy James Donohoe began establishing their own cattle companies, forming partnerships, and registering their own brands. Later, Hennessey and Donohoe each married one of Frank Wallace's six daughters.

Even as Hennessey and Wallace became noted cattlemen in their own rights, the Hash Knife somehow remained an integral part of their lives. Long before Hennessey was elected mayor of Holbrook, newspapers continually recalled his days with the outfit. Wallace later purchased the OW Ranch west of Payson. The ranch was formerly owned by the Blevins family during the 1887 Pleasant Valley War, a notable skirmish involving both the Blevins and some Hash Knife men. When Hennessey died in 1973, he was revered as being the last surviving Hash Knife cowboy.

The descendants of the Hash Knife's many cowboys, as well as a good number of admirers, continue to keep the brand's history alive. A handful of ranches, bed and breakfasts, monuments, clubs, and even a musical group lay claim to the Hash Knife name. Perhaps the best known of these is the annual Hashknife Pony Express Ride, which takes place between Holbrook and Scottsdale each year.

Details on the history of the brand have also been lovingly documented in fine works by Jim Bob Tinsley, Robert Carlock, and Stella Hughes. Tinsley's work, *The Hash Knife Brand*, gives a good overview of the Hash Knife's evolution from a Texas cattle camp to a reigning ranch of Arizona. Carlock, who worked for the Aztec Land and Cattle Company, was able to provide more intimate details in his book, *The Hashknife*. Hughes's husband Mack worked for the Hash Knife during the 1920s. Her book, *Hashknife Cowboy*, provides insight into the brand's later years through Mack's eyes.

In this newest rendition of Hash Knife history, George Hennessey and Frank Wallace also get to tell their stories for the first time. Their history, and that of the Hash Knife, is gathered from a number of books and articles, but also from firsthand accounts written by themselves, their wives, their children, and their grandchildren. Family stories have been passed down. Scrapbooks, photographs, letters, and other memorabilia have been carefully saved. The end result is another facet of history that should be told while there are some who still remember it, and also so that it will not be forgotten.

One

Beginnings of the Brand

Most historians agree that Hash Knife history began in 1874 when John Nicholas Simpson registered his first brand, the "Long S." The Hash Knife brand was certainly in place by 1877 when Simpson and his partner, James Couts, were using it. It was not until 1878, however, that Simpson and Couts first registered the brand in Taylor County, Texas.

Thus began a long and illustrious life for the legendary Hash Knife brand. The first ranch headquarters was a dugout above Cedar Creek that would later become Abilene. Simpson made sure Abilene's first railroad, the Texas & Pacific Railway, would run right by his ranch. He furthermore made sure the town was built directly along the tracks to assure its success. Shortly afterward, Simpson expanded the brand west to Pecos and Baylor County, and formed the Continental Cattle Company.

In Baylor County, Simpson did business with the infamous Millett brothers, the area's own bad boys. Even as he witnessed a bloody shootout at the Millett Ranch while signing the papers, Simpson purchased some land and cattle. He also continued buying smaller outfits around Texas while making even grander plans for a range in Montana.

The Montana holdings, built along the Little Missouri River, were located roughly 20 miles from the tiny community of Stoneville. Puzzling over whether lanky Texas cattle and cowboys could survive Montana's cooler altitudes was soon overshadowed by George Axelby. The Hash Knife cowboy from Texas quit the outfit to form his own gang of outlaws in Montana and sparked a shootout at Stoneville.

Undaunted, the Continental Cattle Company changed its name to the Continental Land and Cattle Company, partnered with the Mill Iron Cattle Company, and expressed a desire to buy ranges in other states. That opportunity came when surveyor Edward Kinsley of the Atlanta & Pacific Railroad spied Arizona's vast lands. The Aztec Land and Cattle Company formed, and the Hash Knife brand moved there with its reputation still under fire. But Arizona had a lot to offer: lots of land at a good price, ample water, a workable climate, and the chance to start over.

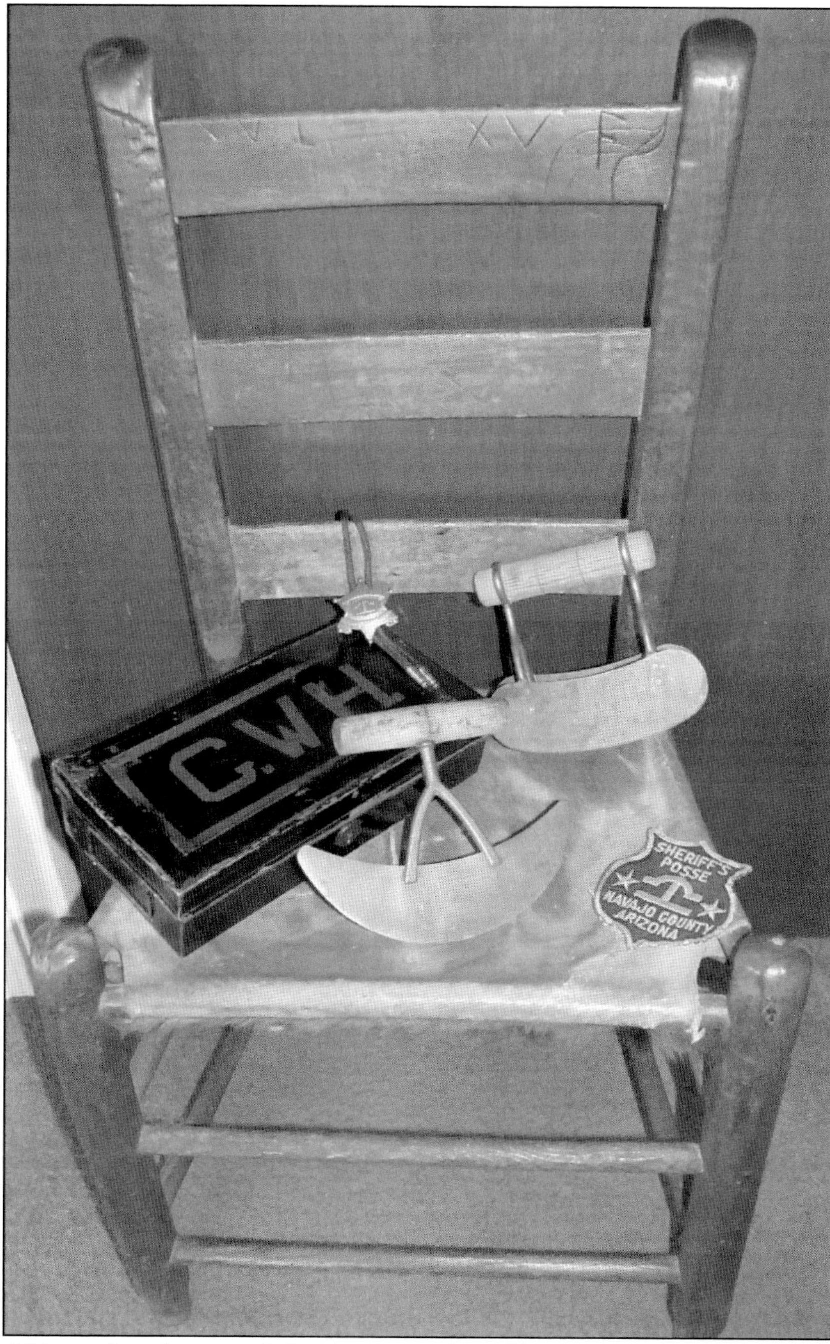

Who would have thought a simple kitchen utensil would spawn one of the best-known cattle brands in the West? The Hash Knife was so named for a handheld tool used to quickly chop or dice large quantities of vegetables or meat, and was a staple on any chuck wagon. Hash knives came in a variety of designs, including the two shown in this image of Hash Knife memorabilia. Other items here include a strongbox belonging to Hash Knife cowboy George W. Hennessey and a patch and badge from the Navajo County Sheriff's Posse bearing the brand. The chair was made by Hennessey and includes carvings of some of the other brands he used.

Tennessee native James Robertson Couts was a farmer when he moved to Weatherford, Texas, in 1865. A year later, Couts used money earned from a cattle drive to California to establish the first bank at Weatherford. By 1872, he was one of the wealthiest men in the region. Couts purchased a half interest in John Nicholas Simpson's cattle outfit in 1877. (First Financial Bank, Weatherford, Texas.)

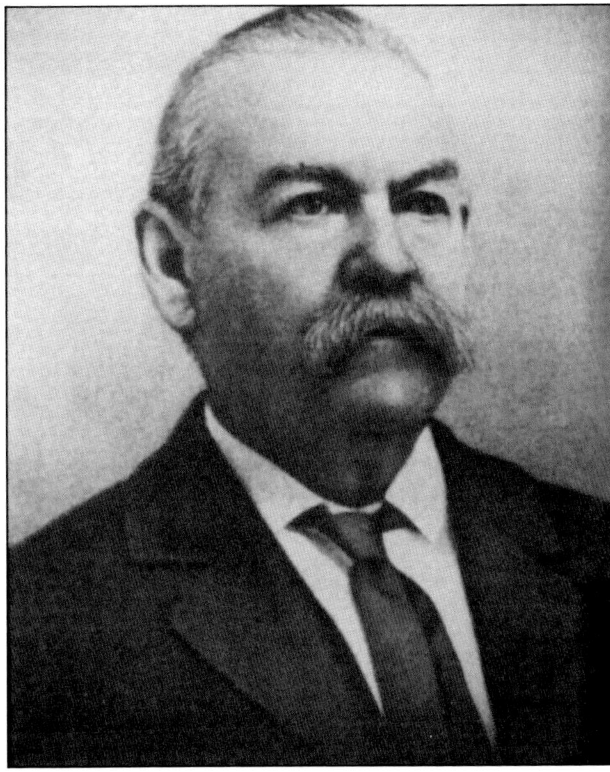

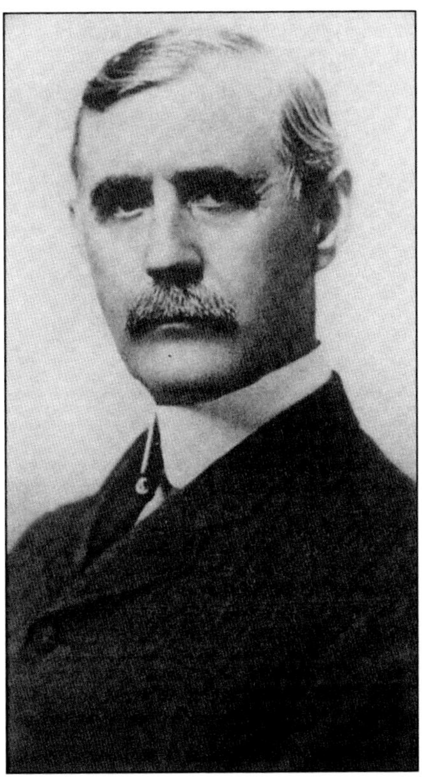

Simpson, also a native of Tennessee, migrated to Weatherford in 1866. Between 1867 and 1872, he operated a dry goods store before turning to cattle. Simpson established the Hash Knife brand in about 1874. Simpson's brother Ed was later a manager of the Aztec Land and Cattle Company before resigning in 1890. (Publicity Department, State Fair of Texas.)

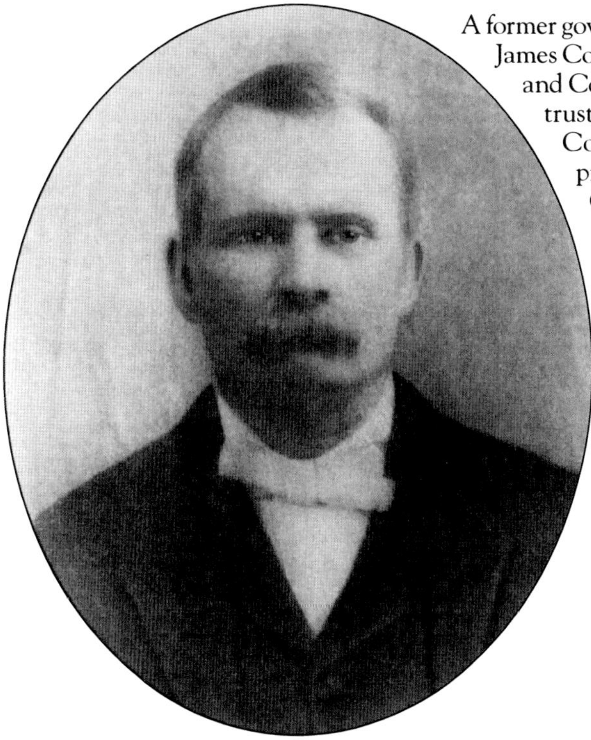

A former government freighter and sometime client of James Couts, Henry Warren was hired by Simpson and Couts around 1877. Over time he became a trustee for the Continental Land and Cattle Company, serving as both manager and president of the Aztec Land and Cattle Company in Arizona. Warren stayed with the Aztec until his death in 1917. (First Financial Bank, Weatherford, Texas.)

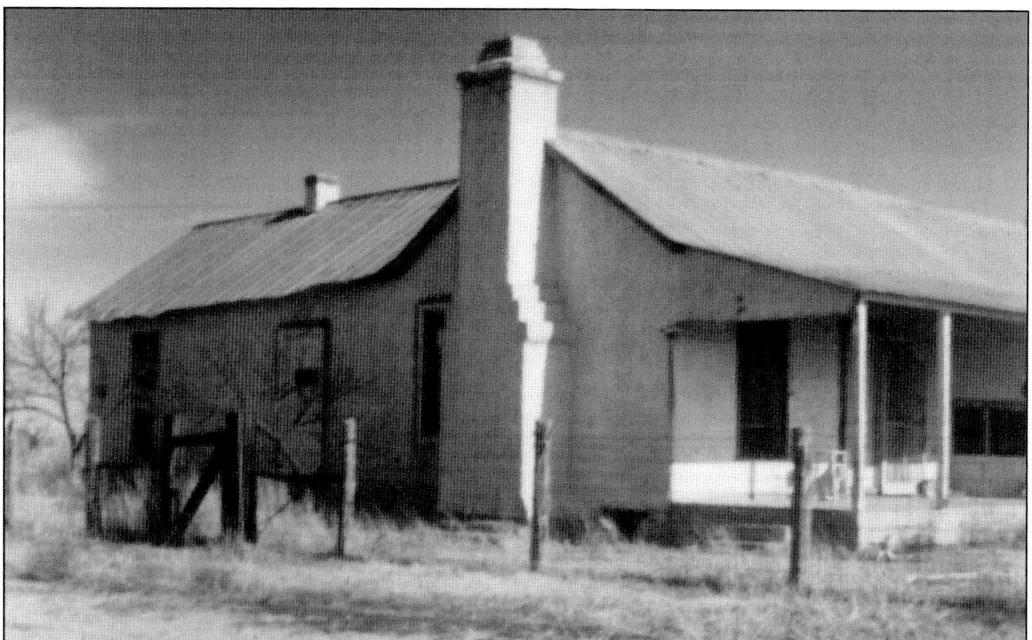

The Millett brothers of Baylor County, Texas, were a rough bunch when John Simpson met them. Citizens of nearby Seymour feared them. Ott Black, who worked for the Milletts and the Hash Knife, called the Millett Ranch (pictured here in 1880) "one of the toughest spots this side of hell" and commented that only "a rustler or gunman could get work with them." (Baylor County Free Library, Seymour, Texas.)

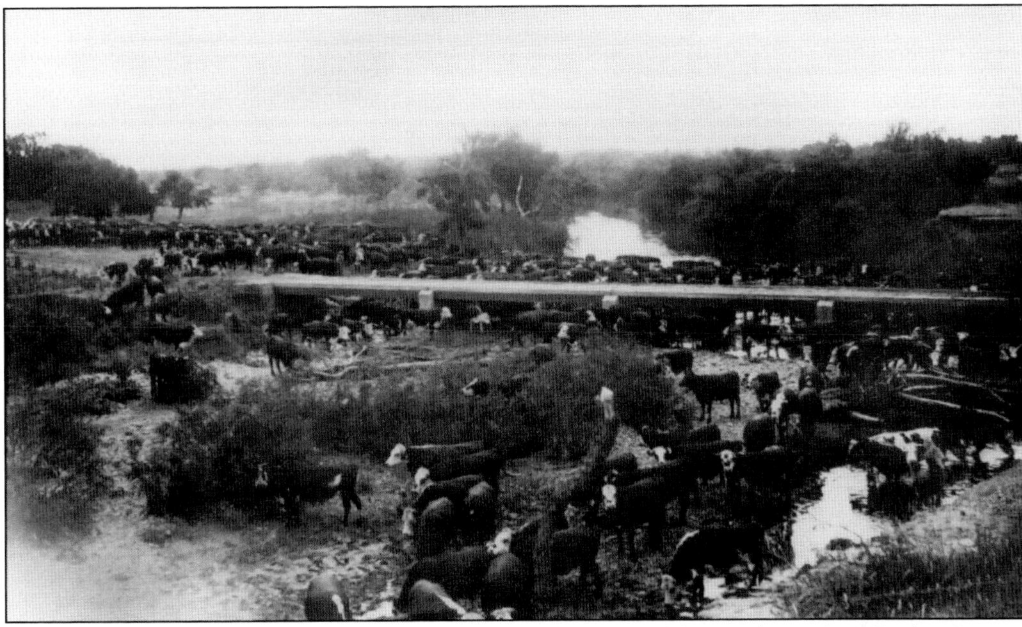

This c. 1882 image is identified as the "last big cattle drive" of the Hash Knife in Baylor County. The cattle were likely being herded toward operations along Box Elder Creek in Montana. Stoneville, located 93 miles away, was the nearest community. Three years would pass before Ekalaka was founded, shortening the distance from civilization to just 20 miles. (Baylor County Free Library.)

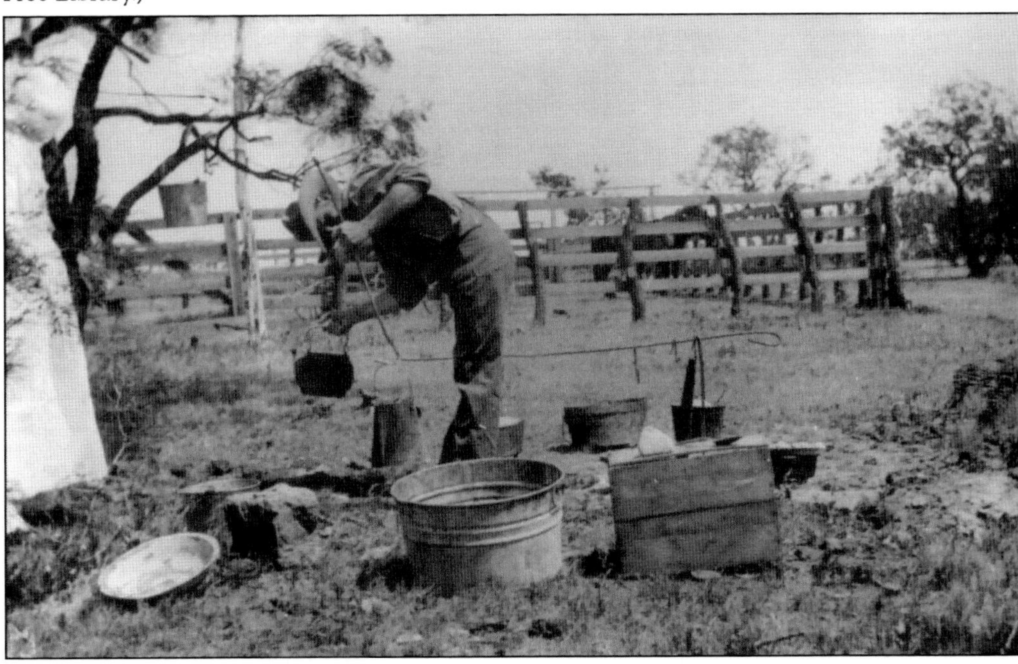

Lowe L. Stout and an unidentified woman (far left) prepare a meal near some corrals in Baylor County around 1917. Stout was employed as ranch foreman for the Stevens Brothers at the Hash Knife Ranch. He and his wife, Alice Robertson, also ranched on Miller Creek for many years. (Baylor County Free Library.)

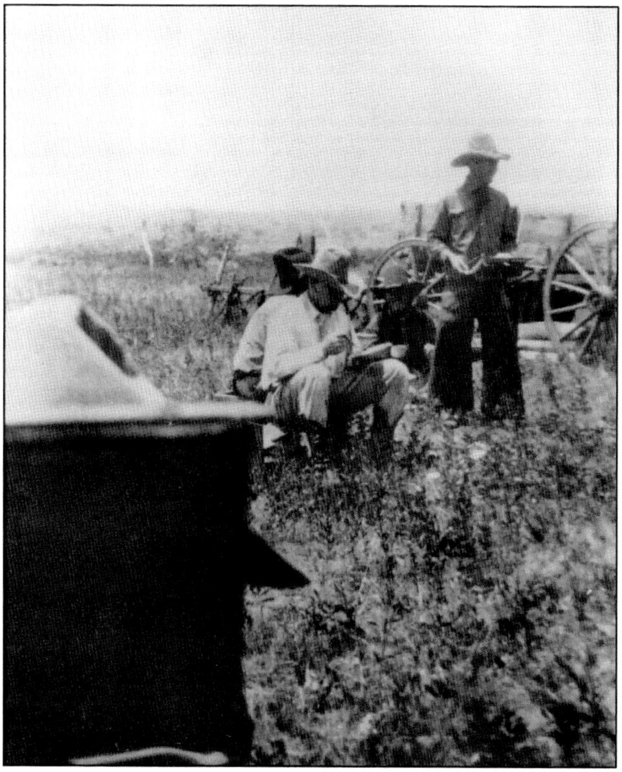

The Hash Knife in Texas continued operations for many years. The Knox Brothers may have owned the ranch before Elmer Stevens (seated) and Roy Stevens bought it in the early 1920s. During the Great Depression, the ranch was turned back to the Knox Brothers, and John D. Mounce (standing) lived at the ranch with his family. Later, a Mr. Anderson leased the ranch. (Baylor County Free Library.)

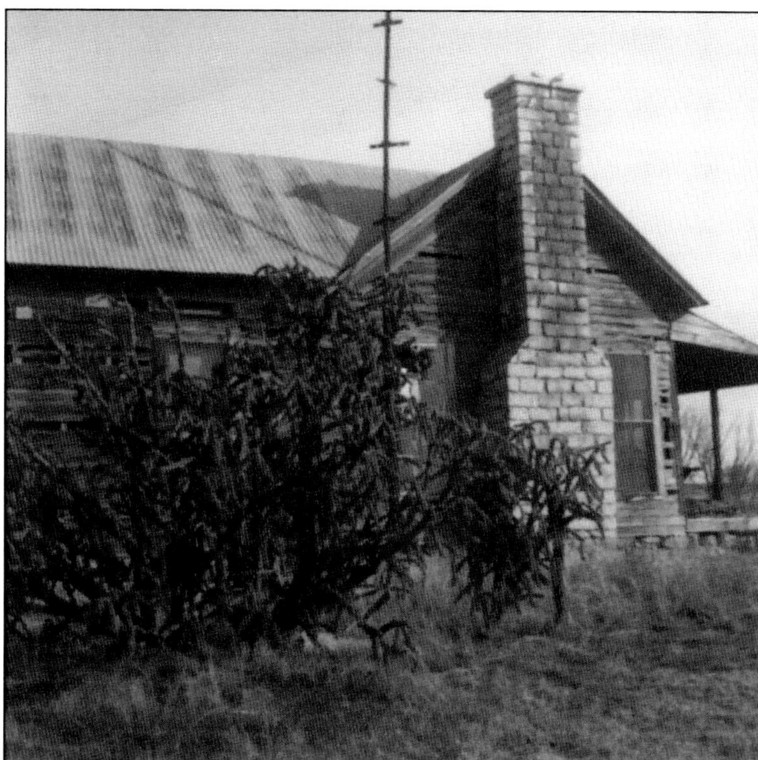

When the Hash Knife in Baylor County decided to build new headquarters overlooking the Brazos River, the old headquarters, pictured here, became home to the Howe family. Aubrey and Mildred Howe Lunsford inherited the house in 1953. According to one source, "It had seen 90 years of service and was pretty well ready for the scrap pile." The Lunsfords tore it down. (Baylor County Free Library.)

Tending the chuck wagon was one of the most important jobs on the trail. Cowboys relied heavily on nourishing grub and strong coffee to make it through the long workday. In 1882, Jacob "Dutch Jake" Heckman served as the cook on the Continental Land and Cattle Company's first jaunt from Texas to Montana. Heckman is pictured here at the age of 90. (Carter County Museum, Ekalaka, Montana.)

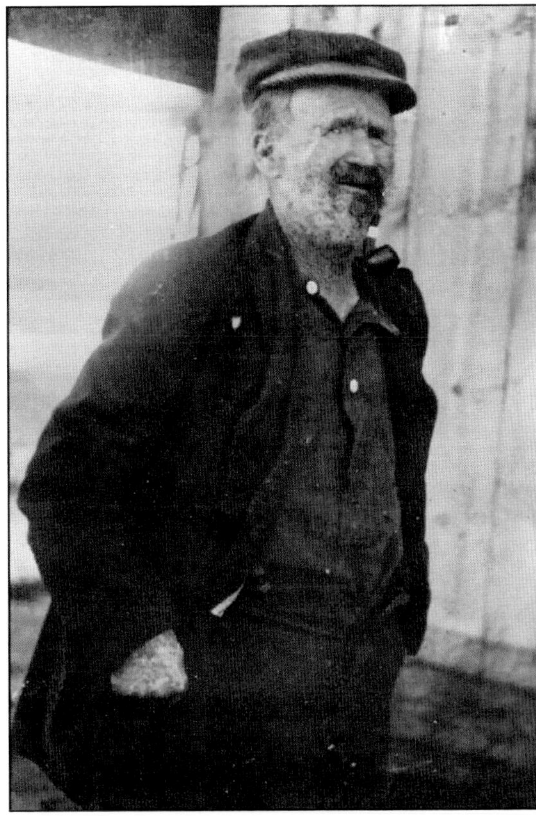

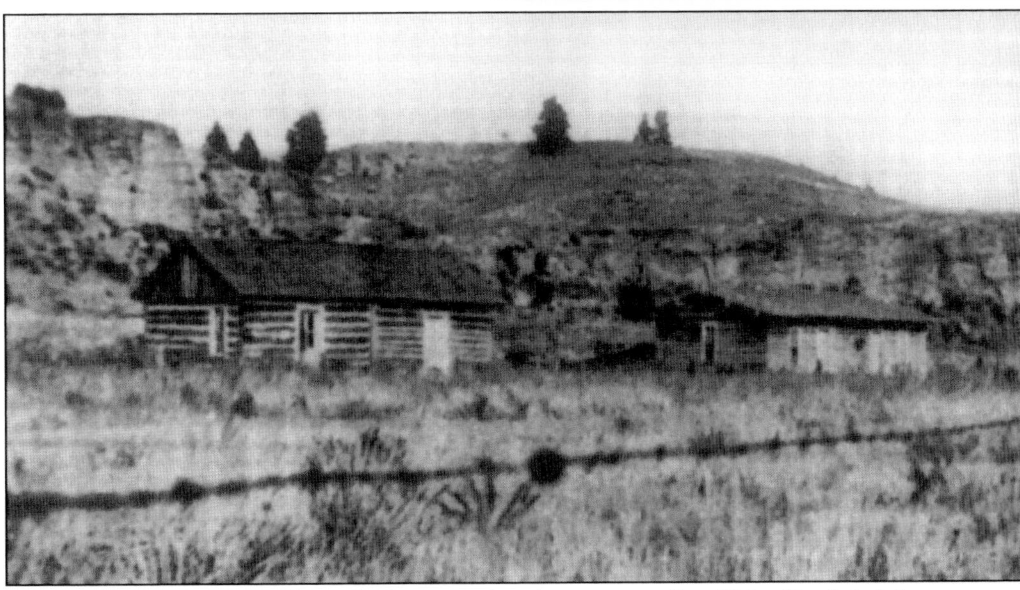

The Continental Land and Cattle Company headquarters on Box Elder Creek in Montana were comfortable enough. When the first herds arrived in the summer of 1882, foreman William Lefors arranged for two cabins to serve as headquarters. The foreman used the cabin on the left for his home and office. Cowboys slept and ate their meals in the cabin on the right. (Carter County Museum.)

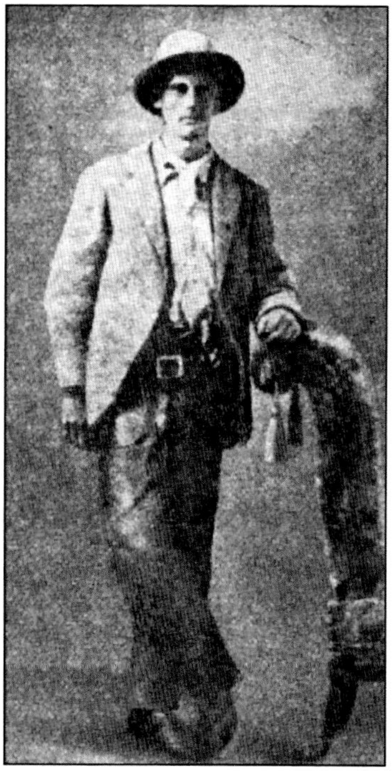

Hash Knife cowboy George Axelby came with the herd from Texas but soon turned rogue. Within a short time, he was hunting buffalo, fighting with Native Americans, and forming a gang with other Hash Knife cowboys-turned-outlaws. Axelby's actions soon caught the attention of authorities, who battled it out with the gang at Stoneville. There were several casualties. Axelby escaped, only to be killed four months later.

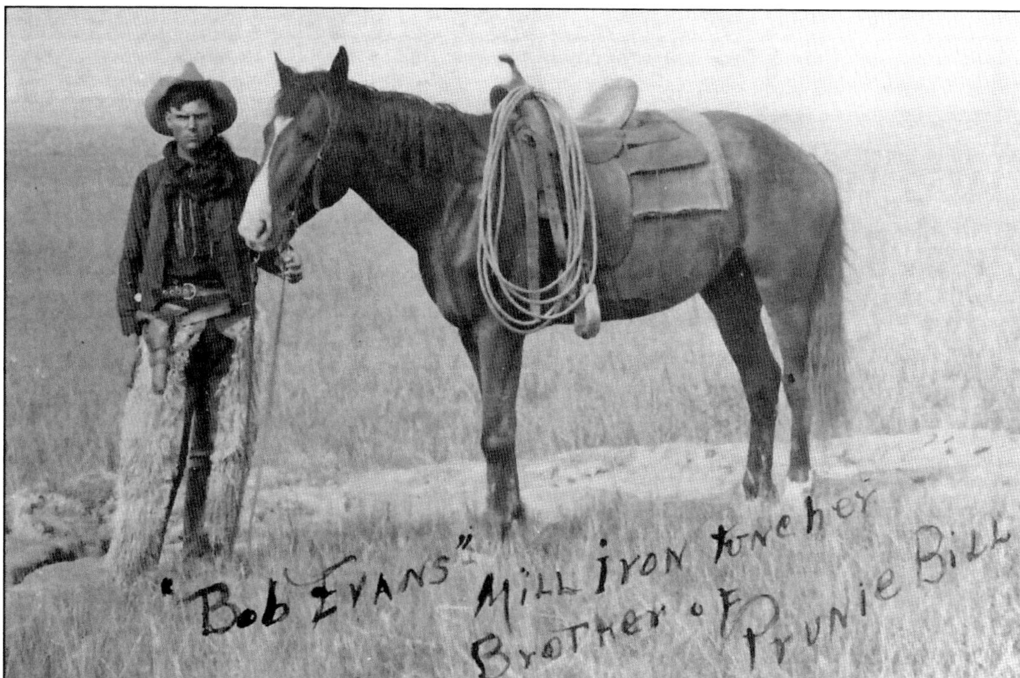

In 1884, the Continental Cattle Company combined its holdings with the Mill Iron Cattle Company in Montana and sported the new name of the Continental Land and Cattle Company. Hash Knife cowboy Bob Evans probably continued working under the brand. Evans was just one of many cowboys who came and went during the Hash Knife's time in Montana. (Carter County Museum.)

Little is known about Hash Knife cowpuncher Clarence Sisley, pictured here during the 1880s, including whether he was part of the Texas bunch that migrated to Montana. Cowboys there looked upon Texas cattle as poor stock; worse yet, their keepers appeared equally lanky in stature. Cowboy Walt Colburn noted that Texas cowboys "were a different breed of cowhand for the most part." (Carter County Museum.)

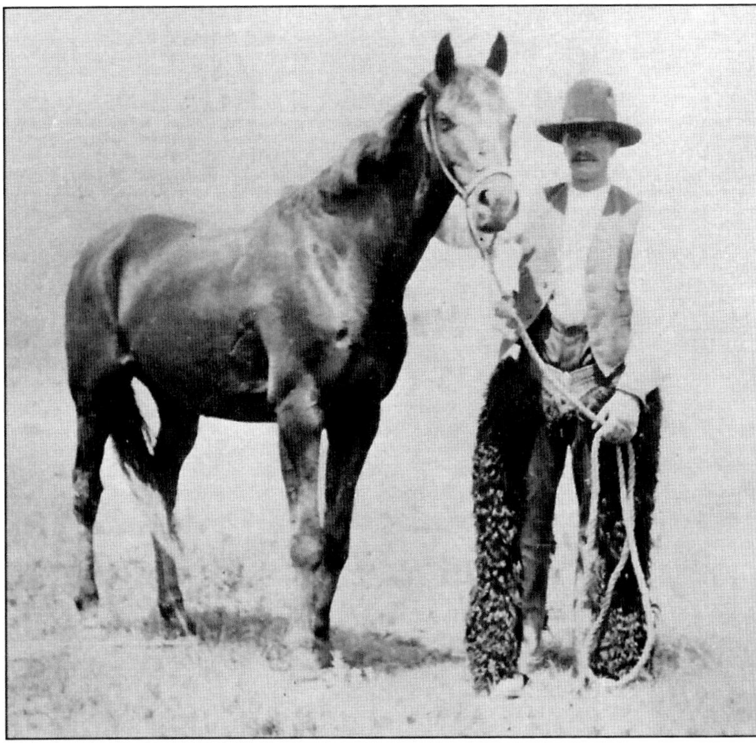

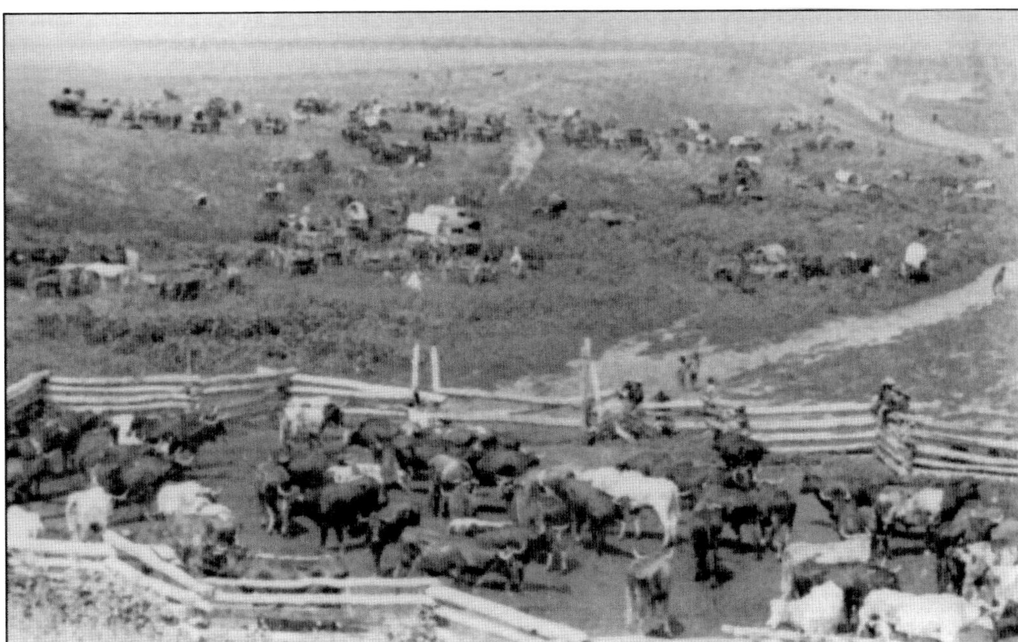

During the 1880s, the federal government rationed beef to various Indian reservations in Wyoming, Dakota Territory, and Montana. This allowed the Hash Knife to sell their beef at government prices. The largest shipment was likely 2,500 head delivered to Fort Yates, North Dakota, in 1883. Here, Hash Knife and Mill Iron cattle are being corralled at Standing Rock Indian Agency in Dakota Territory around 1884. (Carter County Museum.)

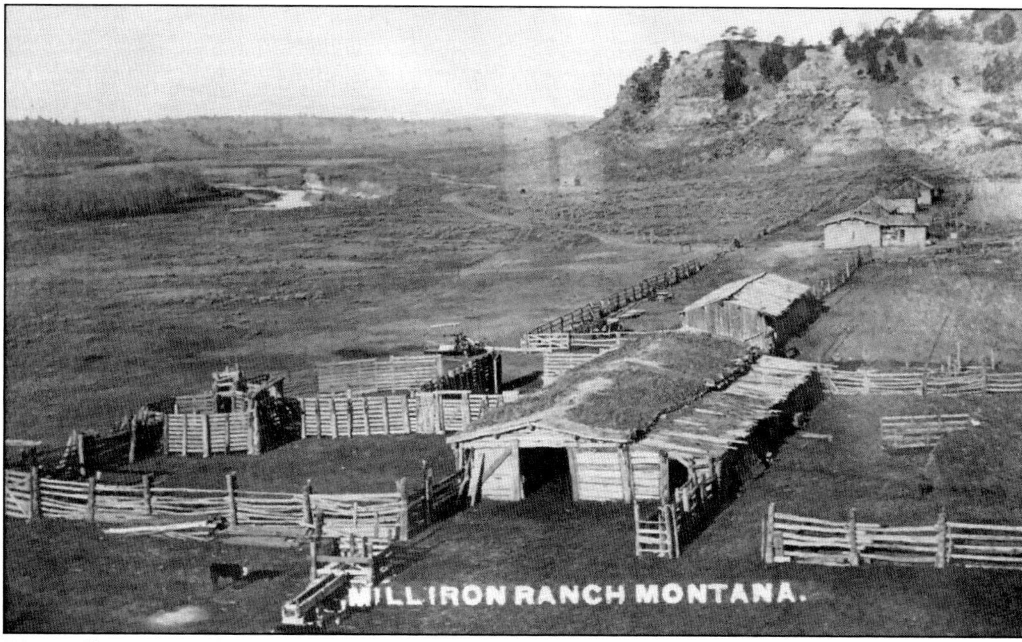

The Mill Iron Ranch was located roughly 80 miles from Stoneville, with the Continental Land and Cattle Company somewhere between the two places. The Great Western Cattle Trail from Texas ended at Stoneville, but Hash Knife cattle still needed to be pushed on to one of the two ranches. Still, the Mill Iron Ranch, pictured here in 1884, benefited greatly from the Western Trail. (Carter County Museum.)

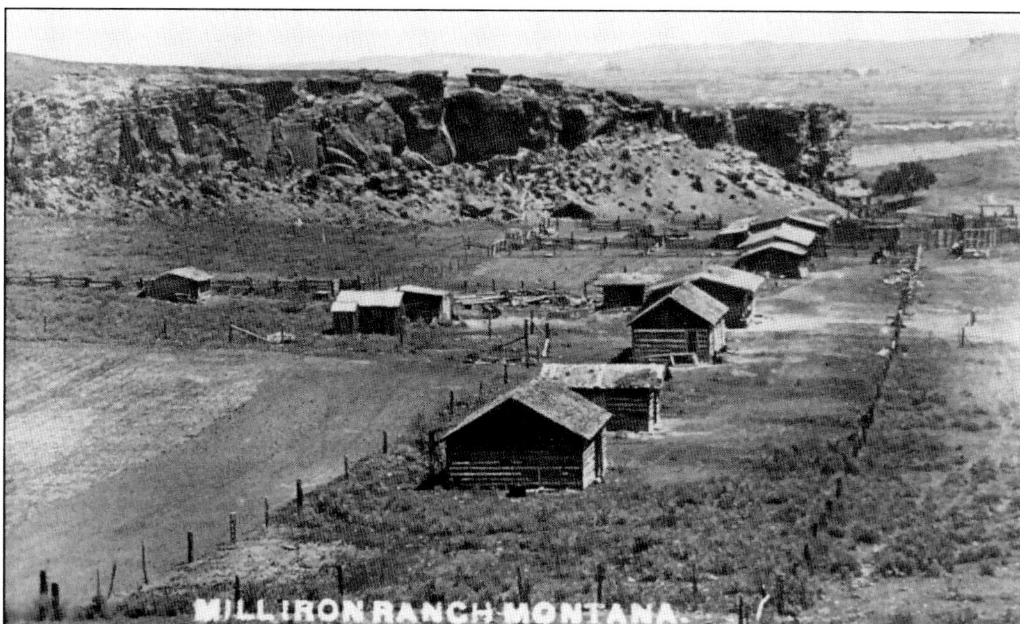

A view from the opposite end of the Mill Iron Ranch shows how large the operation was. There is little doubt that Hash Knife cowboys appreciated a night at the Mill Iron, whose bunkhouse likely offered better lodging than the cabin on Box Elder Creek. Henry Warren, the ever-flexible employee of the Hash Knife, was in charge of the Mill Iron operations. (Carter County Museum.)

As dapper as he appears in his fancy suit and fur coat, virtually nothing is known about Hash Knife cowpuncher Pete Buzman. Pictured here in 1884, Buzman may have been running under an alias when he worked in Montana. This image was taken in Rapid City, South Dakota. (Carter County Museum.)

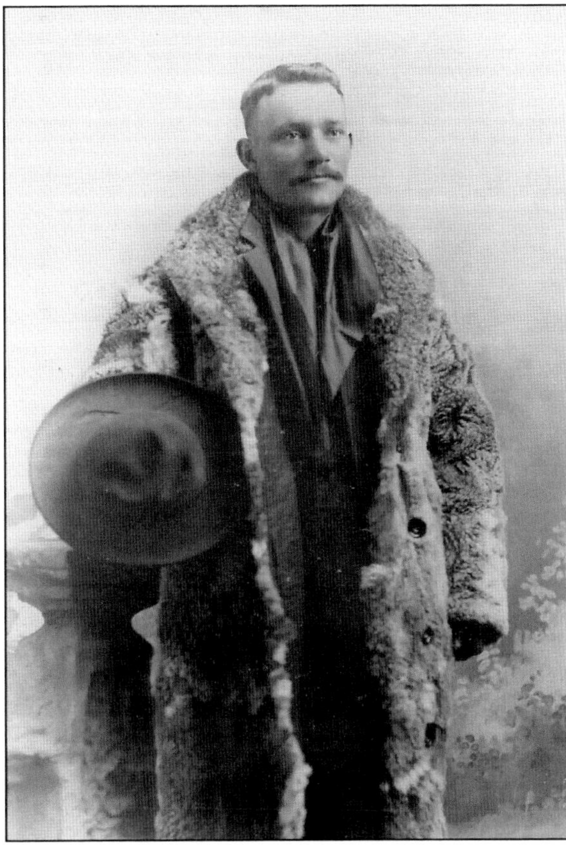

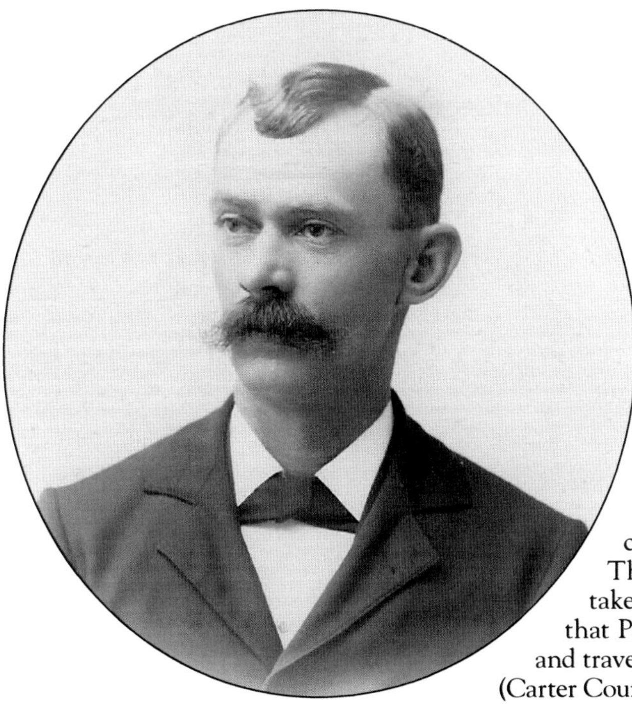

Like Pete Buzman, information is also scant on fellow Hash Knife cowpuncher Johnnie Pannel. Also like Buzman, Pannel is wearing clothing not suited to herding cattle. The fact that this c. 1884 image was taken in Fort Worth, Texas, may indicate that Pannel worked for the brand in Texas and traveled on one of the drives to Montana. (Carter County Museum.)

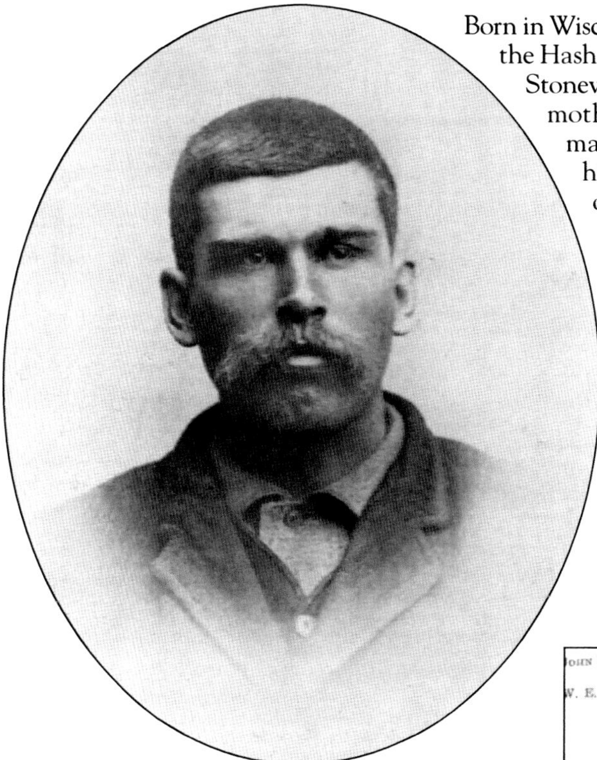

Born in Wisconsin in 1860, Jay Griffen Shelden joined the Hash Knife outfit at Box Elder Creek. In 1885, Stoneville was renamed Alzada in honor of his mother, Laura Alzada Flagg. Shelden later married and homesteaded at Alzada, but his wife could not bear the loneliness of ranch life and left him. Shelden died in Belle Fourche in 1912. (Carter County Museum.)

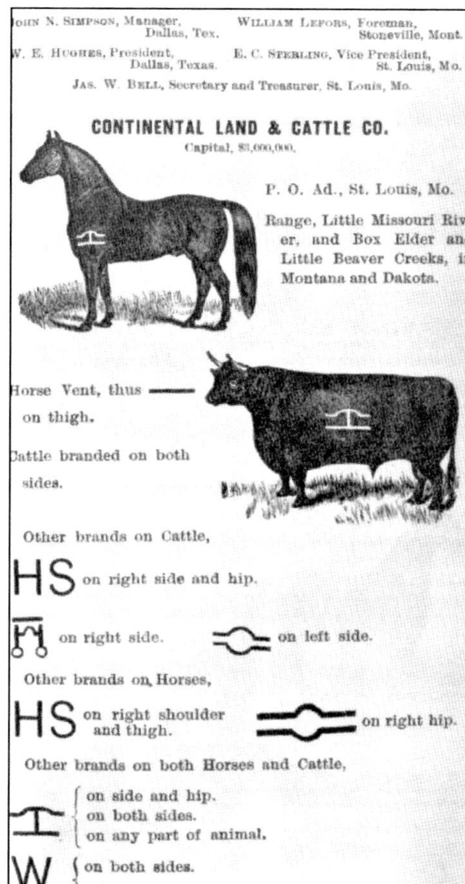

JOHN N. SIMPSON, Manager, Dallas, Tex.
WILLIAM LEFORS, Foreman, Stoneville, Mont.
W. E. HUGHES, President, Dallas, Texas.
E. C. SPERLING, Vice President, St. Louis, Mo.
JAS. W. BELL, Secretary and Treasurer, St. Louis, Mo.

CONTINENTAL LAND & CATTLE CO.

Capital, $3,000,000.

P. O. Ad., St. Louis, Mo.

Range, Little Missouri River, and Box Elder and Little Beaver Creeks, in Montana and Dakota.

Horse Vent, thus —— on thigh.

Cattle branded on both sides.

Other brands on Cattle,

HS on right side and hip.

on right side. on left side.

Other brands on Horses,

HS on right shoulder and thigh. on right hip.

Other brands on both Horses and Cattle,

on side and hip. on both sides. on any part of animal.

W on both sides. on either side.

The 1885–1886 *Brand Book of the Montana Stock Growers Association* illustrates the brands used by the Continental Land and Cattle Company. Included here are the Hash Knife brand (top) as well as other brands John Simpson and his partners purchased. Cattle were often branded on several sides, including the back, to be easily identified on the trail. Such identifying marks were known as road brands.

The Continental Land and Cattle Company's letterhead in 1885 included both the Hash Knife and Mill Iron brands. The main office was located in Dallas, with a branch office in St. Louis. Principal officers of the company occasionally left their cushy suites in these big cities to visit Hash Knife ranches in Texas, Montana, and, later, Arizona. (Pierce Collection, Dolph Briscoe Center for American History, Austin, Texas.)

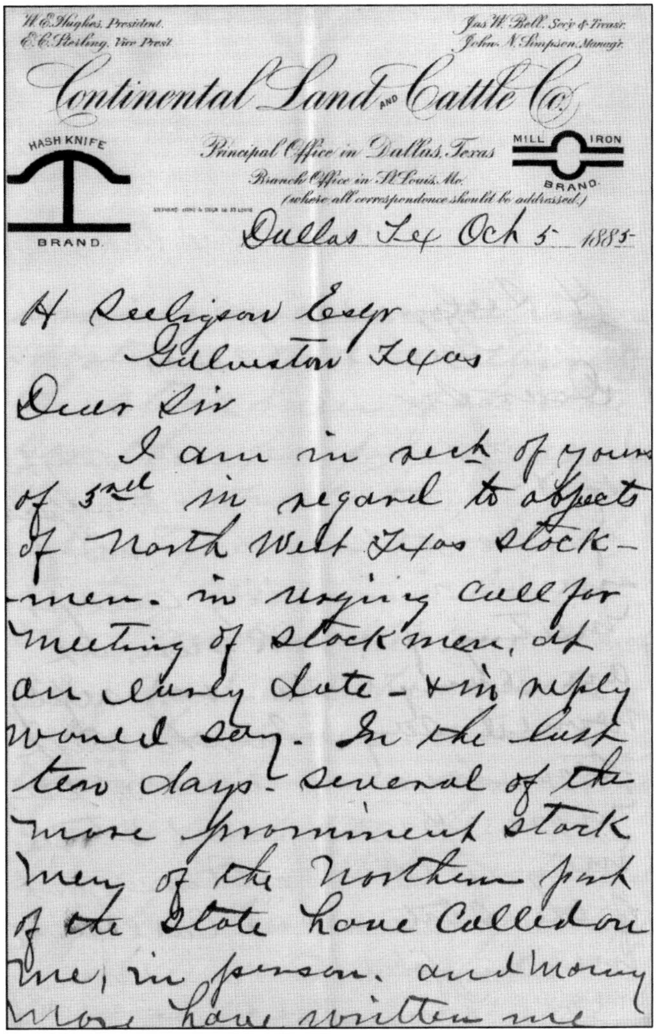

W. E. Hughes, President.
E. C. Sterling, Vice Prest.

Jas W. Bell, Secy & Treasr.
John N. Simpson, Managr.

Continental Land and Cattle Co.

HASH KNIFE BRAND

Principal Office in Dallas, Texas
Branch Office in St. Louis, Mo.
(where all correspondence should be addressed.)

MILL IRON BRAND

Dallas Tex Oct 5 1885

H Seeligson Esqr
Galveston Texas

Dear Sir

I am in rect of yours of 3rd in regard to aspects of North West Texas stock-men. in urging call for meeting of stockmen, at an early date - & in reply would say. In the last ten days several of the more prominent stock men of the Northern part of the State have called on me, in person. and many more have written me

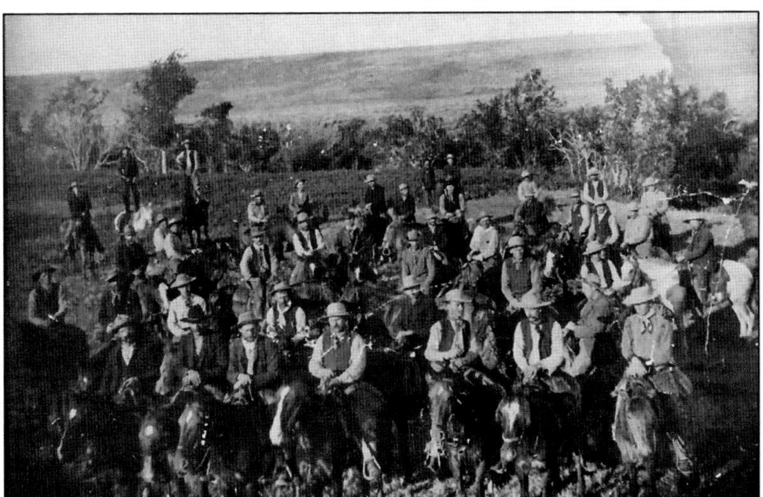

After the Aztec Land and Cattle Company formed to open up new range in Arizona, the Hash Knife continued operations in Montana. This image of an early morning round-up on the Little Missouri River, in May 1890, portrays cowboys who chose to keep working at the Montana outfit. (Carter County Museum.)

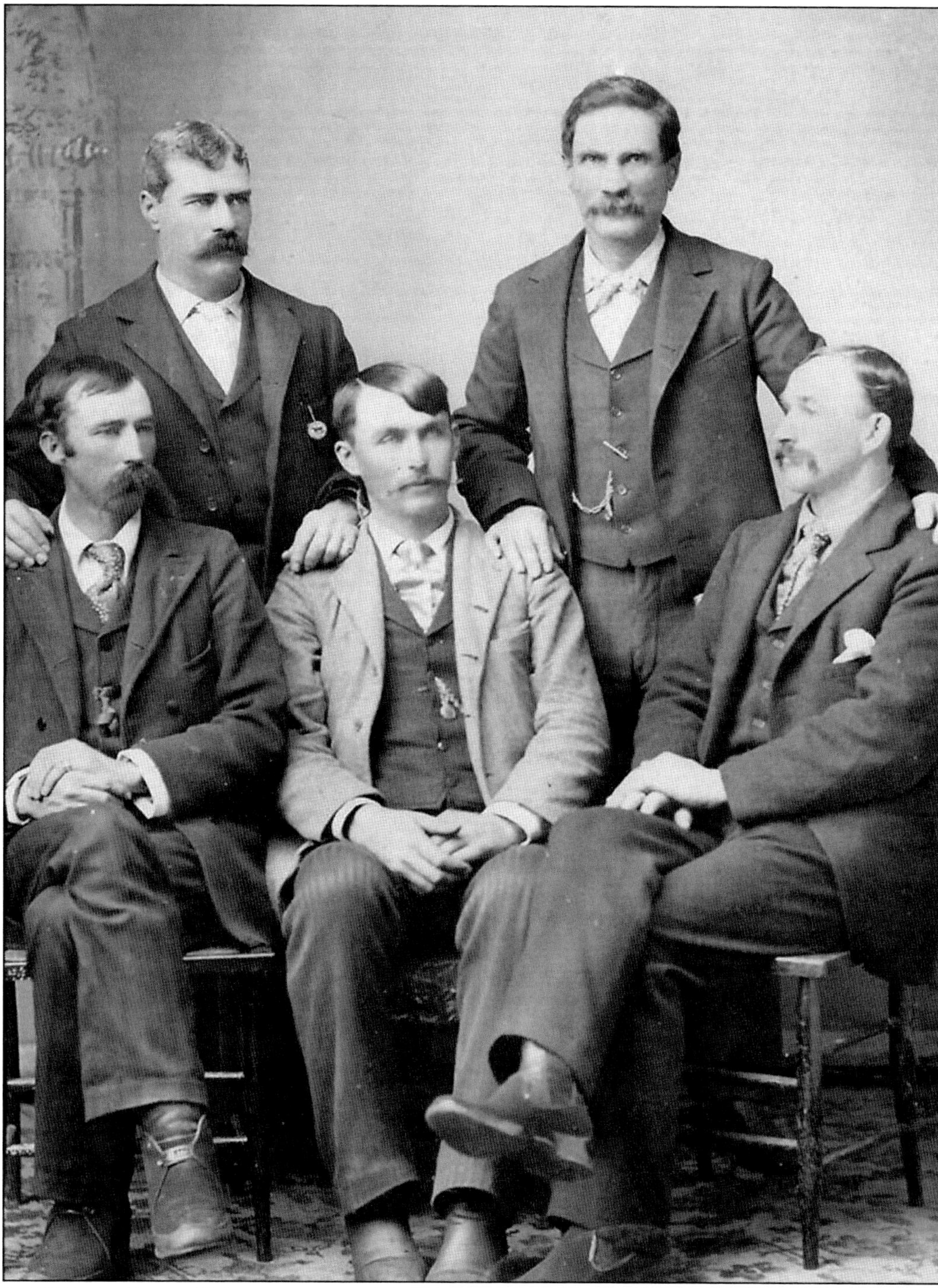

In 1897, the State of Montana accused the Continental Land and Cattle Company of failing to pay enough taxes. Hash Knife cowboys who were witnesses at the trial decided for some reason commemorate the occasion with a photograph in Helena. The men, from left to right, are Phil DeFrand and Ed Ramsberg (standing), Jim Connley, Frank Castleberry, and H.H. Floyd. (Carter County Museum.)

Two

Holbrook

Arizona Territory was established in 1863. By the 1870s, communities and ranches were springing up along major water sources, including the Little Colorado River. New settlers to the region included Mexican families, Mormons from Utah, and pioneers from the East.

Near the confluence of the Little Colorado and the Rio Puerco was a place called Horsehead Crossing. At this remote spot, Juan Padilla built a house and Berado Frayre, or Frayde, ran a trading post and saloon. The trading post was also owned by Santiago Baca & Company for a time. It was said that "nobody left without food, even if they could not pay."

Edward Kinsley of Boston first laid eyes on Arizona as part of a survey team for the Atlantic & Pacific Railroad. At the time, the railroad was planning to lay tracks from Albuquerque, New Mexico, to Mojave, California. The new rails would run very near Horsehead Crossing. When Kinsley returned to Boston, his mind was still on the abundant land he had observed in Arizona. Such a vast area would be the perfect place to raise cattle.

The Atlantic & Pacific Railroad made it to the Little Colorado in September 1881. A year and a half later, Baca, along with Pedro Montano, Henry H. Scorse, and F.W. Smith, filed a plat for the town of Holbrook two miles west of Horsehead Crossing and right along the tracks. Holbrook quickly became a popular shipping point and center of commerce in the region.

In December 1884, Ed Kinsley partnered with nephew Henry Kinsley, Frank Ames, James McCreery, and a New York bank—Seligman & Seligman—to form the Aztec Land and Cattle Company. The men purchased 1 million acres from the Atlantic & Pacific for 50¢ per acre. By buying only the odd-numbered sections of land from the railroad, the company prevented other cattle companies from accessing the even-numbered sections. Thus the Aztec Land and Cattle Company owned the million acres they bought, and also had undisputed and sole access to another million acres.

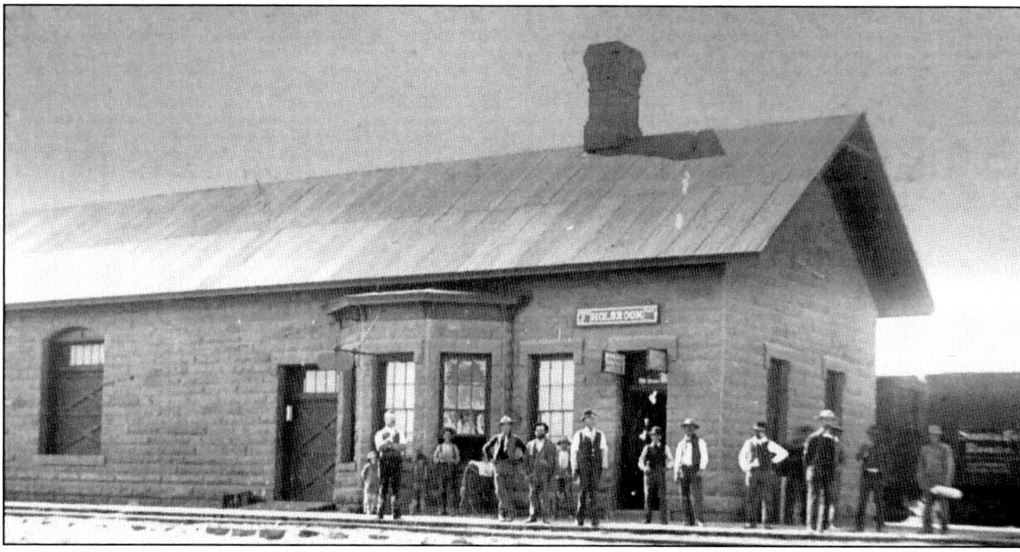

One of the first structures built at Holbrook was the depot. The community grew quickly as the Atlantic & Pacific Railroad made Holbrook a regular stop. The Aztec Land and Cattle Company saw an immediate opportunity to use Holbrook as a shipping point. Beginning in 1884, the company began bringing stock cars filled with cattle from Hash Knife operations in Texas. (Navajo County Historical Society, Holbrook, Arizona.)

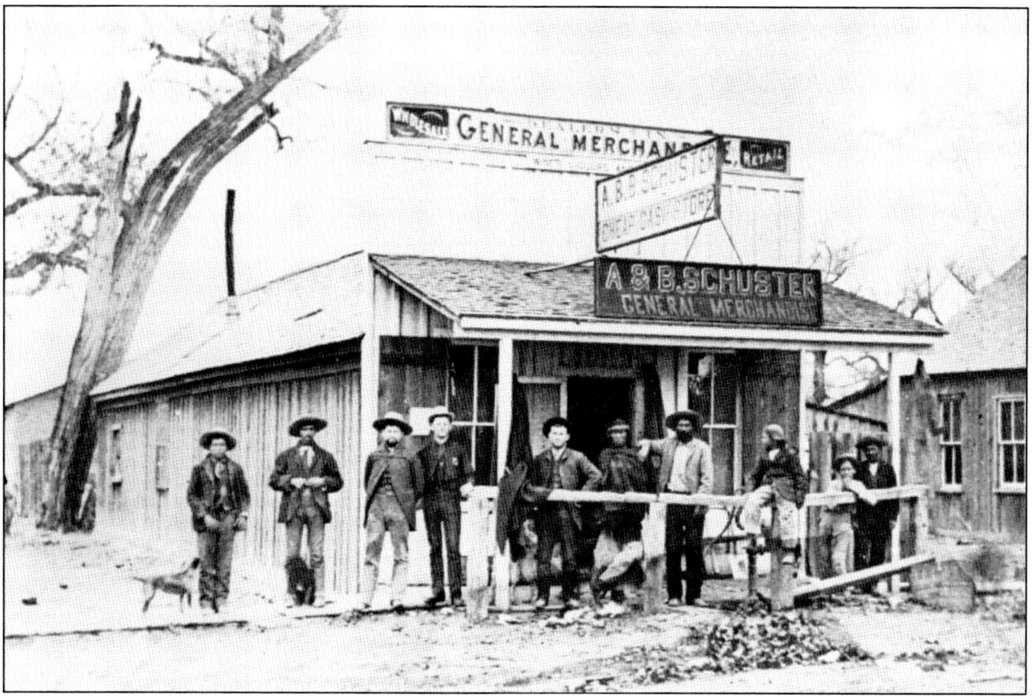

Twin brothers Adolph and Ben Schuster opened their A & B Schuster Company at Holbrook in 1884. Adolph is third from the left; his brother is fifth from the left. For decades, the Schusters reigned as prominent businessmen in Holbrook. The business later expanded to include a third brother, Max. (Navajo County Historical Society.)

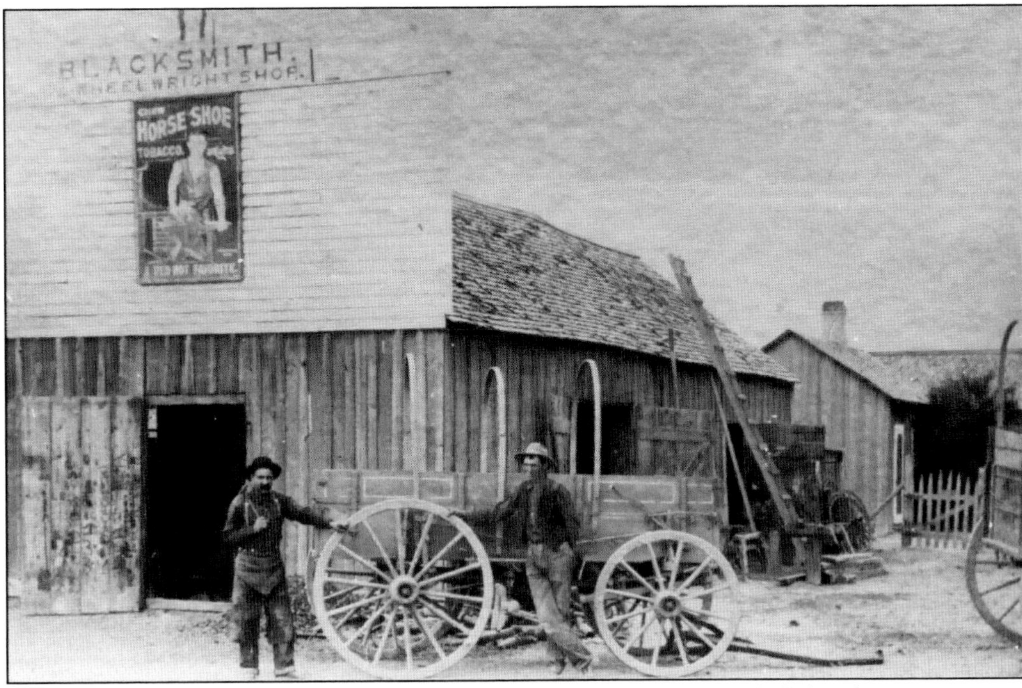

Holbrook's business district grew up around its depot. Early businesses included a Chinese restaurant, two saloons, a drugstore, A & B Schuster's grocery, a mercantile, and William Armbruster's blacksmith and wheelwright shop. A German immigrant, Armbruster first came to Arizona in about 1875. He flourished for over 25 years in Holbrook but was advertising his business and a five-room house for sale in 1910. (Navajo County Historical Society.)

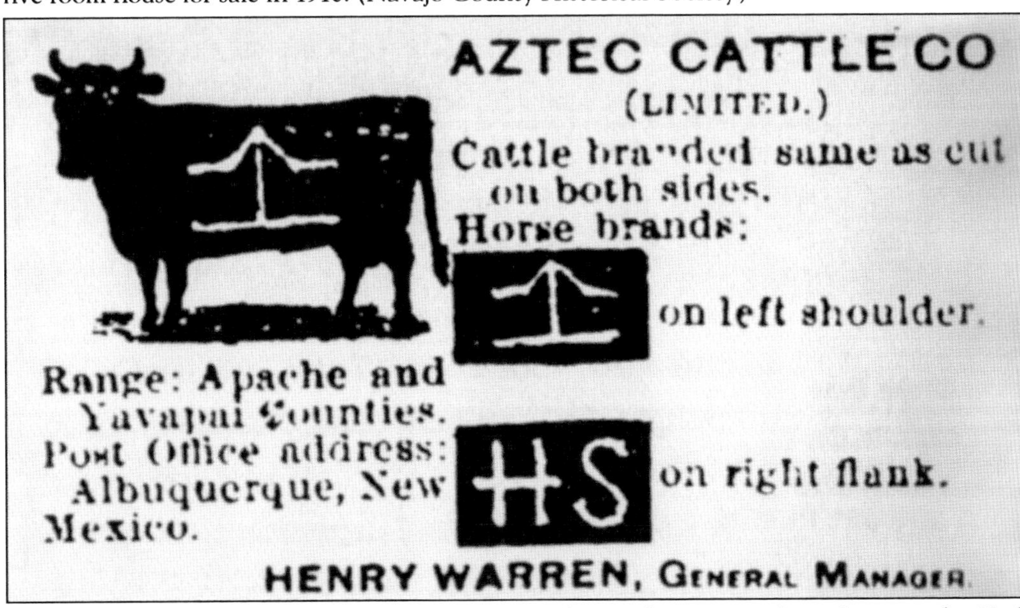

Shortly after the Aztec Land and Cattle Company began shipping cattle to Arizona, the Hash Knife brand was registered in Apache County on June 2, 1885. Henry Warren filed the paperwork and published this advertisement in the June 11 edition of the *St. Johns Herald* newspaper. The brand was also registered in Yavapai County on August 22.

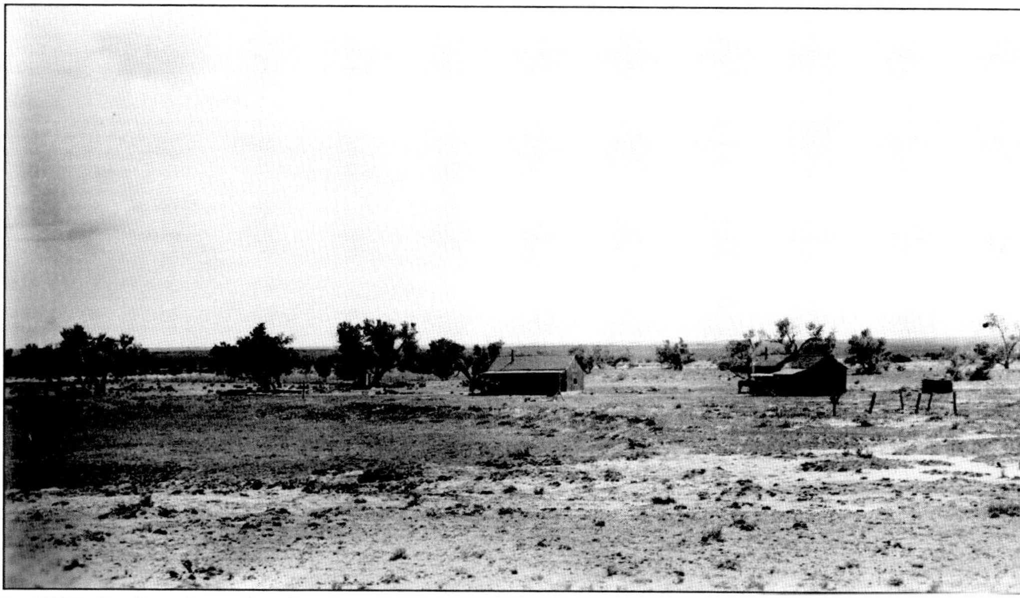

In 1885, the first Aztec headquarters was constructed 10 miles west of Holbrook, on the south side of the Little Colorado River. The company spent $850 to construct a small ranch house measuring 14 feet by 24 feet, a tiny cookhouse, and one or two outbuildings. Hash Knife cowboys were obviously not meant to spend much time here, but rather out on the range. (Arizona Historical Society, 96-2117.)

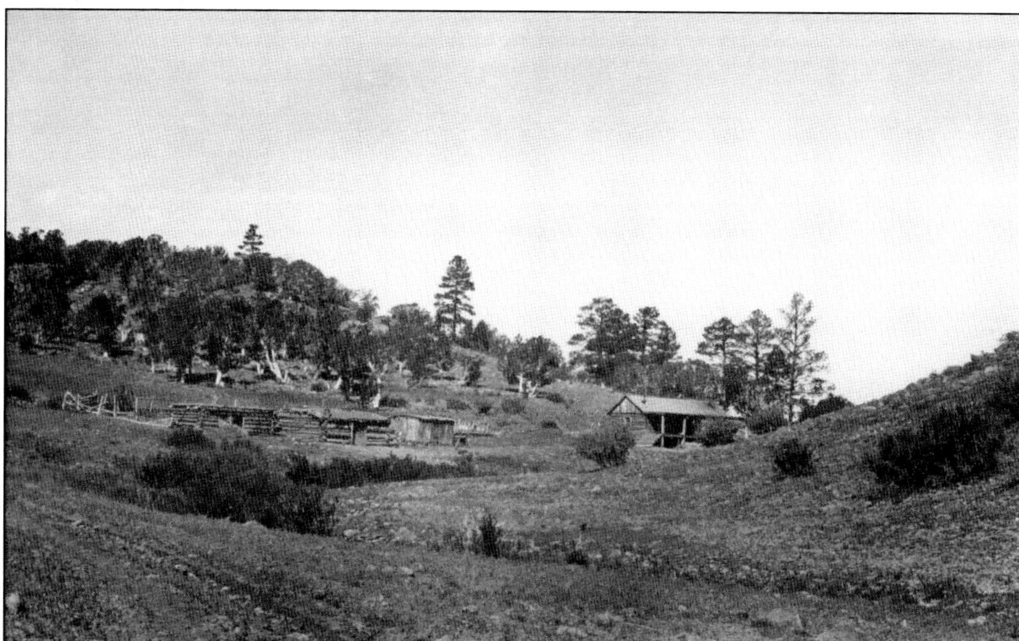

At the line camps scattered across the Aztec Land and Cattle Company range, cowboys could rest, corral cattle, brand, and perform other chores. This camp, built around 1885 on Chavez Pass near Payson, looks at least as comfortable (if not more) than the headquarters. Other line camps were located at Pine Springs, Mormon Mill, Sycamore, and near Winslow, to name a few. (Arizona Historical Society, 96-2130.)

Edward Kinsley hired his nephew Henry to work for the Hash Knife in Texas before appointing him assistant treasurer of the Aztec. Despite allegedly receiving only room and board his first year, the Boston city boy appears to have taken to cowboy life quickly even if he was occasionally spoiled by his uncle. Young Kinsley is pictured here in 1886, just after joining the Hash Knife in Arizona.

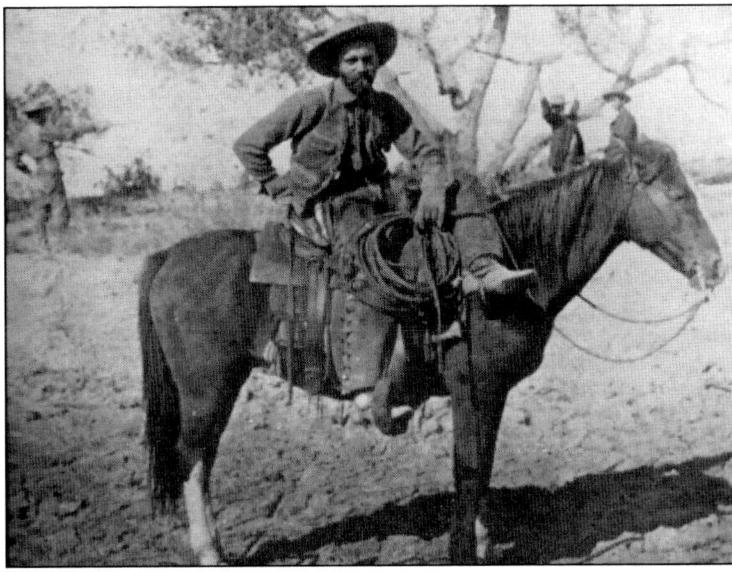

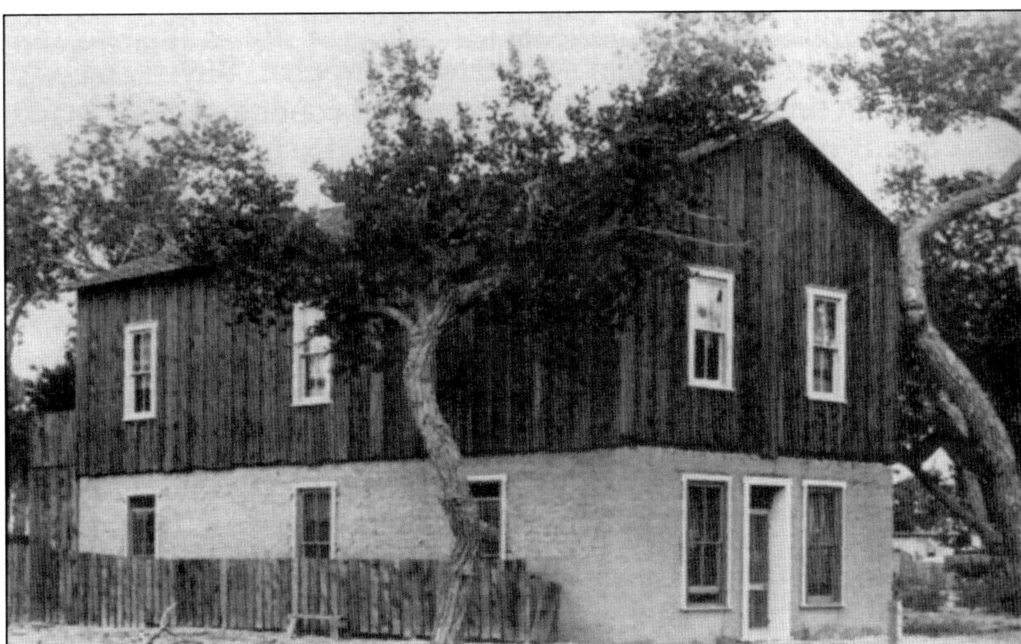

In 1887, a second Aztec headquarters was located on Washington (later Santiago and then Alvarado) Street in Holbrook. The company shared quarters with the Masonic lodge, renting the bottom floor for $150 annually. Henry Kinsley was living at the headquarters in 1888. Old-timers say the Hash Knife also used the nearby Brunswick Hotel as a headquarters, but the hotel was not known by that name until the 1890s.

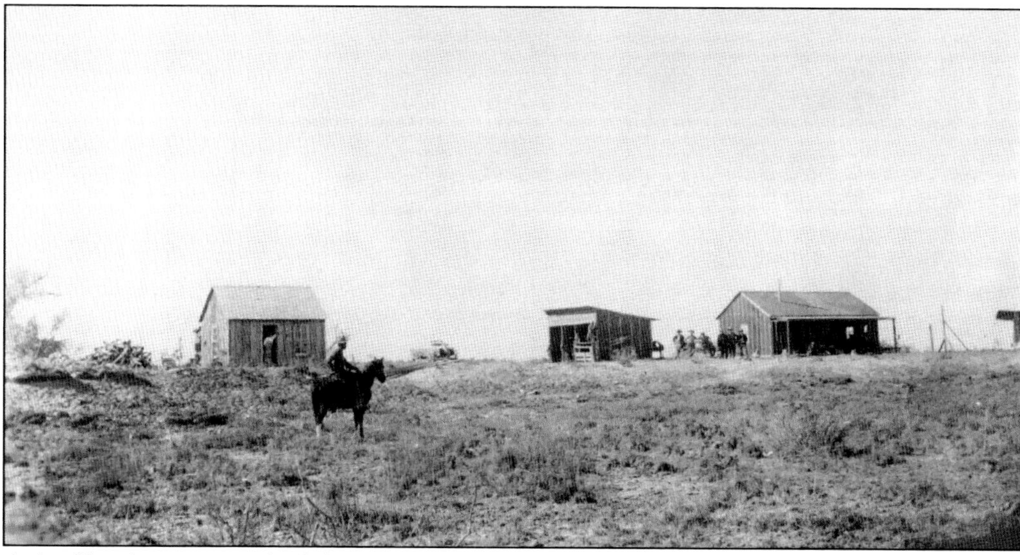

A third headquarters was built four miles south of Joseph City not long after, or even in conjunction with, the headquarters at Holbrook. Most historians identify the date of this image as 1886. The buildings are identified, from left to right, as the kitchen and dining room, the grain house, and the main office. Henry Kinsley is on the horse. (Arizona Historical Society, 03-1365.)

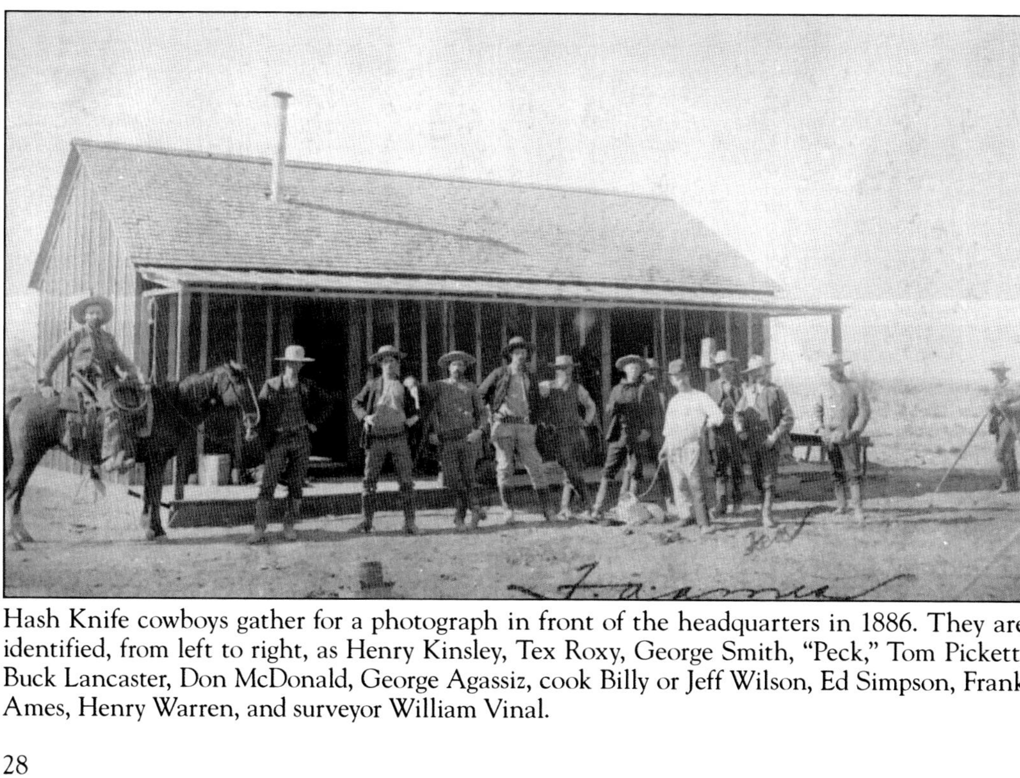

Hash Knife cowboys gather for a photograph in front of the headquarters in 1886. They are identified, from left to right, as Henry Kinsley, Tex Roxy, George Smith, "Peck," Tom Pickett, Buck Lancaster, Don McDonald, George Agassiz, cook Billy or Jeff Wilson, Ed Simpson, Frank Ames, Henry Warren, and surveyor William Vinal.

The Aztec Land and Cattle Company had plenty of neighbors with large spreads in their own right. Some of them later became involved with the Hash Knife. Pictured in 1888 from left to right are ranchers Burt Potter, Jug Jackson, and Joe Woods. Potter was Woods's nephew. Both men did business over the years with the Hash Knife; Woods later ran the Pioneer Saloon in Holbrook. He also served as sheriff there.

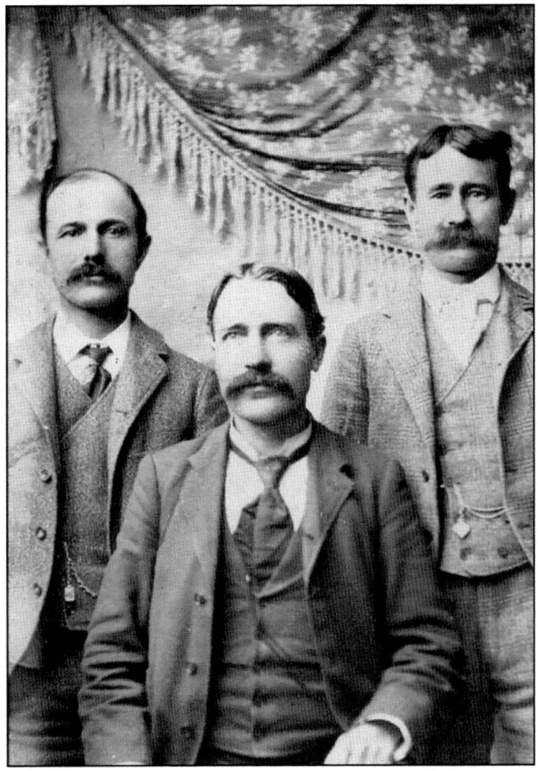

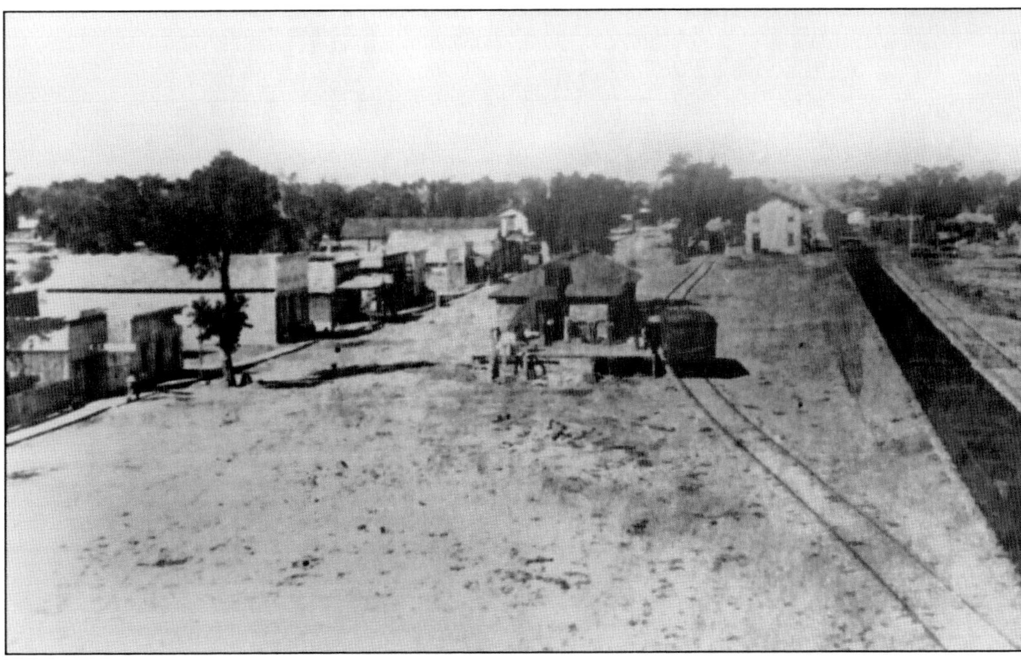

As the Aztec settled into Arizona, Holbrook continued to grow. The far white building on the right in this view, looking east, is the Atlantic & Pacific Railroad depot. A number of other businesses blossomed along the south side of the tracks. Holbrook's population was about 250 citizens, with homes scattered around the downtown area. (Navajo County Historical Society.)

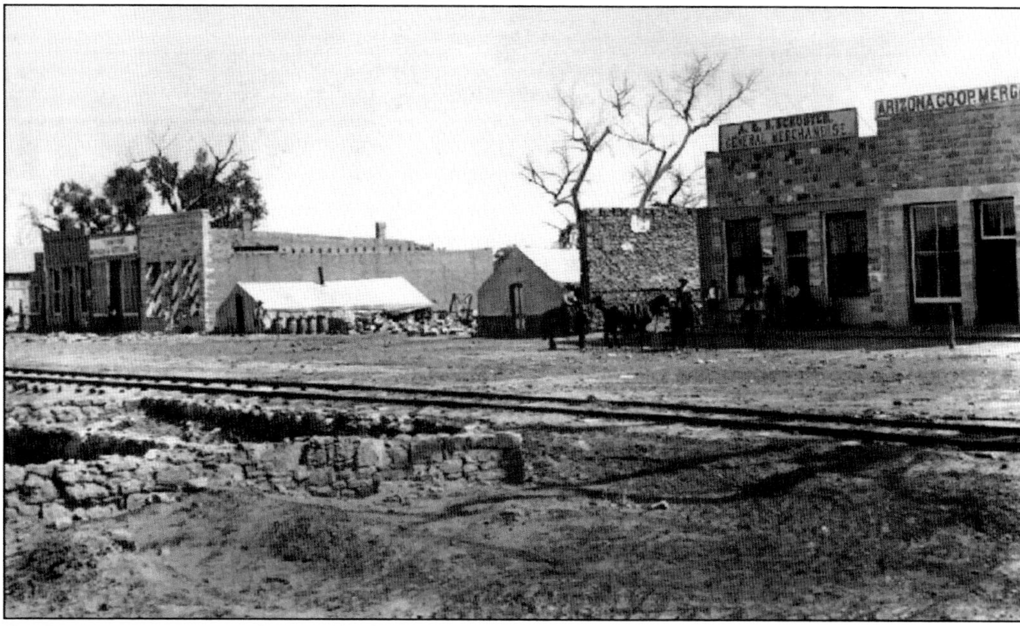

On June 26, 1888, a warehouse filled with wool inexplicably burst into flames at Holbrook, burning most of the downtown. Reconstruction efforts are pictured here in the burned out buildings. They include A & B Schuster's on the right. The white tent served as a tavern while the Cottage Saloon was rebuilt next door. Frank Wattron's drugstore is next to the saloon. (Navajo County Historical Society.)

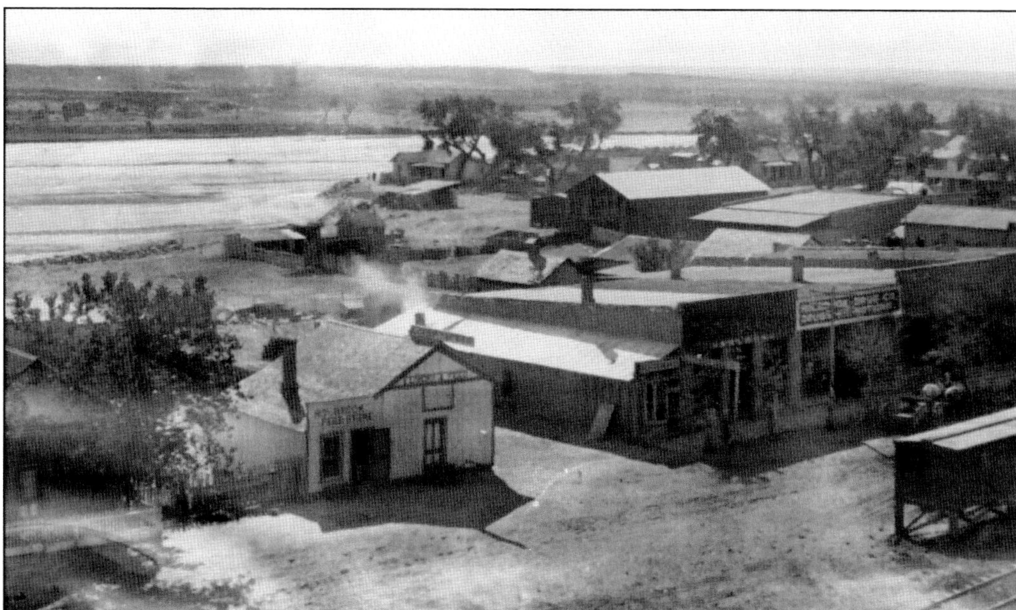

The Little Colorado River provides a scenic backdrop behind the new and improved downtown Holbrook. Within a year, rebuilt businesses included a feed store, livery stable, restaurant, the Cottage Saloon, Wattron's drugstore, and the Mormon Arizona Cooperative Mercantile Institution. Houses, some of which survived the fire, are visible in the small neighborhoods adjacent to the downtown area. (Navajo County Historical Society.)

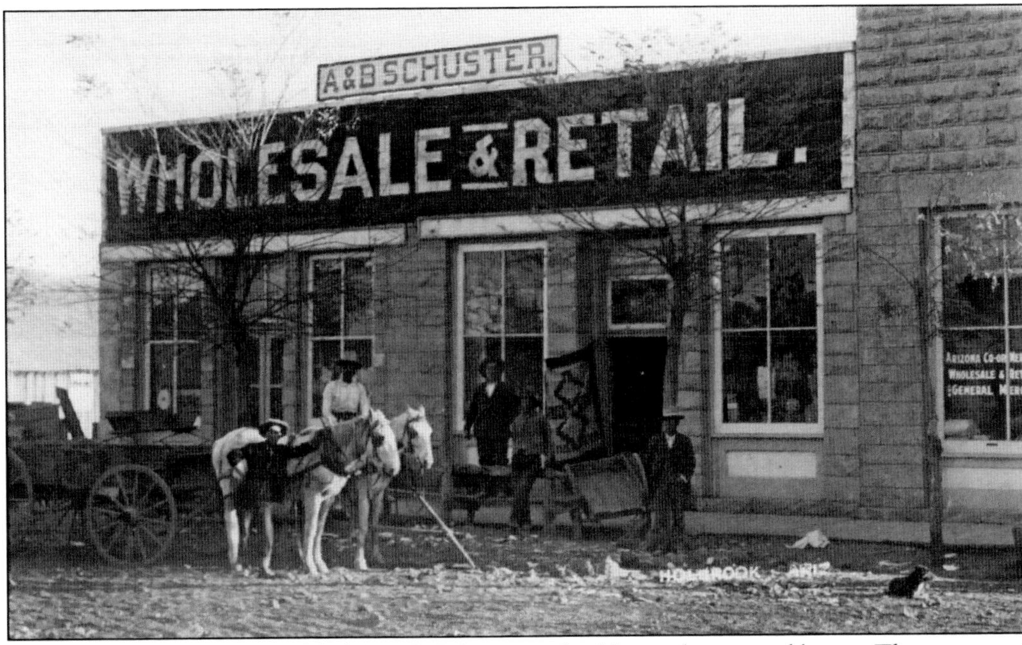

Holbrook's fire actually enabled A & B Schuster to build even bigger and better. The company's success eventually allowed the brothers to open branch stores and trading posts, hiring managers to run them. The Schusters eventually moved to Los Angeles. Ben died in 1911 and Adolph died in 1934. In 1952, A & B Schuster in Holbrook was recognized as the oldest continuously operated grocery outlet in Arizona.

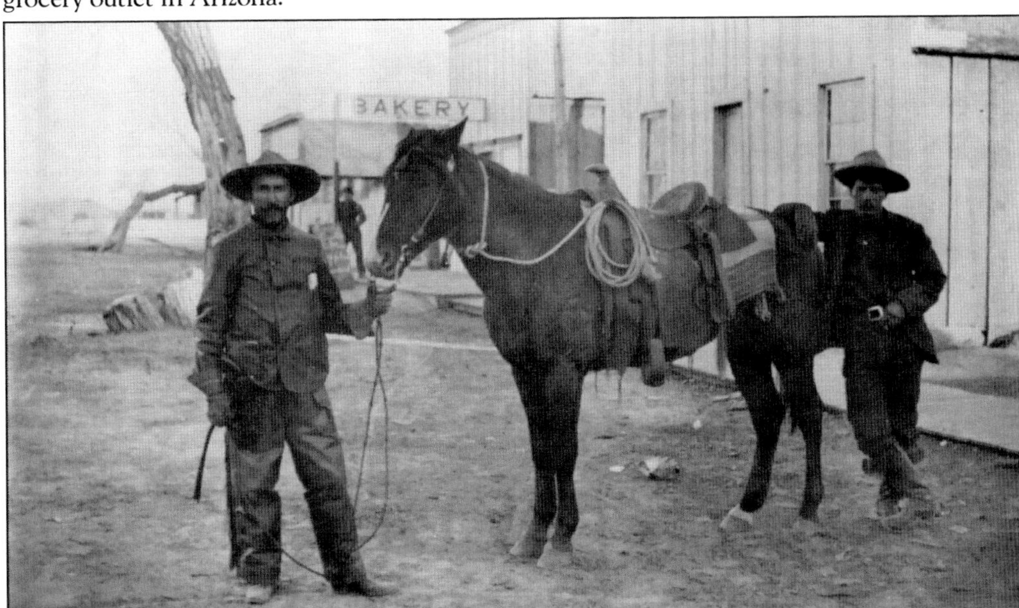

Frank Ames, his horse Dandy, and Hash Knife wagon boss Ed Rogers pose at Holbrook around 1888. Ames, from a well-to-do Massachusetts family, hired on in Texas, came to Arizona, and eventually became the Aztec's land agent. Rogers was working for the outfit by 1885 and was respected as a top hand. He left the outfit, married, and moved to Oklahoma in 1888. (Arizona Historical Society, 96-2119.)

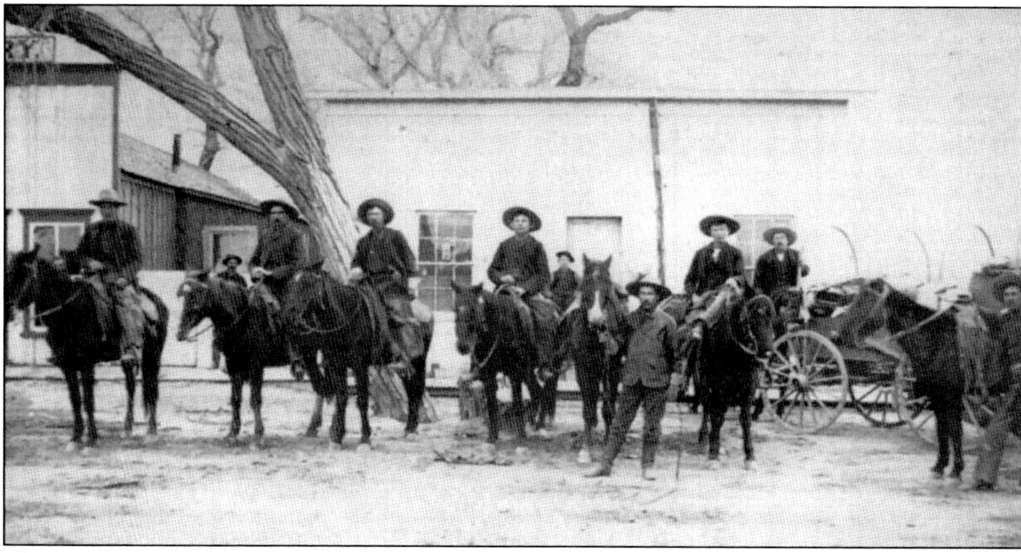

This image was likely taken the same day as that of Frank Ames and Ed Rogers in 1888 (see page 31). Hash Knife cowboys in the foreground are Rogers, John Taylor, Charlie Baldridge, Jim Burdette, Ames, Don McDonald, Bill Smith, and a man identified as either Tom Smith or Tom Beach. Both photographs may have been taken for publicity purposes; at least one of them is credited to photographer J.C. Burge of Flagstaff.

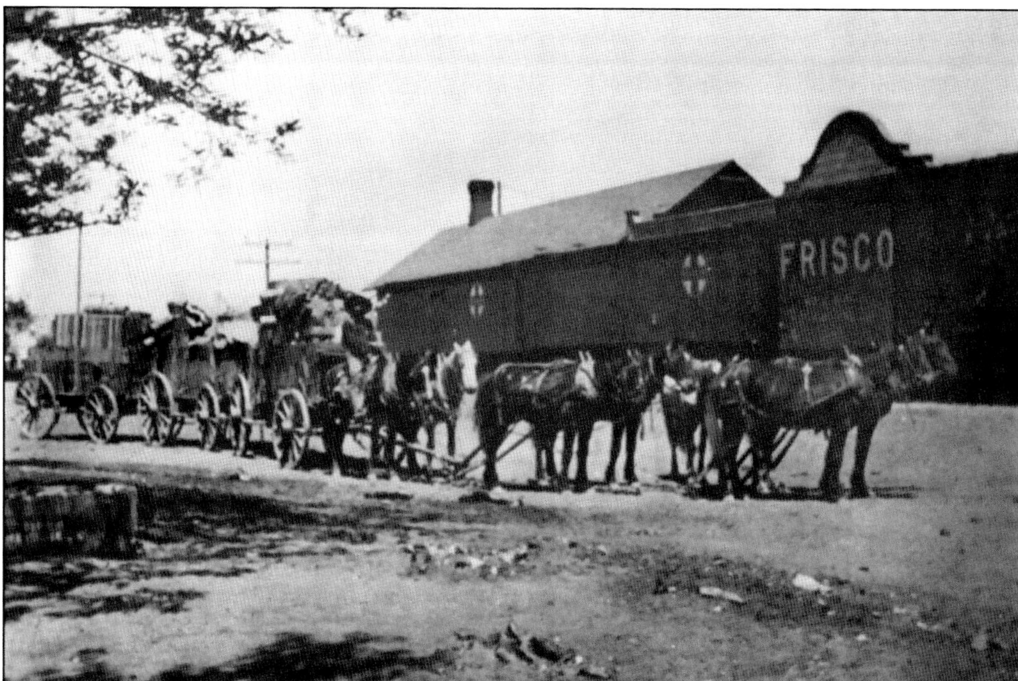

By 1892, the Atlantic & Pacific Railroad depot had been rebuilt at Holbrook and the town was back in full swing as a busy transportation center. Pack trains such as the one pictured here hauled wool and other goods to and from the station. The rail stop was also used to haul sheep and thousands of Hash Knife cattle. Passenger service was available, too. (Arizona Historical Society, 96-2111.)

Three

An Unsavory Reputation

No history of the Hash Knife is complete without inclusion of the brand's notorious outlaw characters and their deeds. Unfortunately, however, a number of writers have glamorized the brand's infamy to the extent that its "history" has become the stuff of Hollywood fodder.

Admittedly, the Hash Knife did experience some rough beginnings upon arriving in Arizona. The cowboys of Texas and Montana found themselves in a strange new world of high desert climates, Native Americans, staunch Mormon settlers, and a lot of hot, unforgiving territory between towns and camps. Ranchers resented being thrown off land they had used but which now belonged to the Aztec Land and Cattle Company. There was no fencing; by accident or design, both sides made dire mistakes in claiming the wrong land or cattle. Enemies were made fast. The notorious Pleasant Valley War was the result of such misunderstandings.

The conditions were most trying for those few cowboys who were hoping to hide their notorious pasts once they got to the new range. Saloons at Horsehead Crossing and Holbrook provided the only break from an otherwise monotonous cowboy life. The combination of cowboys and alcohol on a night livened up an otherwise complacent railroad town. In those early days, Hash Knife boys were credited with galloping "through the town with their guns blazing" and shooting holes "through the kerosene lamps at dance halls" while residents cowered in their homes. Still, the scene is hard to picture given that Holbrook in 1884 only spanned about one city block.

As Holbrook grew, rustling, hangings, and shootouts did become more commonplace. Some of the incidents—but not all—involved Hash Knife cowboys. Saloon skirmishes at Holbrook and nearby Canyon Diablo, the Pleasant Valley War, and other incidents eventually added up to give the brand a bad name. By 1898, stories of "that Hash Knife outlaw outfit" were circulating far and wide. Never mind that the Aztec was battling drought, feed shortages, and record winters while trying to raise cattle. The more colorful tales were what journalists and reporters would later love capitalizing upon.

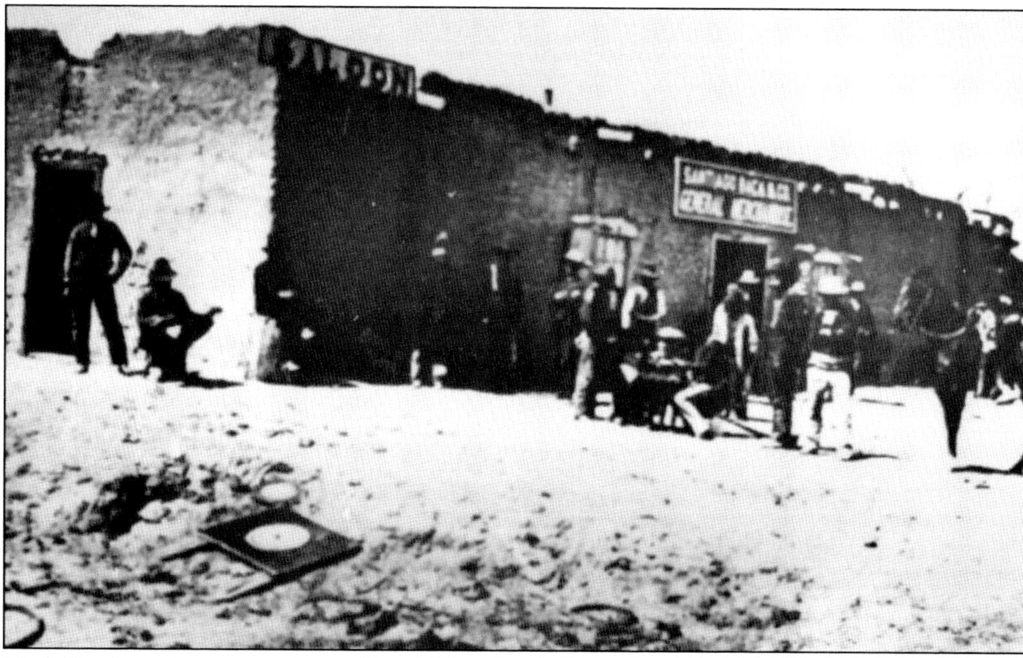

Hash Knife cowboys spent time at Baca's Horsehead Crossing saloon, which had been built in the late 1870s. The sign to the right reads "Santiago Baca & Co. General Merchandise." The saloon was still standing when this image was captured in 1888, and it was later alternately known as the Pioneer Saloon. (Navajo County Historical Society.)

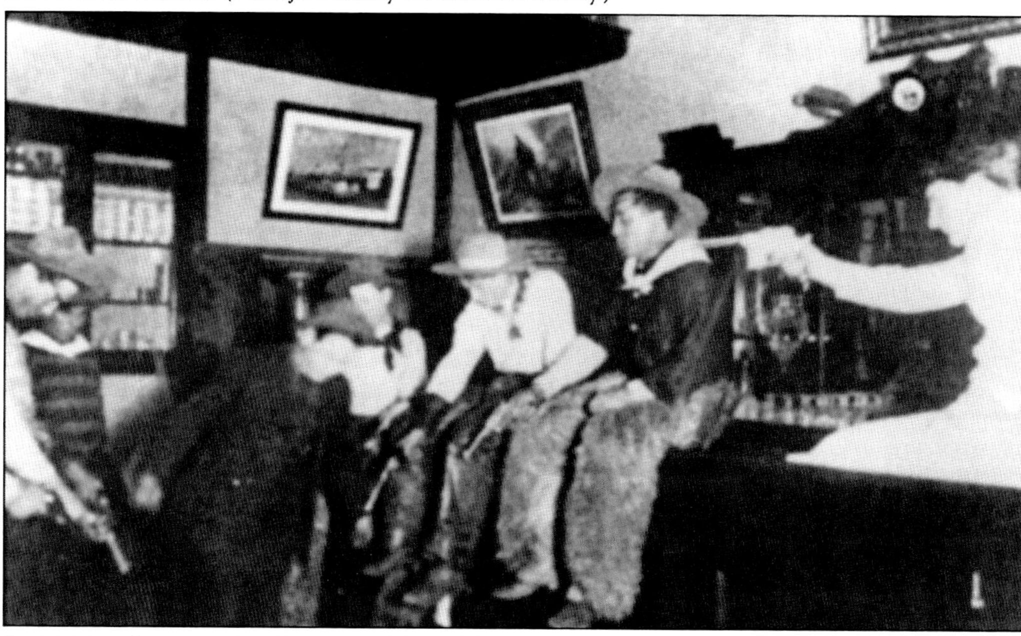

By M. Terrill owned the Cottage, Holbrook's best-known saloon in the heart of town, in 1886. Throughout time, the bar was owned by several people and was also known by many other names. The tavern earned its nickname, the "Bucket of Blood," following a bloody gunfight in its early years. Hash Knife cowboys and roughnecks favored drinking at the Cottage. (Navajo County Historical Society.)

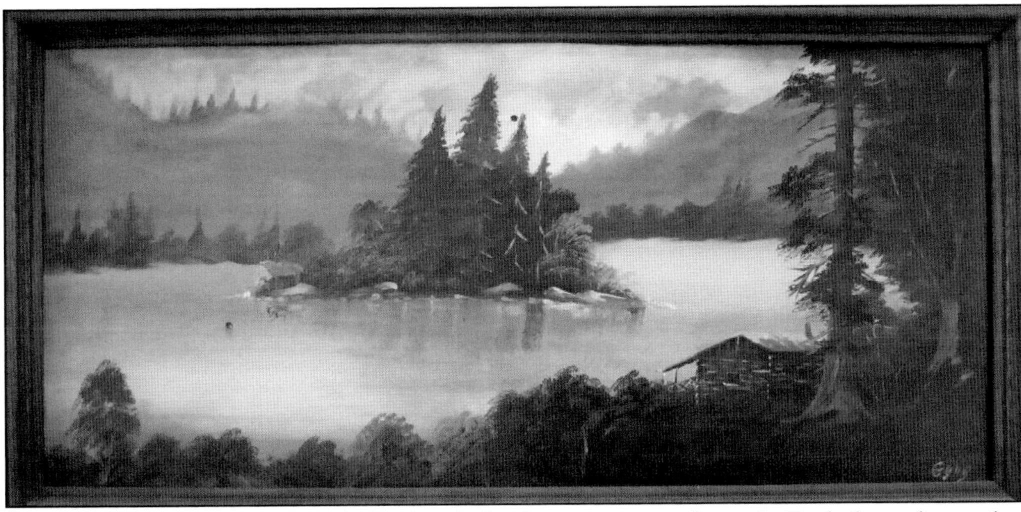

Memorabilia from the Bucket of Blood includes this painting with two bullet holes—the result of poor target practice. The holes are visible at the bottom left and the top center. After the saloon closed, the painting hung in the Holbrook Hotel for several years before being given to barbershop owner Louis Turley. Later, Turley donated the painting to the Navajo County Historical Society, where it is on display today.

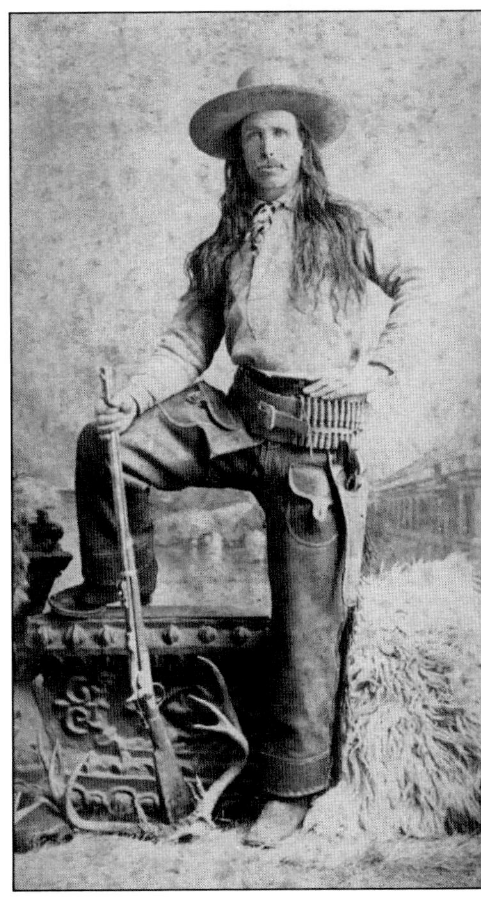

Cowboy and crack shot Commodore Perry Owens worked for ranchers James Houck and A.E. Hennings before being elected sheriff of Apache County in 1886. His territory included Holbrook, where, it was hoped, Owens would help clean up the town. The new sheriff set about arresting drunks and serving 14 warrants left by his predecessor. Unfortunately, Owens ultimately caused more problems than he solved. (Navajo County Historical Society.)

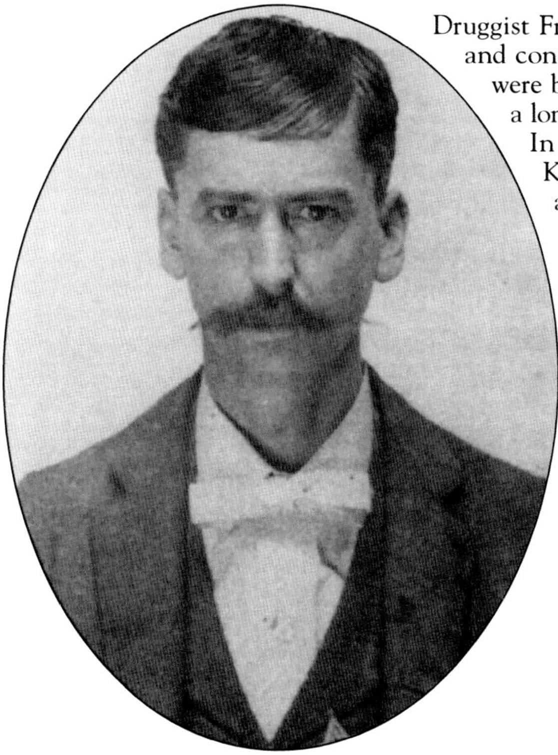

Druggist Frank Wattron alternately acted as deputy and constable for Sheriff Perry Owens. Both men were blatantly aware of the Pleasant Valley War, a longtime range war raging south of Holbrook. In 1887, rancher Hamp Blevins and Hash Knife cowboys Bob Gillespie, John Paine, and Tom Tucker had a shootout with the Tewksburys as part of that war. Blevins and Paine were killed, and Tucker and Gillespie were wounded.

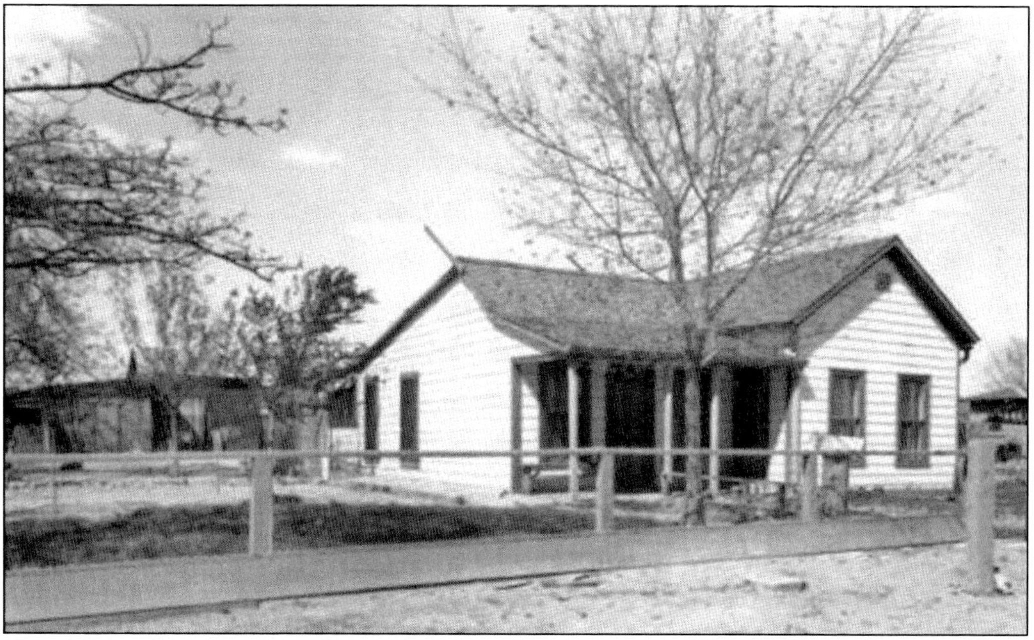

Shortly after the Blevins-Tewskbury shootout, Sheriff Owens served a warrant in Holbrook on Andy Cooper of the Blevins clan. Meeting resistance, Owens killed Cooper, Mose Roberts, and teenager Sam Blevins at what is now called the Blevins House. Holbrook pioneer Julia Scorse recalled in 1981 that this house (pictured in 1947) was actually built after the old bullet-ridden cottage was torn down. (Navajo County Historical Society.)

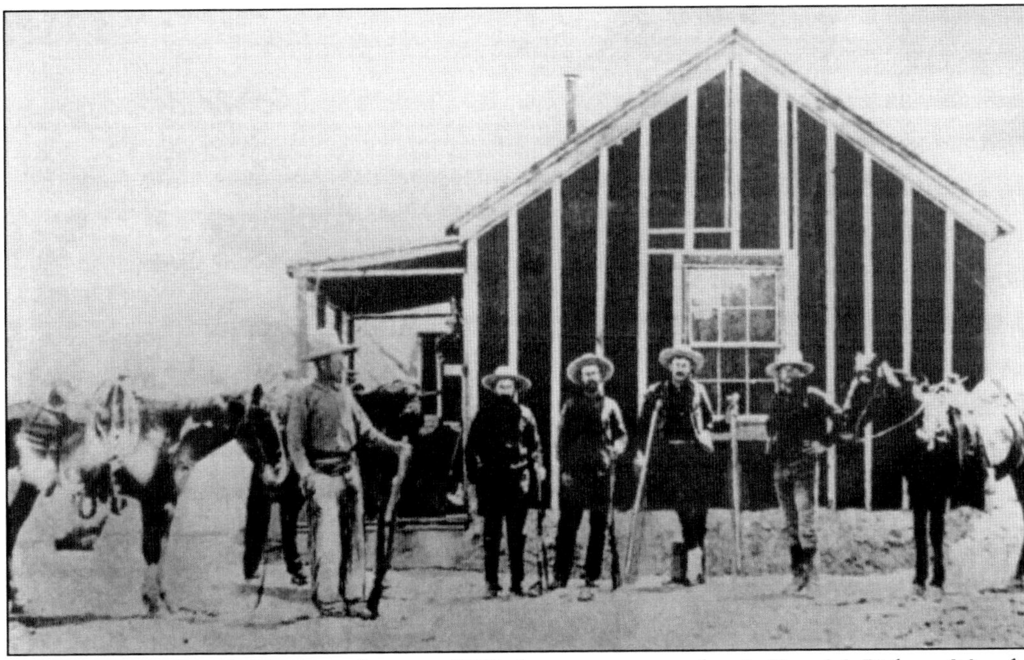

In this image of Hash Knife cowboys in 1887, the man on crutches is Tom M. Pickett. Months earlier, he was shot in the ankle during a fray at Holbrook. Pickett worked for the brand for over 10 years. Later, another Tom Pickett—known to be associated with Billy the Kid—also migrated to Arizona but never worked for the brand. The two are often confused by historians.

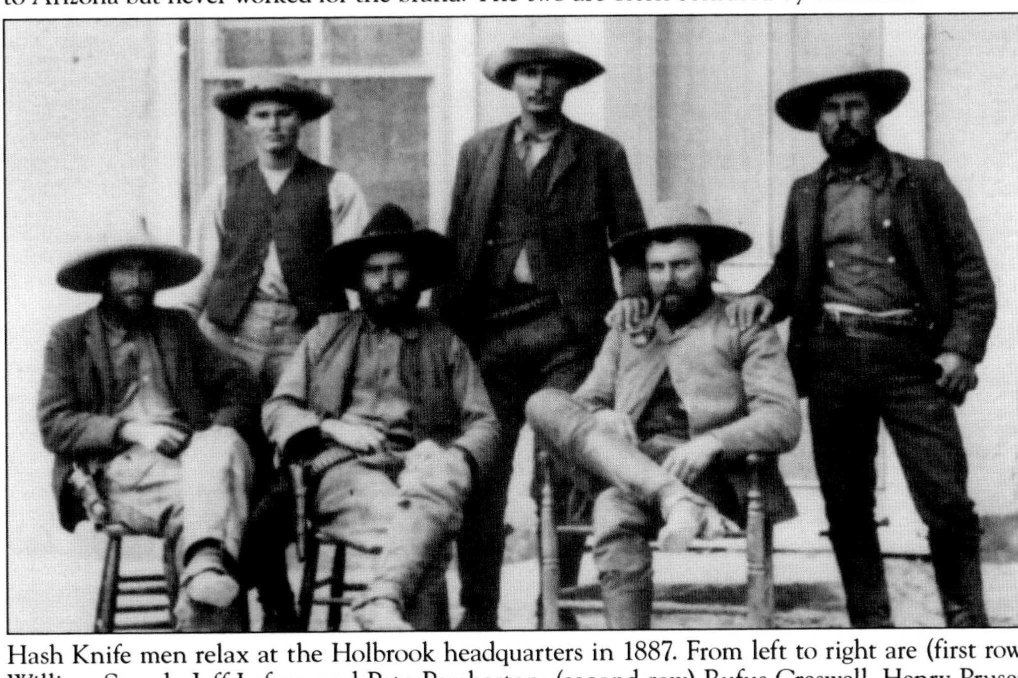

Hash Knife men relax at the Holbrook headquarters in 1887. From left to right are (first row) William Swank, Jeff Lefors, and Pete Pemberton; (second row) Rufus Creswell, Henry Pruser, and Charlie Moss. Lefors's brother was Montana range manager William Lefors. Pemberton came with the brand from Texas. Pruser was killed in a fight near Wilford in 1894. (Old Trails Museum, Winslow, Arizona.)

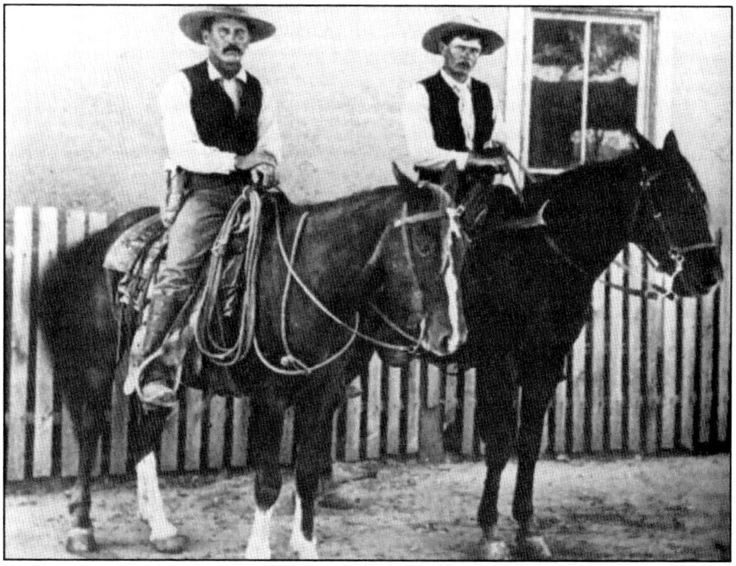

Two unidentified men pose in front of the Holbrook headquarters around 1887. By then, so many cowboys came and went at the Hash Knife that it was difficult to keep them straight. Several used nicknames, a common practice amongst cowboys, but a few were aliases too. Some of the more colorful monikers included Windy Bob, Long Bill, Rimmy Jim, Loco Tom, Ace of Diamonds, and Poker Bill.

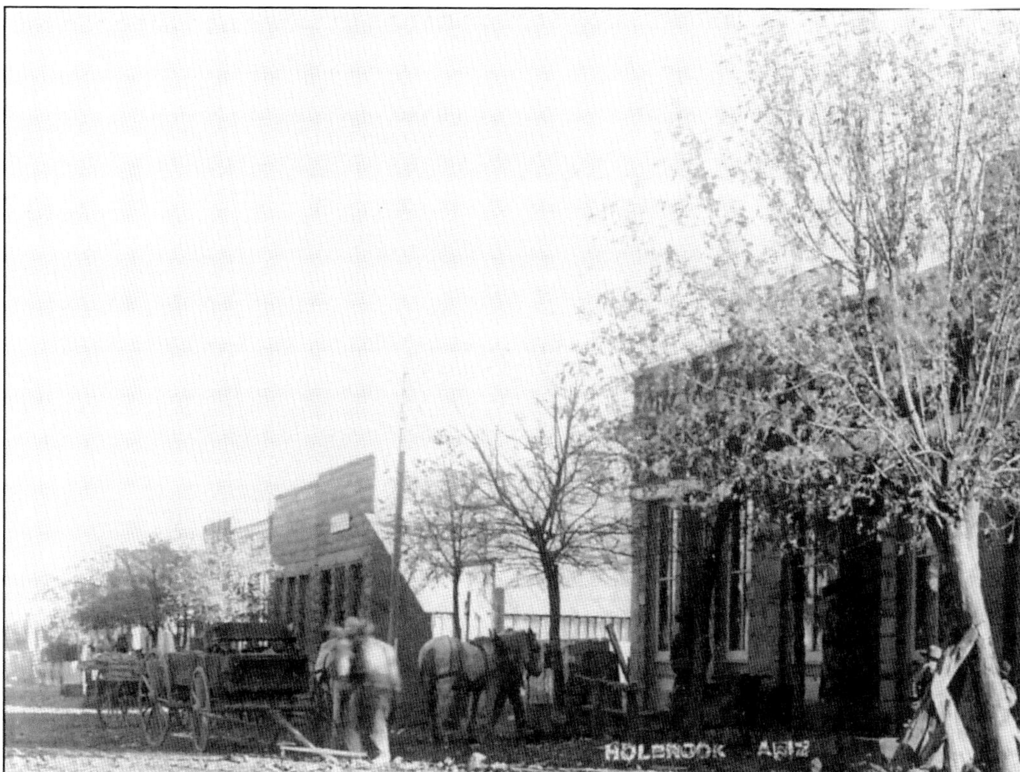

Downtown Holbrook was looking quite civilized by 1888. Several businesses flourished along Central Avenue. Of particular interest to Hash Knife cowboys were A & B Schuster's, Adamson & Burbage general merchandise, A.M. Boyer's Apache House, the Cottage, F.M. Zuck's Holbrook House, F.X. Schreiner's Bakery, Leser Rehfeld's barbershop, Little and LaForce's Saloon, and Henry Scorse's Pioneer Saloon which had been relocated from Horsehead Crossing. (Navajo County Historical Society.)

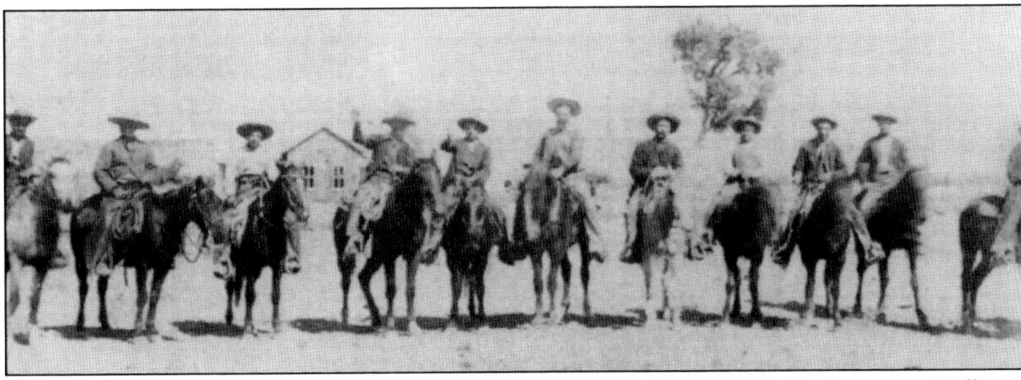

Longtime cowboy Mose Tate is sixth from the left in this image of Hash Knife men at Holbrook in 1888. A veteran of such well-known outfits as that of Charles Goodnight and the Waters Cattle Company, Tate joined the Aztec Land and Cattle Company in about 1886 with stellar references. His years of experience likely helped to quell at least some of the outlawry among his fellow cowboys.

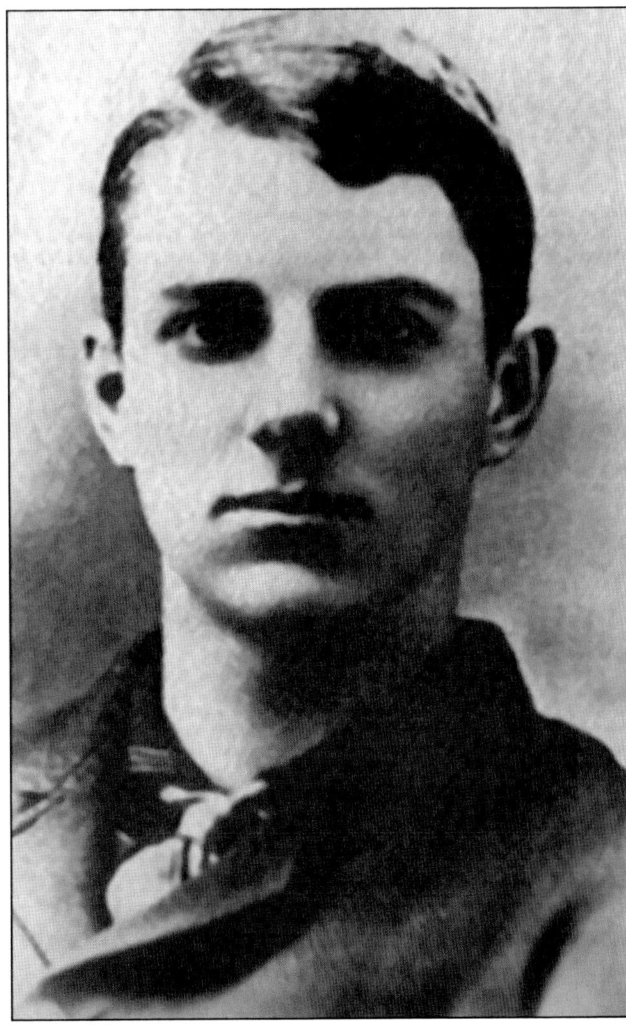

Rancher James Stott was friends with Hash Knife cowboys who frequently stopped by his Circle Dot Ranch near Pleasant Valley. In 1888, a posse led by James Houck rode up to Stott's ranch with a "fictitious" warrant for horse stealing. Stott and Hash Knife boys James Scott and Jeff "Billy" Wilson were arrested. Houck later claimed that masked men took charge of the prisoners and forced the posse to move on.

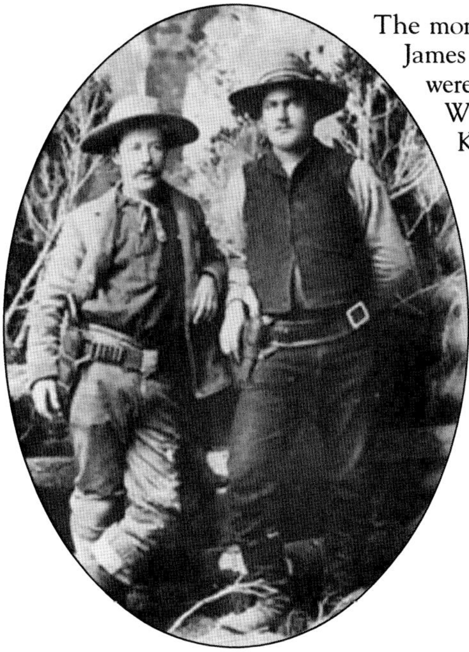

The morning after James Houck's claim that outlaws took James Stott, Jeff Wilson, and James Scott, the three men were found hanging from a tree near the Circle Dot Ranch. Wilson is pictured here on the left, with fellow Hash Knife cowboy Tom Tucker. The boys' killers were never caught. The powerful Houck, whom everybody knew had a grudge against James Scott, was never formally questioned about the incident.

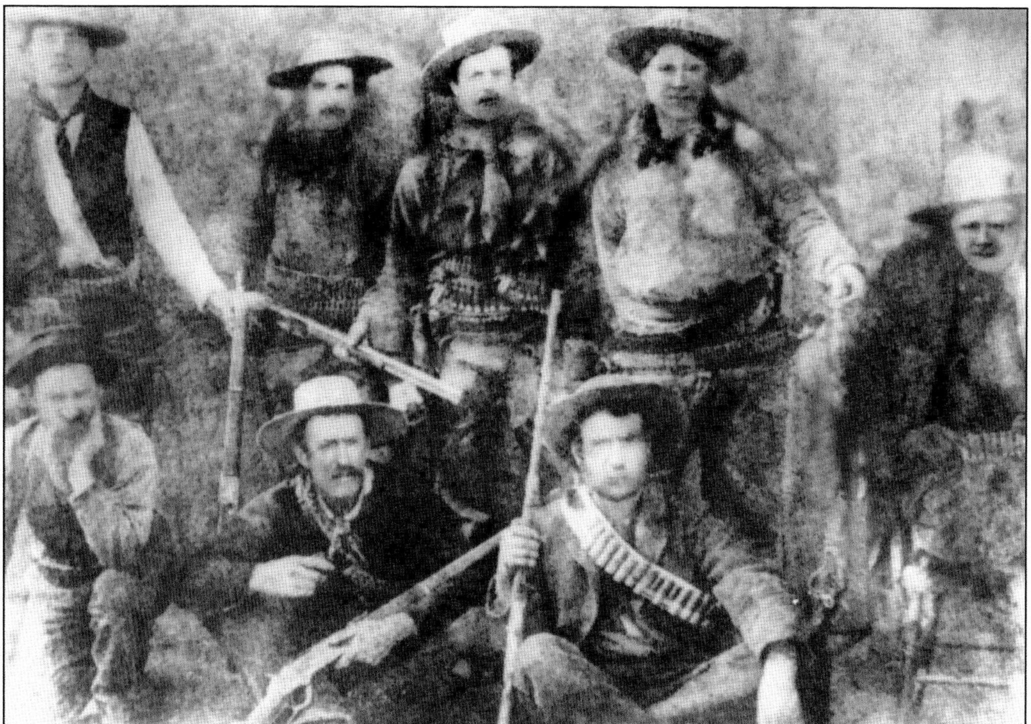

Hash Knife boys were not the only rough bunch around Holbrook. This quarrelsome-looking group is identified as, from left to right, (first row) convicted forger Sol Barth; St. George Creaghe, who beat Commodore Perry Owens in election for sheriff in 1888; and John Lee; (second row) Carr Blassingame, of Pleasant Valley War fame; Tom Perez, who was also defeated by Creaghe; Commodore Perry Owens; Dan Dubois; and "Dolby." (Navajo County Historical Society.)

Ranchers often fought with Mexican sheep herders over land. Once, Dick Greer and his cowboys were invited to a fiesta at St. Johns with the promise of cheap cattle for sale. The party turned out to be an ambush for, from left to right, Joseph Woods, "Nigger Jeff," Nat Greer, and Hi Hatch. The men survived; Albert Potter joined the group for this photograph. (Navajo County Historical Society.)

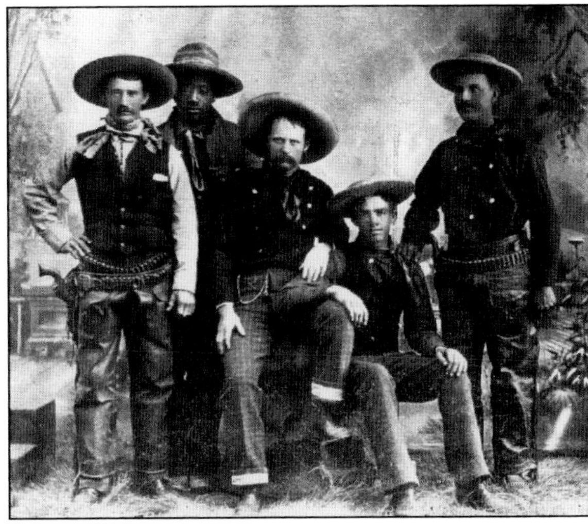

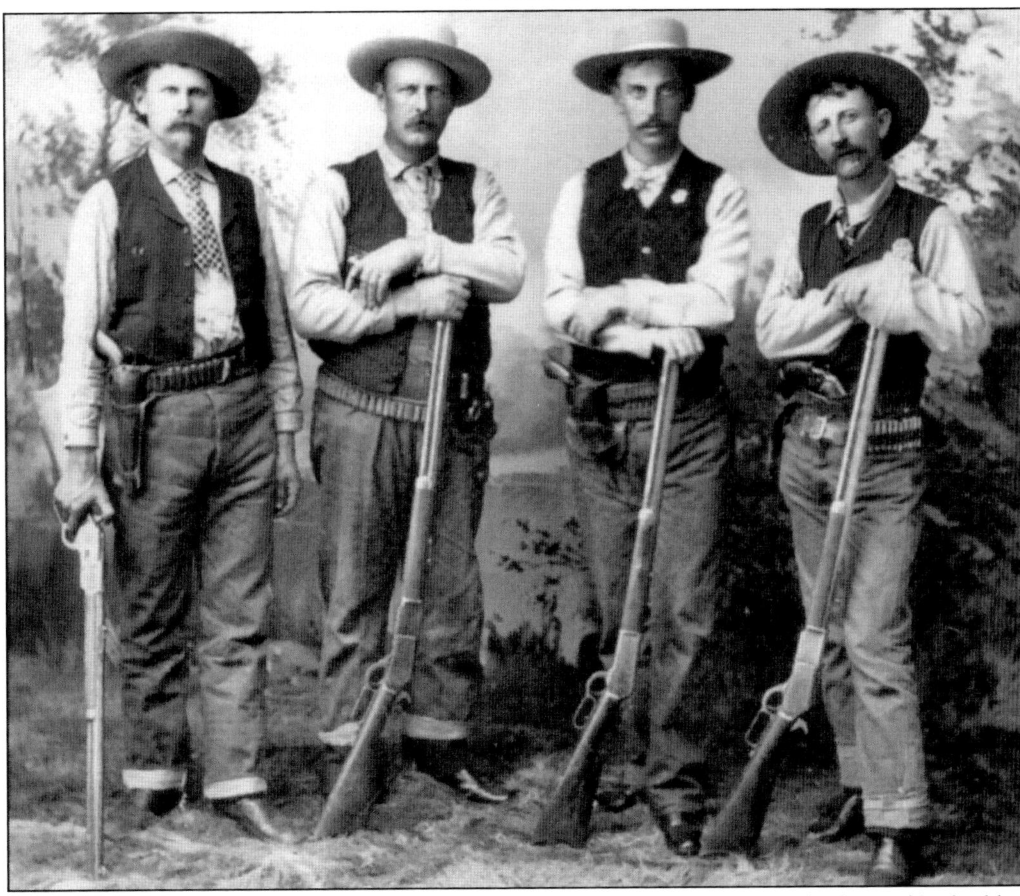

In 1889, Hash Knife cowboys Dan Harvick, Jack Smith, William Sterin, and John Halford robbed the Atlantic & Pacific train at Canyon Diablo. A posse consisting of, from left to right, Carl Holton, Jim Black, William "Bucky" O'Neill, and Ed St. Clair caught the robbers near the Utah border. Despite an attempted escape by Smith, all four men were tried at Prescott and sentenced to the Territorial Prison at Yuma.

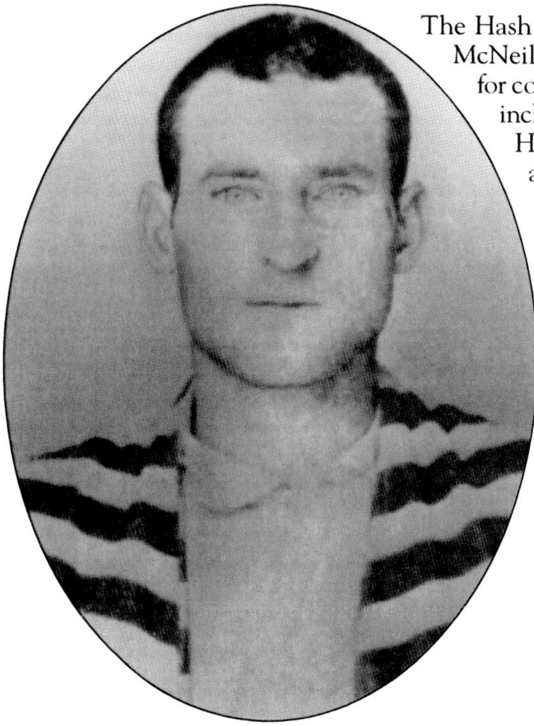

The Hash Knife's most colorful outlaw was W.R. "Red" McNeil, the "Rhyming Robber." McNeil was known for commemorating his robberies by leaving a poem, including one to the Schuster brothers of Holbrook. He also left Commodore Perry Owens some verse after the sheriff unknowingly shared a bedroll with the outlaw while pursuing him. McNeil was finally caught in 1889 and served time in Utah. (Utah State Prison.)

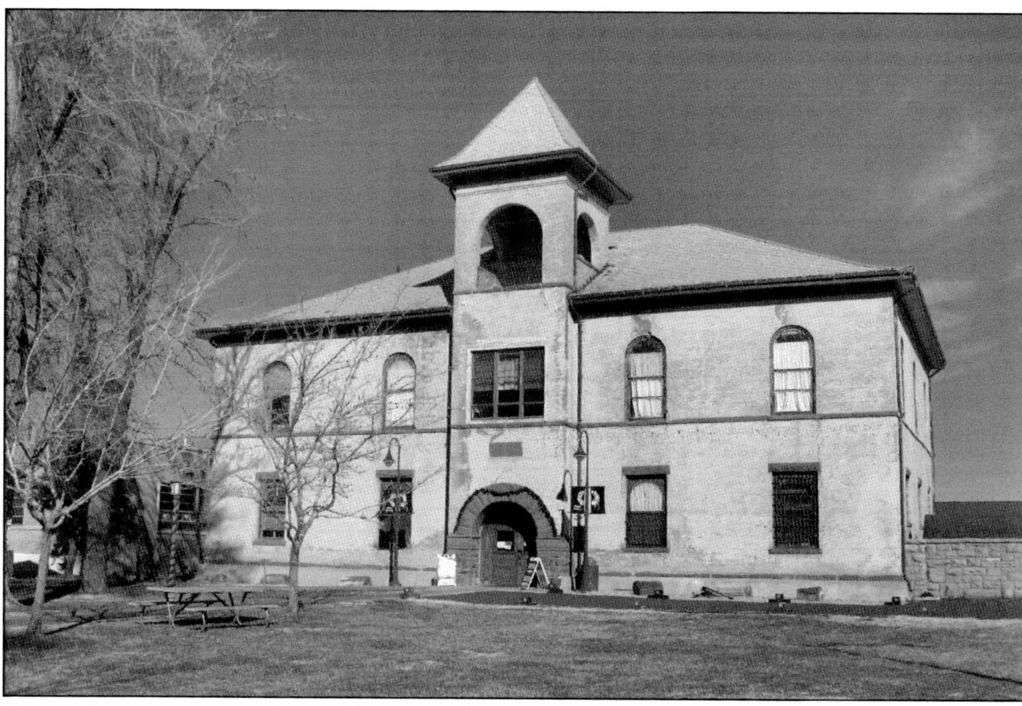

Navajo County was formed in 1895. In 1898, the Navajo County Courthouse was built in Holbrook. The town was growing, and the new building was located several blocks from the old downtown. The imposing structure brought a sense of law and order to town. Numerous outlaws were tried here, and one hanging took place in the courtyard.

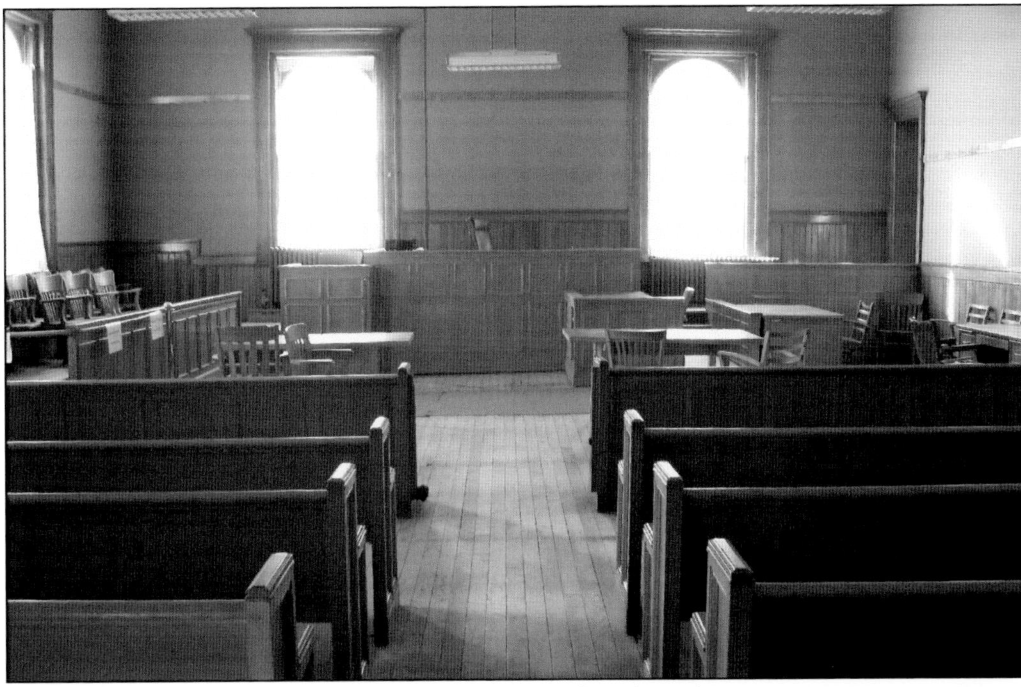

Lawbreakers who were tried at the new courthouse found an elegant, no-nonsense courtroom that was vastly different than anything they had seen before in frontier Holbrook. City officials were likely reinforced and even emboldened by the new surroundings.

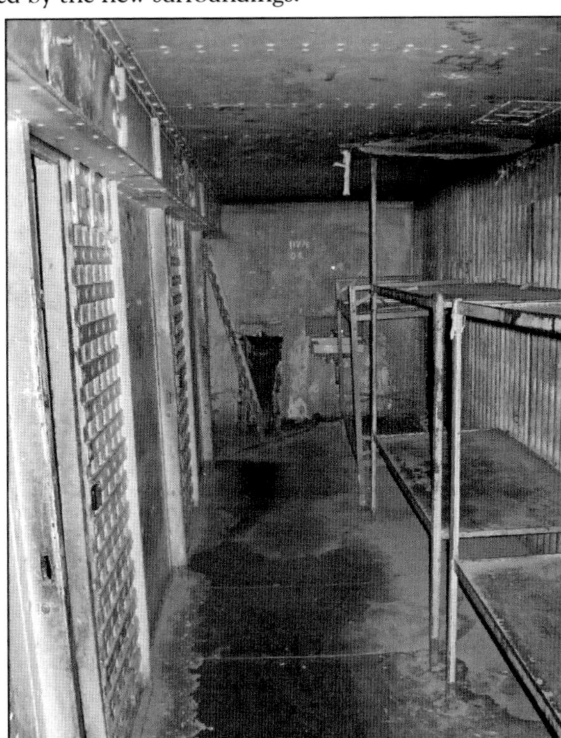

Prisoners of the jail in the basement of the courthouse were met with stark metal and cement. The cells were manufactured in St. Louis, Missouri. They were mostly small, dark places with metal bunks and nary a window. There was little hope for escape, since Sheriff Frank Wattron's office was kept there as well. The courthouse was used until 1976 and became the Navajo County Historical Society in 1981.

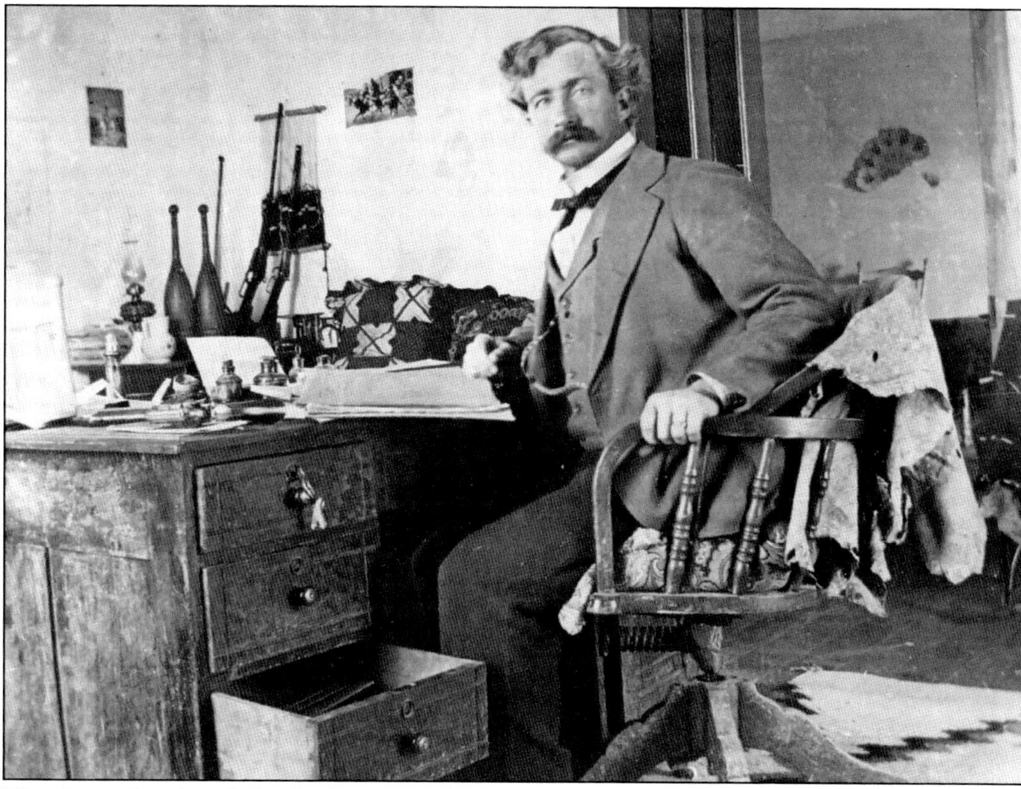

The Aztec Land and Cattle Company furthered cleanup efforts by hiring Burton T. "Cap" Mossman, formerly of Texas and New Mexico, in 1898. Mossman later claimed that his first day of work included capturing three rustlers who stole some Hash Knife cattle. He also fired Hash Knife range manager Bob Morris and 52 other cowboys. In doing so, he restored an amazing amount of order to the Hash Knife.

Holbrook, Arizona,......................1899.

Mr. ....

You are hereby cordially invited to attend the hanging of one

George Smiley, Murderer.

His soul will be swung into eternity on Dec. 8, 1899, at 2 o'clock, p. m., sharp.

Latest improved methods in the art of scientific strangulation will be employed and everything possible will be done to make the proceedings cheerful and the execution a success.

F. J. WATTRON,

Sheriff of Navajo County.

In 1899, Sheriff Frank Wattron overstepped his boundaries by sending out this tongue-in-cheek invitation to the hanging of George Smiley. Such invitations were required by the Arizona penal code, but many were offended by Wattron's crude joke. Presiding judge Richard Sloan chastised Wattron for his "perverted sense of humor." The sheriff dutifully produced a second, more composed invitation. Smiley was the only man to be legally hanged in Holbrook.

A Holbrook cowboy, likely from the Hash Knife, harmlessly entertains a dog around 1900. Folks were starting to forget the Cimarron Kid, a young renegade befriended by Hash Knife cowboys who met a sorry end in Holbrook. Other memories, like the time a wounded Joe Crawford rode 12 miles from the Cottage Saloon to Bert Potter's cow camp, and the day John Taylor was killed at Page's Saloon in Winslow, were fading. People hardly recalled Tom South, the Hash Knife cook who stole some cattle, sold them in Colorado, and opened a saloon, returning to his job when he went broke. By the turn of the 20th century, most of the Hash Knife boys were now good, honest men. "It wasn't a mean bunch," recalled George Hennessey, who later worked for the outfit, "just happy to return trouble."

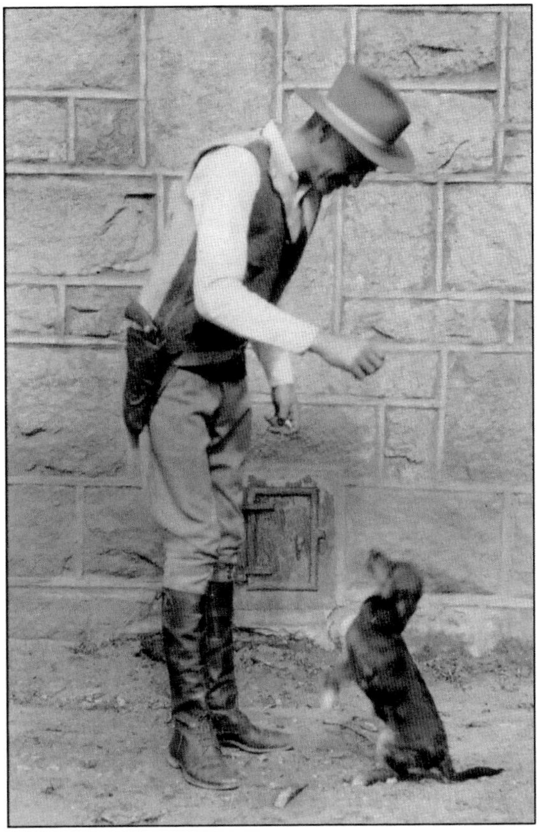

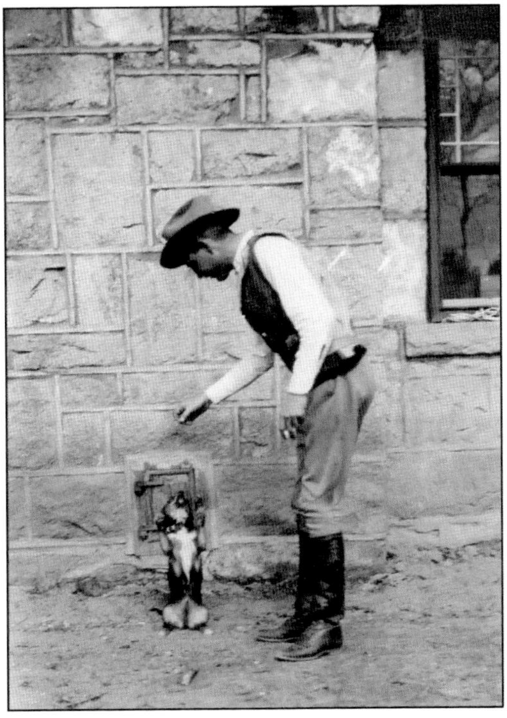

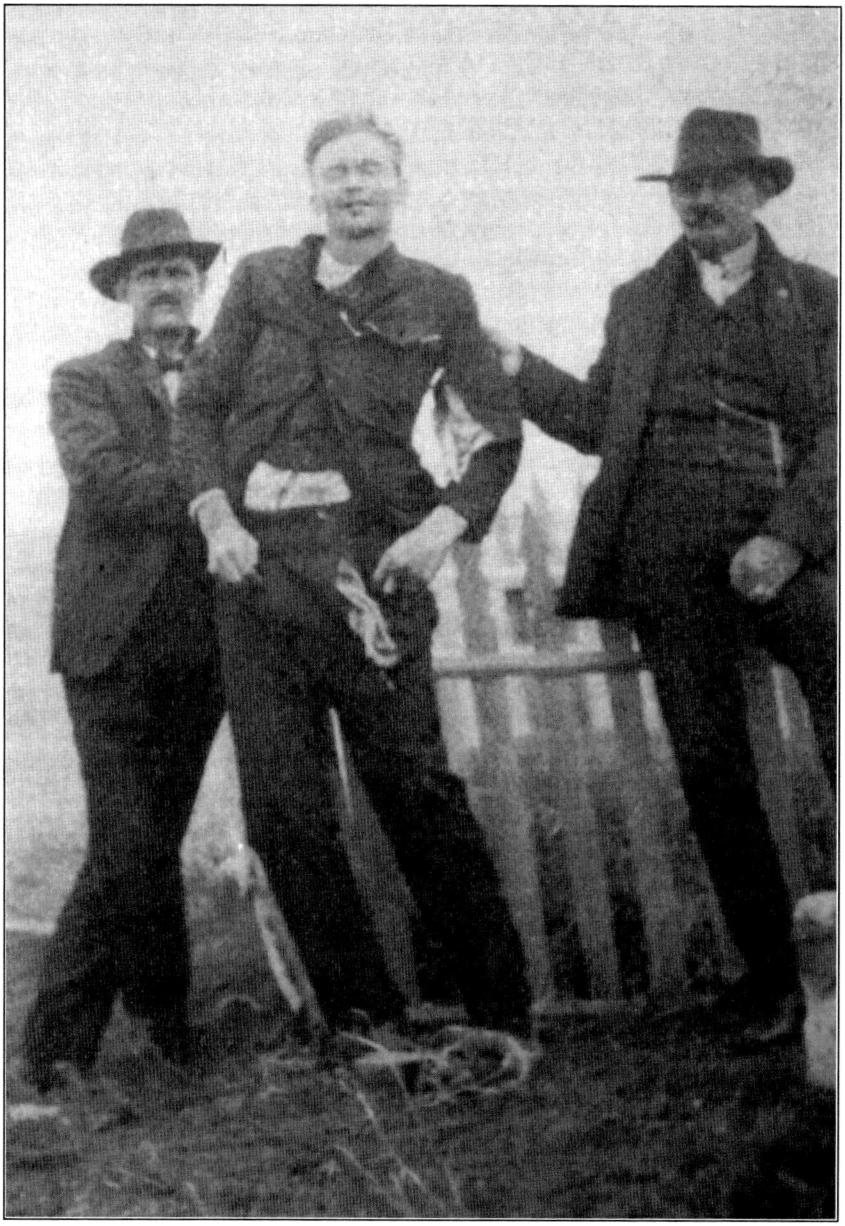

One other notable incident involving the Hash Knife occurred in 1905. Lucien Creswell and Tex Roxy were in the Wigwam Saloon in Winslow when William Smith and John Shaw robbed the place. All were said to be current or former Hash Knife hands, as well as Deputy Sheriff Pete Pemberton, who helped track Smith and Shaw to Canyon Diablo and killed the latter man. The outlaw was buried by the tracks. The following night, more Hash Knife cowboys were drinking at the Wigwam. It was brought up what a shame it was that Shaw never got to have the drink he left on the bar before the robbery. Fifteen men, including Pemberton, duly caught the train to Canyon Diablo and dug up the outlaw. The sight of Shaw's face sobered everyone present. Two men lifted Shaw from his grave, and a final drink of whiskey was poured into his mouth. Witness Jack LeBarron later defended the group's actions, explaining that "it seemed to us that giving him a drink for his last trail was proper."

Four

Frank Wallace and George Hennessey

Benjamin Franklin Wallace was born at Lone Oak, Texas, in 1860. When his father came home from the Civil War in 1865, it was the first time Wallace remembered seeing him. It was also the first time he rode a horse.

By the age of nine, Wallace was unhappy with his home life. He began working odd jobs, including the ranches of his uncles where he learned to break horses. Upon his father's death in 1874, Wallace left Lone Oak. He learned to read and write during his first cattle drive along the Chisholm Trail in 1876. By 1885, he had traveled all around Texas, mostly working for ranches. His employers included Elam Harold, R.A. Hagan, the V-P outfit, Ira Haven, and Tom and Ike Stevens. In 1886, George Brookshire hired him at the Hash Knife outfit near Pecos City. Fellow cowboys included Barney Stiles, "Brush Joe," and Bill Russell.

At election time, Brookshire threatened to fire the cowboys if they did not vote his way. Wallace quit in disgust and took work at Joe Nations' Bar N Cross ranch, herding cattle to New Mexico. During his travels, he met Burt Mossman, who would become his boss at the Hash Knife in Arizona, and also Cora Taylor Forbes, who would become his wife. The couple married in 1888, and the following year Cora gave birth to a son. When Wallace was offered a job with the Waters Cattle Company, the family moved from New Mexico to Winslow, Arizona.

When Waters Cattle Company sold to the Aztec Land and Cattle Company in 1896, Wallace rejoined the Hash Knife. In 1898, the family relocated to the Hash Knife headquarters south of Joseph City. Wallace was promoted to foreman, and in 1899 he hired George William Hennessey. Like Wallace, Hennessey came from Texas and had also left home at the age of 14 to become a cowboy. Little did the two men know they were destined not only to be lifelong friends but also family.

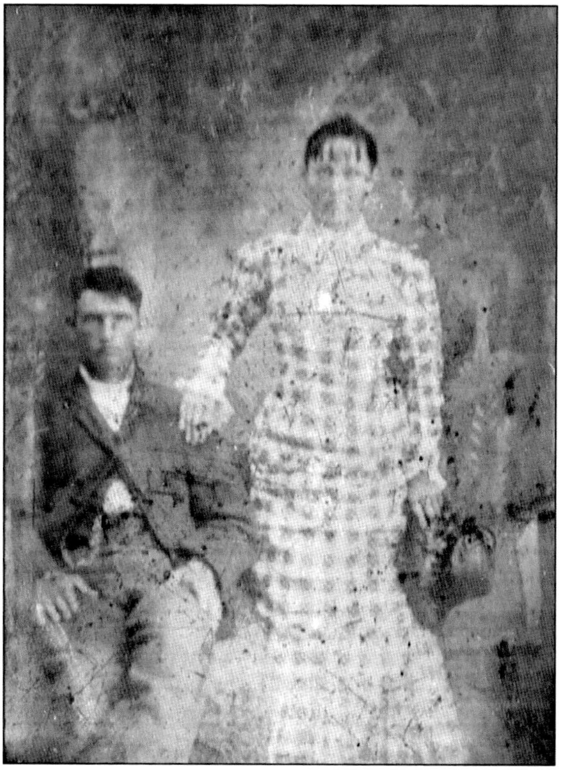

Frank Wallace's early years were spent in a typical dysfunctional household of the frontier. He was the youngest of four children. His mother died while he was a baby, and his father's second wife lived only a year. A third wife bore two more children. The man in this tintype from the family album is probably Wallace's half-brother Jack; the woman remains unidentified.

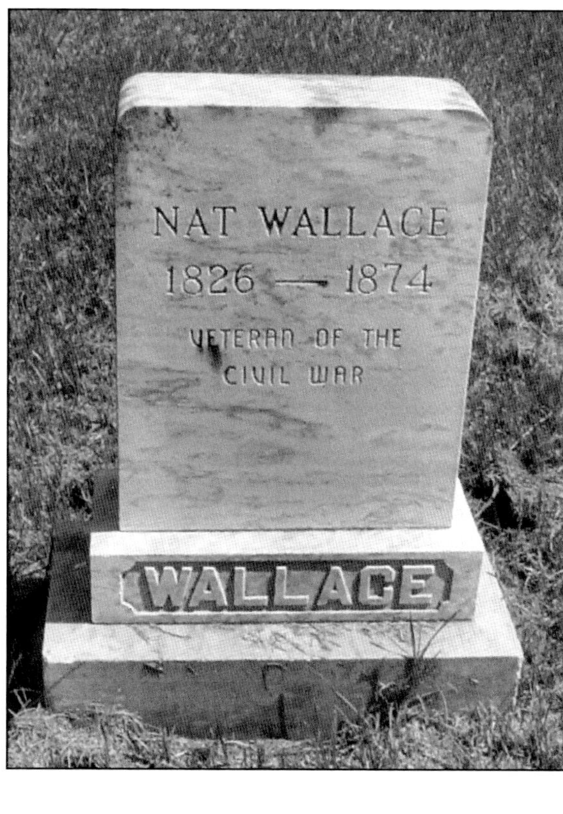

Wallace's father, Nat, was shot to death in 1874 while trying to break up a fight. Frank referred to himself as "orphaned" after that time and struck out on his own. He visited his family in Lone Oak at least twice, once in 1876 and again in 1885. Following the latter visit, he went to Pecos City and was hired to work for the Hash Knife.

In 1877, Frank was at "Lowno [*sic*]," Texas, with his cousin Jim Wallace and his uncle Isham Wallace, who had founded Lone Oak. Jim got in a knife fight with Frank's employer from the Chisholm Trail, John Sullivan. Frank hit Sullivan in the head with a wagon spring, likely saving Jim's life. This image of Jim (seated) and Frank was taken many years later.

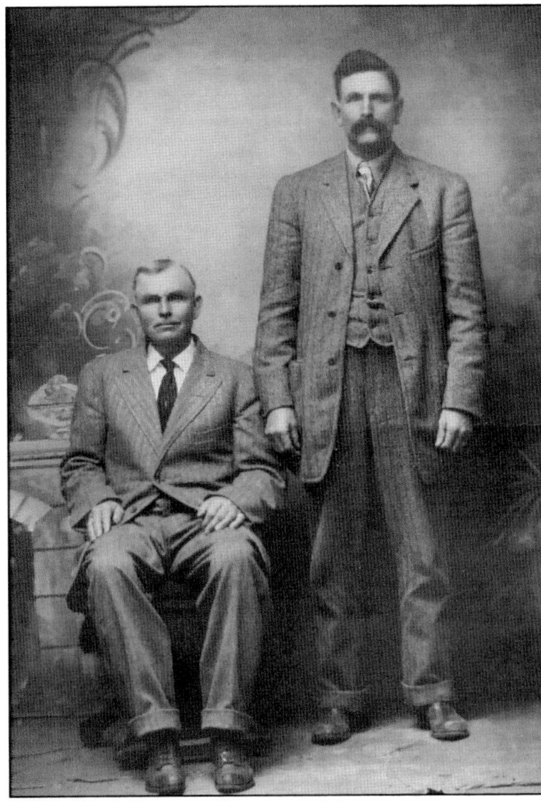

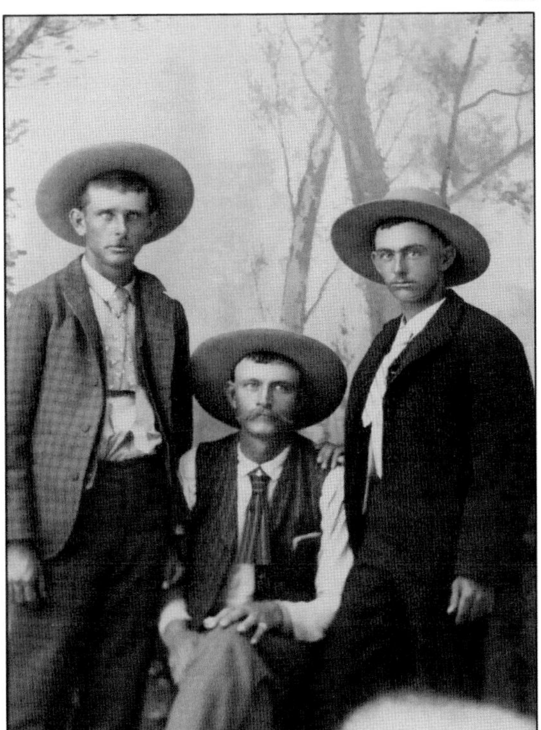

Frank, seated, poses with two unidentified friends at Albuquerque, New Mexico, around 1887–1888. He was probably herding cattle for John Nations. A favored meeting point was El Paso, Texas. In New Mexico, Frank traveled to American Bend, Dona Ana, Fort Selden, Las Cruces, and Mesquite. In 1887, he was living at a place he called Tenuca.

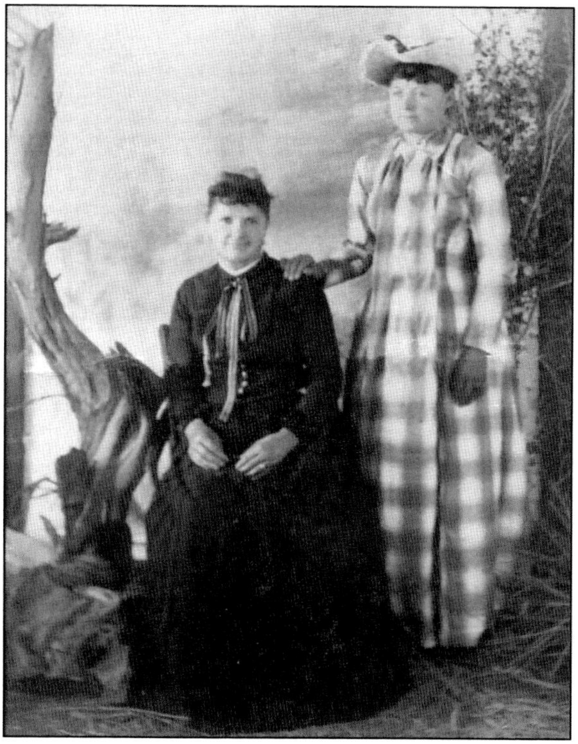

In February 1888, Frank Wallace met Cora Taylor Forbes (pictured on the right with an unidentified woman) near Dona Ana. Forbes was born in Arkansas in 1870 to Emma Taylor and James Monroe Forbes. She was proud to be the great niece of Zachary Taylor, 12th president of the United States on her mother's side, and a distant cousin of James Monroe, fifth president, on her father's side.

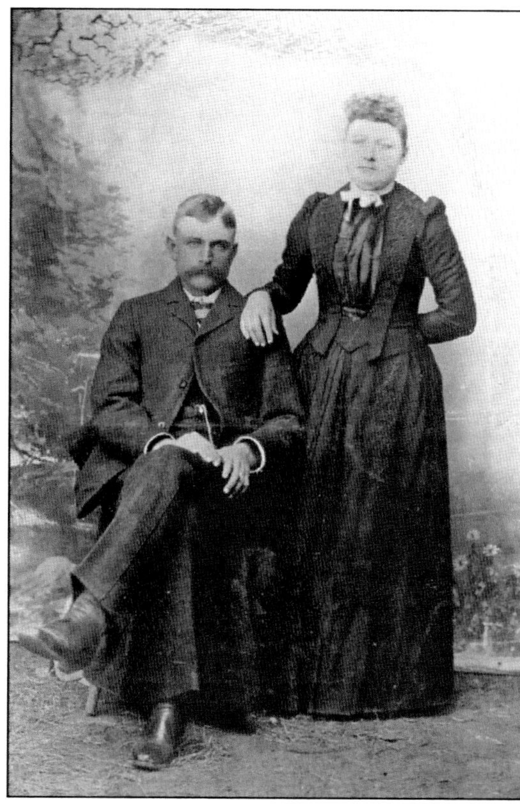

Wallace was taking horses to Mesquite, New Mexico, when he met Forbes. He stayed the night at the Forbes ranch before going on to Mesquite and delivering the horses. He soon returned, marrying Cora at American Bend on February 9, 1888. Frank took more jobs punching cattle, sometimes as manager. The couple lived at Tenuca, Aleman, a place called Agnel, and also Engle for the next few months.

Cora and Frank Wallace's son Emmet was born June 27, 1889, in Rincon, New Mexico. The young family moved to Winslow soon after Emmet was born. This image of Cora, Frank, and Emmet was likely taken a few months after they arrived. Note the adobe bricks of their first home in Winslow.

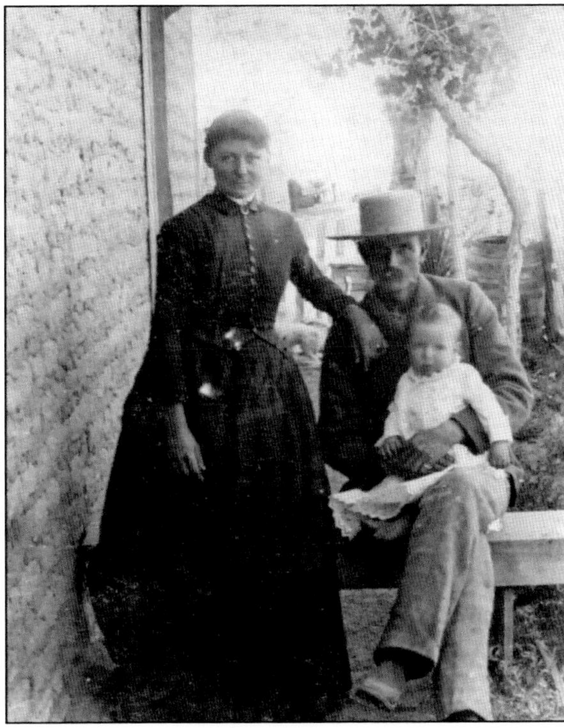

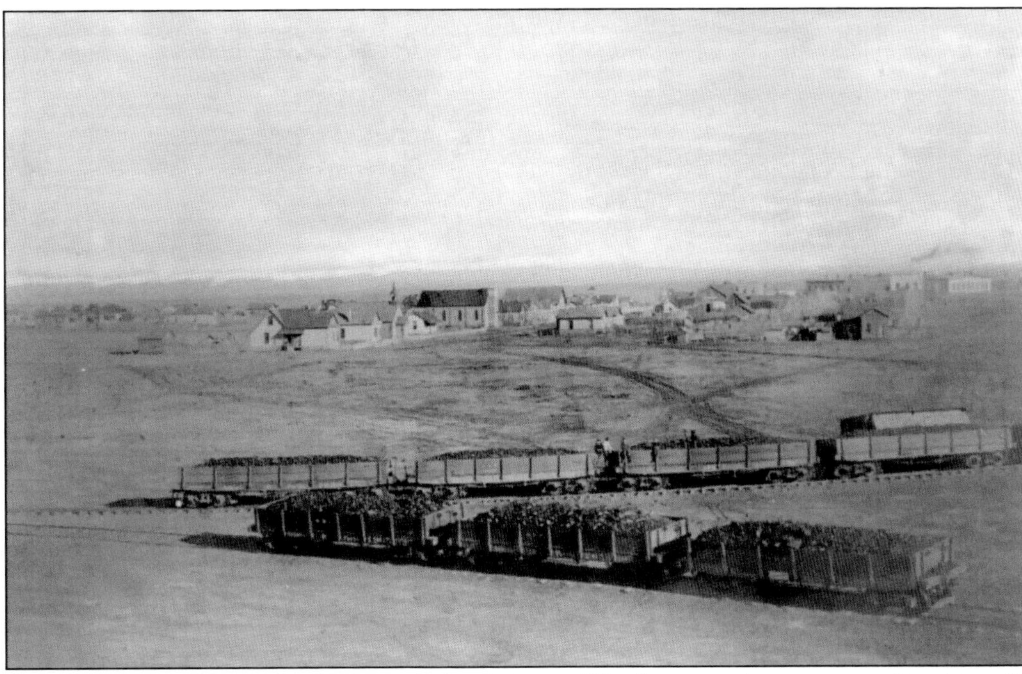

Compared to the barren landscapes of New Mexico, Winslow must have appeared inviting. By the time the Wallaces arrived, Winslow businesses included the Arizona Central Hotel with its restaurant and saloon, a blacksmith, a grocery, the Hotel Navajo, a newspaper, the Ohio Restaurant, the Parlor Saloon, the Peoria Restaurant and Saloon, the Reception Saloon, and Richardson's Trading Post.

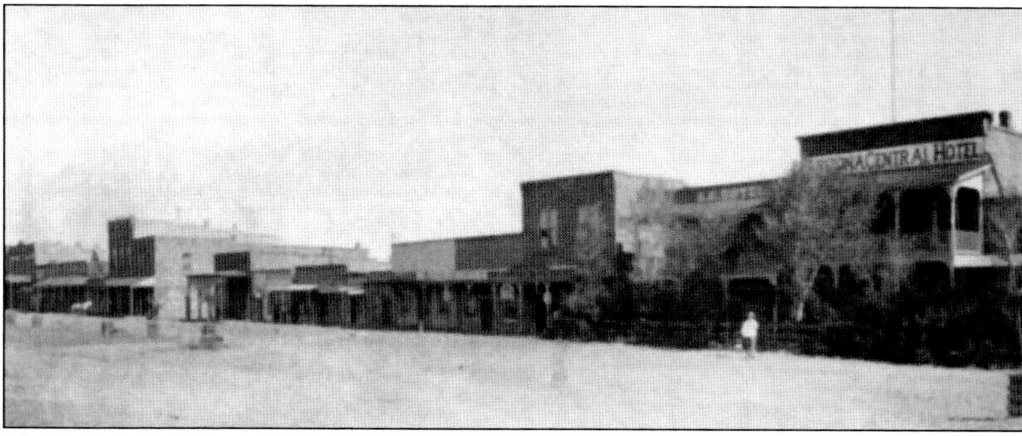

The Waters Cattle Company range ran right next to that of the Aztec Land and Cattle Company. Frank Wallace's new job likely included keeping things peaceful between the cowboys of each company. Although the Waters company headquarters was 40 miles south of Winslow, the Wallaces chose to stay in town. Cora likely appreciated being able to go to downtown Winslow for things when she needed them.

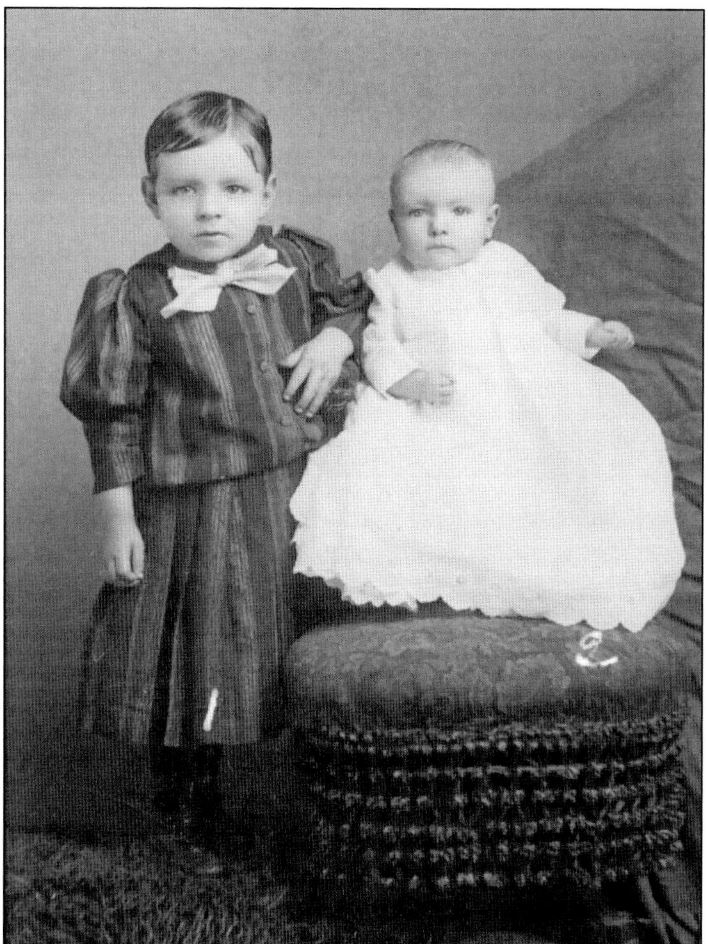

In 1891, Cora gave birth to her second child, Frances. Frank was probably out working on the range when Cora took Emmet (left) and Frances to E.W. Baker's photography studio in Flagstaff or Williams to pose for this image. Frank was running the Waters Cattle Company and making better money, which would have enabled Cora to make the trip by train.

In 1893, the Wallaces purchased two empty lots in Winslow from the Atlantic & Pacific Railroad and built their first home. Two years later a second daughter, Margery, was born. Frank was still working for Waters Cattle Company but also partnered with Johnnie Merritt, who had migrated with the Wallaces to Arizona. The men purchased their own small herd of cattle, which Merritt looked after.

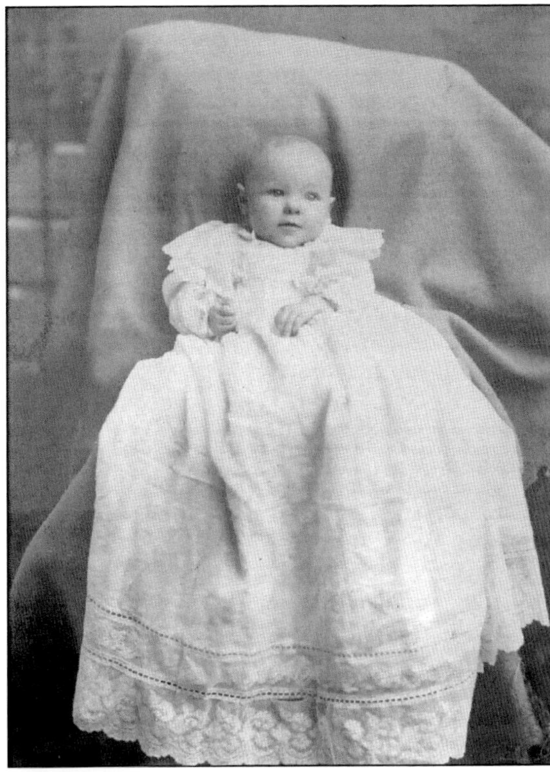

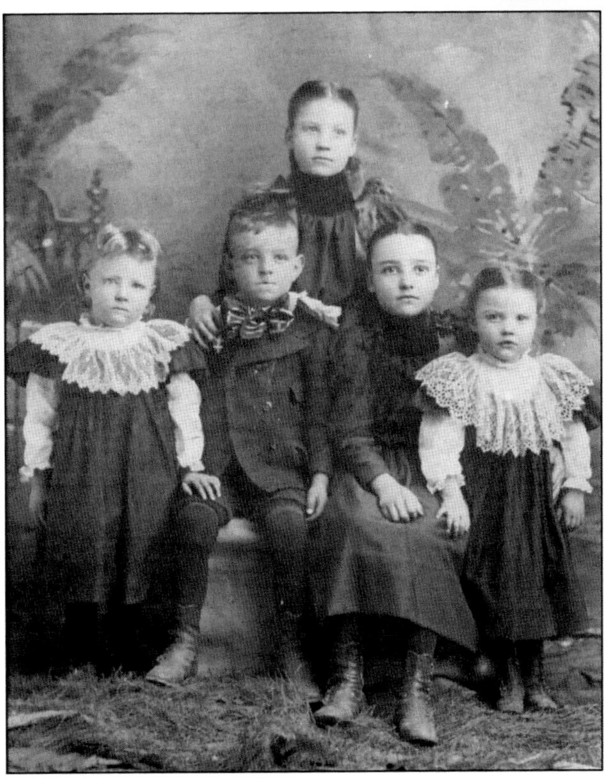

Frank Wallace's daughter Ruth recalled that her mother, Cora, took in some children who had lost their own mother, and that they "were brought up as she raised her own." The girls may have been the Rand children, featured in this c. 1896 image. From left to right are (first row) Frances and Emmet Wallace, and Ruth and Mildred Rand. Nellie Rand stands behind the group.

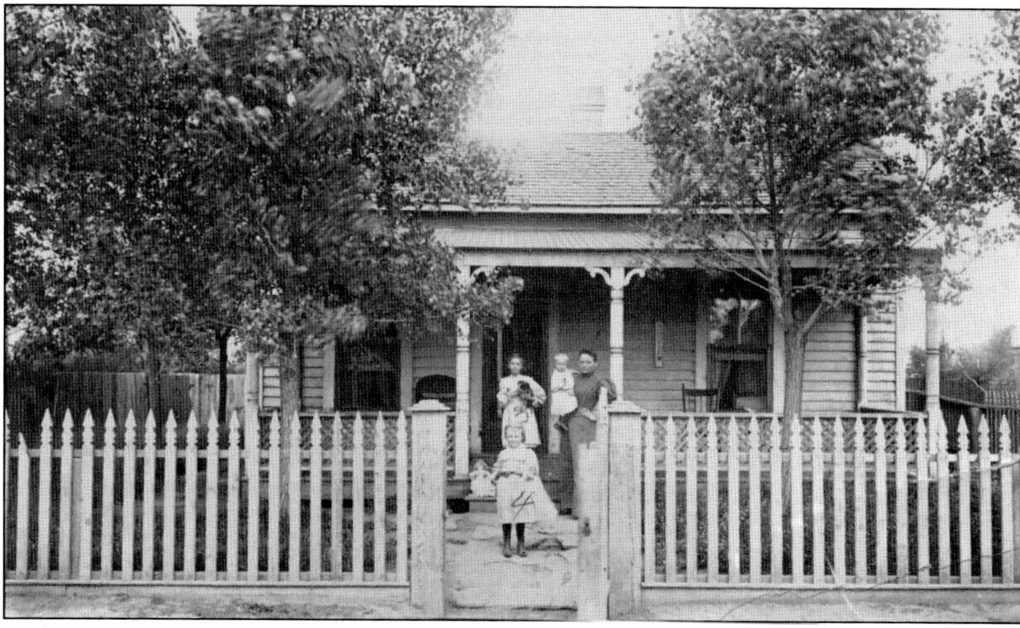

In the spring of 1896, the Waters Cattle Company sold out to the Aztec Land and Cattle Company. Frank Wallace sold his own cattle interests to Johnnie Merritt and went back to work for the Aztec. The Wallaces were living at 317 North Kinsley in Winslow when this c. 1897 photograph was taken. Frances Wallace is in front; behind her are Nellie Rand and Cora Wallace, who is holding daughter Margery.

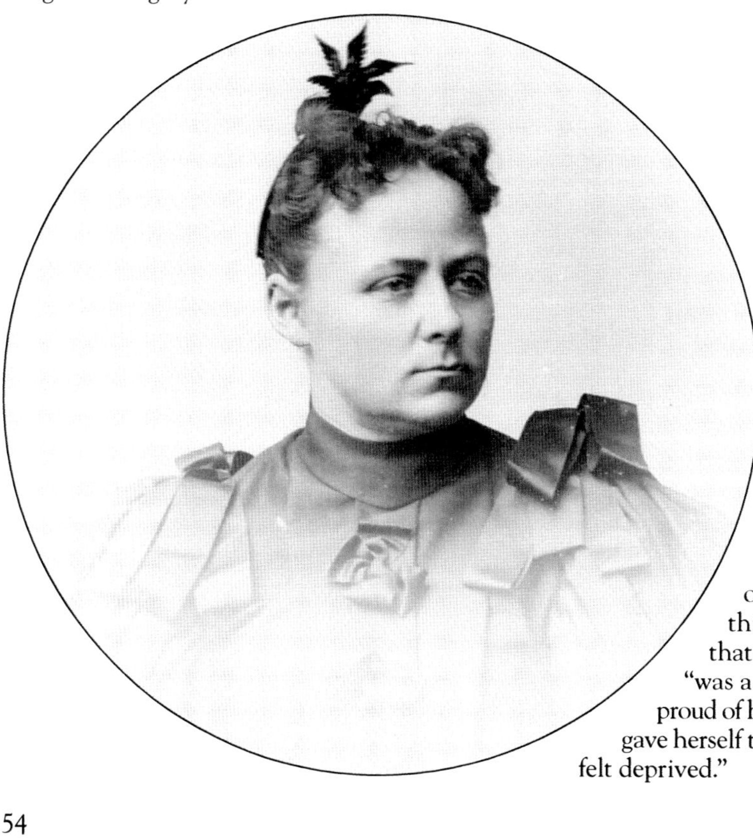

Being the wife of a cattleman was not easy. Cora Wallace's daughter Ruth commented that ranchers "would be gone weeks at a time leaving their wives to take care of the children and keep things going." Ruth also said that her mother, pictured here, "was a cheerful person and very proud of her heritage," also that "she gave herself to all around her. We never felt deprived."

George Hennessey, whom Frank Wallace hired in 1899, was born July 4, 1877, in Mason County, Texas, to Matilda Jane Martin (pictured) and Thomas Hennessey. Matilda was born in Texas, marrying Hennessey in 1874. Their eldest child, Henry Edward, was born in 1875. Matilda would give birth to 10 children in all, but George had left home by the time his two youngest brothers, Ben and James, came along.

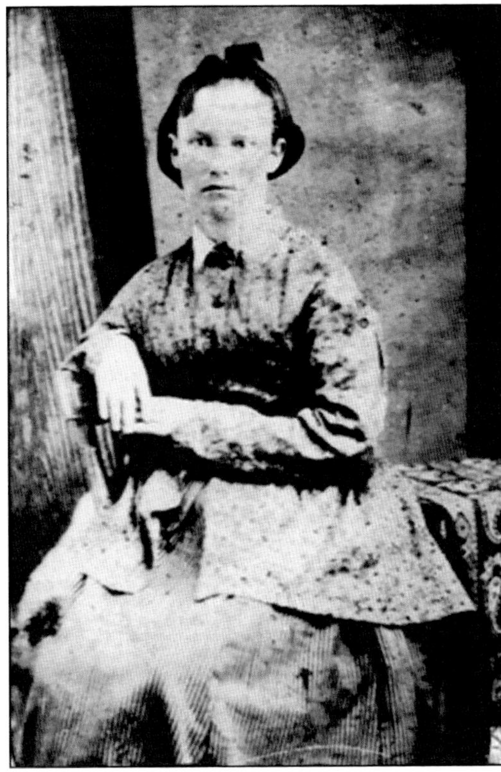

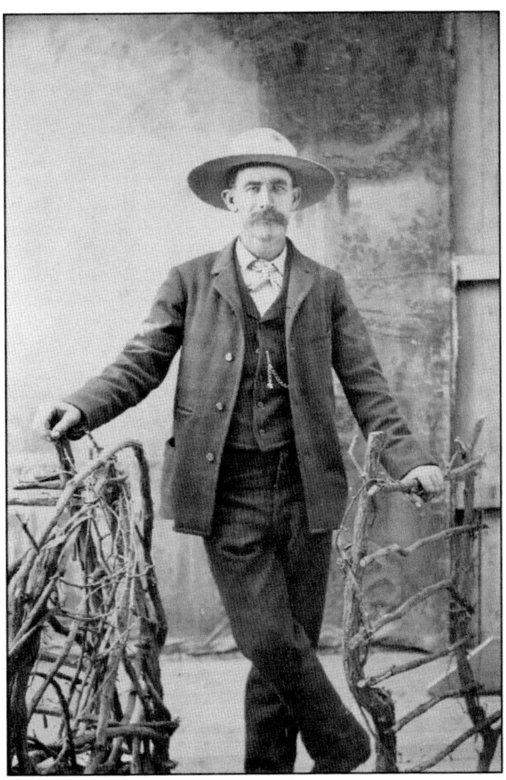

Thomas Hennessey, pictured here, was born in England, immigrated to America in the 1860s, and took up ranching sheep and cattle in Texas during the 1870s. Going by the birthplaces of his children, the family evidently moved around a lot. Between 1877 and 1891, they lived in Mason, Fort Davis, Uvalde County, San Angelo, Bronte, and Turkey Creek.

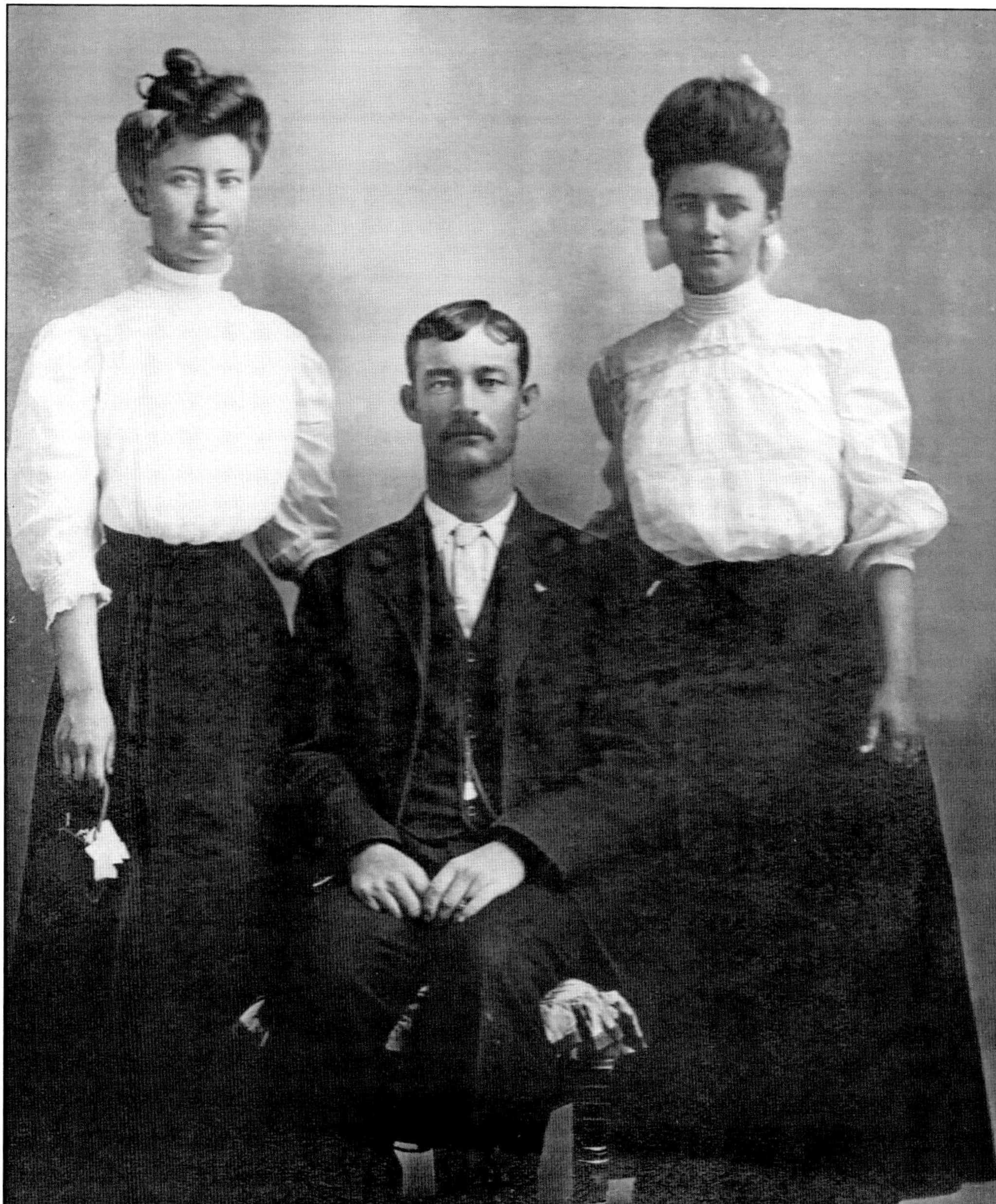

George Hennessey's childhood was not the easiest to bear. He once got in trouble for chopping the toes off of his tight shoes, and his father made him wear them that way all winter. His first job was building fence and wrangling cattle for $12.50 per month. His next job paid $30 per month. Hennessey moved to Arizona in 1898. Shortly before his departure, he took this photograph with his sisters, Nancy and Rose, at San Angelo. Upon his arrival in Arizona, Hennessey first worked for rancher Johnnie Paulsell near Holbrook. He may have known Paulsell or even Frank Wallace, since all three men came from Texas. The similarities between the backgrounds of Hennessey and Wallace are striking: both were born and raised in Texas, both experienced a rough childhood, and both left their family homes at the age of 14. All that is known for sure, however, is that Wallace hired Hennessey to work for the Hash Knife brand in 1899.

Wallace and Hennessey met and worked with hundreds of cowboys during their careers. Some are remembered in history books today, while others have faded into the past and been forgotten. This portrait of Willy Mayes, taken at Harper & Company's studios in Texas, is one of many from the family albums. Mayes must have been important enough to the family to merit keeping his picture.

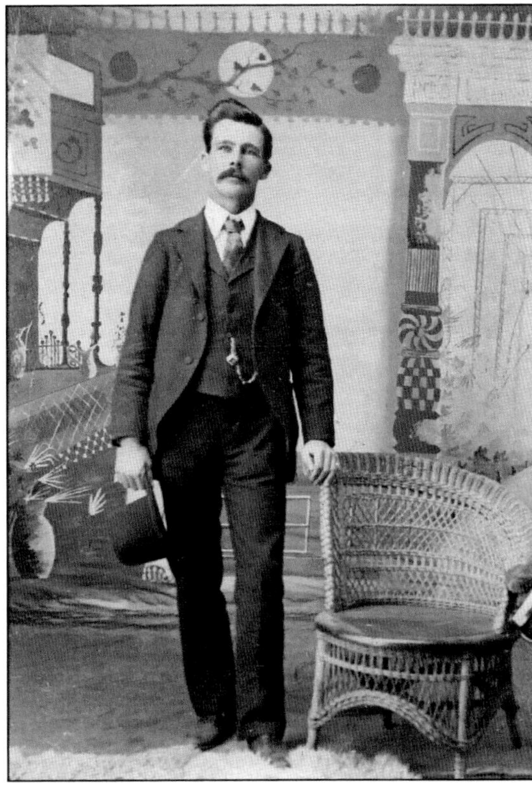

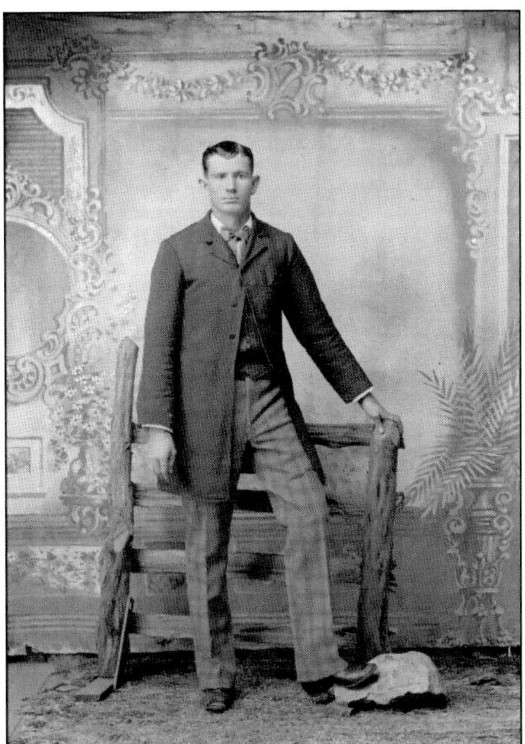

Another family friend, Red Rogers, is even harder to trace, given his colorful but common nickname. This portrait was taken in Ballinger, Texas. Given that Ballinger is very near San Angelo and Bronte where George Hennessey resided, Rogers was most likely a friend of the Hennessey family.

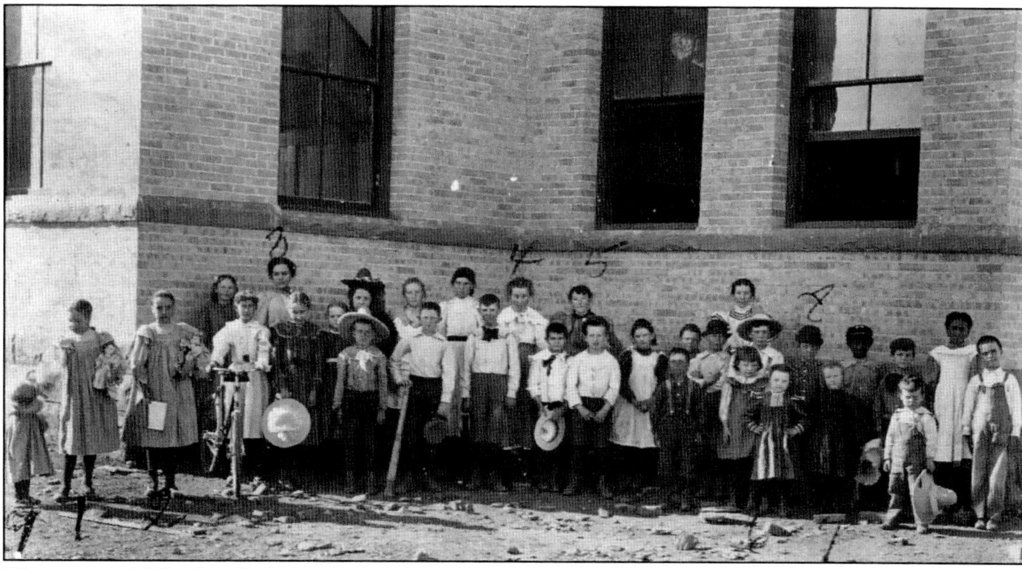

The town of Winslow built a large, rather impressive school in 1897. The older Wallace children attended school there, and some of their classmates were other ranchers' children. Only the children with numbers in this image are identified. They are 1. Nellie Rand, 2. Ruth Rand, 3. Hattie Henderson, 4. Mercy McAlister, 5. Nellie Kelly, 6. Mildred Rand, 7. Frances Wallace, 8. Emmet Wallace, and 9. Margery Wallace.

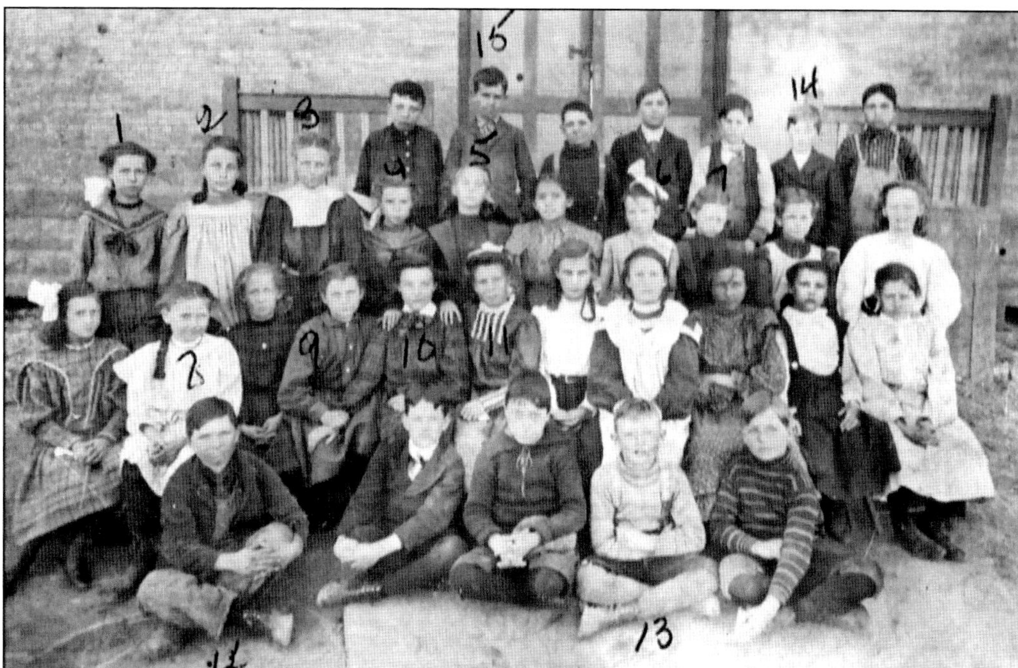

In 1898, Winslow schoolchildren included 1. Lona Norman, 2. Amy Dagg, 3. Frances Wallace, 4. Alma Norman, 5. Jessie Buttner, 6. Martha Downs, 7. Grace Buttner, 8. Cora Creswell, 9. Margaret Morrison, 10. Mildred Rand, 11. Adah Taylor, 12. George Creswell, 13. Elmer Henderson, 14. Bill Wyrick, and 15. Lyn Duncklin. The Creswells were also children of Hash Knife cowboys; Wyrick's father, Charles, later became part owner of the outfit.

Five

Working for the Brand

In 1890, the Aztec Land and Cattle Company's final headquarters was built just south of the Mormon community of St. Joseph. Burt Mossman and the Wallace family moved there in 1898. In turn, Wallace hired George Hennessey at a salary of $35 per month. It was a busy time; George Hennessey remembered that by June, 11,000 cattle had been shipped from the Aztec range due to drought. He also guessed that around 16,000 calves were branded during that year.

Hennessey remembered a typical workday: "We ate breakfast about 4 a.m. and wrangled our horses. Sometimes we'd circle for 20 miles in a day, bringing the cattle in. Generally, we got a little rest in the afternoon. We'd come in at night in time to get the herd together and hold it overnight. Then everybody would stand three hours guard at night."

Unfortunately, the Hash Knife was facing a relentless drought and problems with cattle thieves. No sooner had Frank Wallace apprehended murderer George Smiley in 1899 than Mossman caught a band of three rustlers on the outskirts of the Hash Knife range. The Aztec ultimately decided to sell out, and Mossman began liquidating the cattle. By September 1900, the *Holbrook Argus* commented, "This company has but few cattle left, and will soon be out of business altogether."

Mossman resigned in December, and Wallace continued shipping cattle. By the end of 1901, 40,000 cattle had been sold. In April 1902, the Hash Knife brand was purchased by Hash Knife cowboy Barney Stiles and Babbit Brothers of Flagstaff, who had come to Arizona from Ohio and established the C O Bar Ranch. The men purchased both the brand and the remaining cattle for $3,000.

The Aztec allowed Wallace to continue working as caretaker of the headquarters ranch in exchange for free board, plus hay for his cattle. Another daughter, Ann, was born in 1902, and in 1903 Wallace sold his house at Winslow. At Christmas, Frances Wallace received a beautiful autograph album. The first person to sign it was George Hennessey.

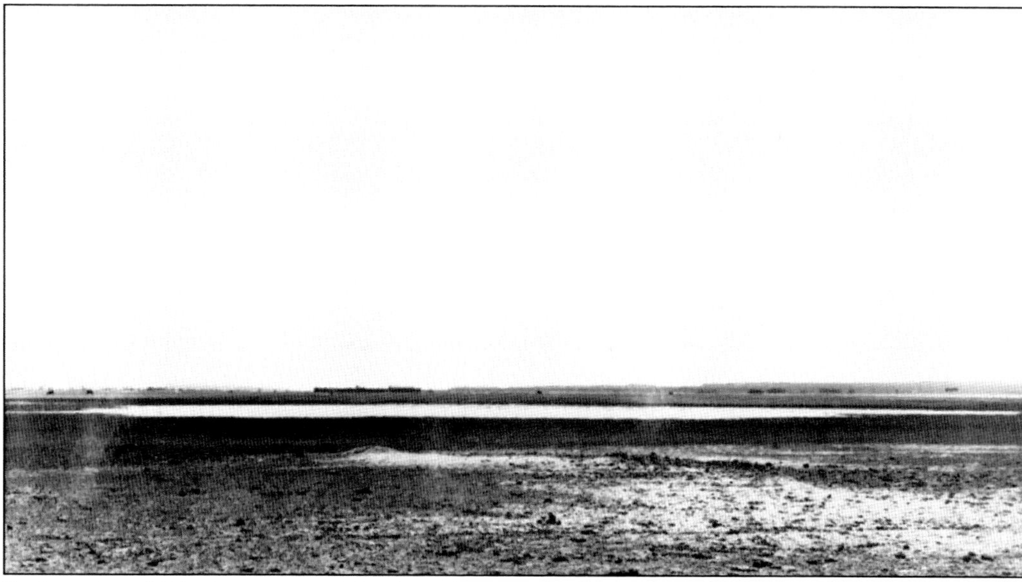

St. Joseph and Obed were two of the four Mormon settlements established on the Little Colorado River. Obed and its nearby lake, pictured here, were abandoned by the time the Aztec Land and Cattle Company built their fourth headquarters there. The outfit may have used some existing buildings they found at Obed, including a stone corral. (Navajo County Historical Society.)

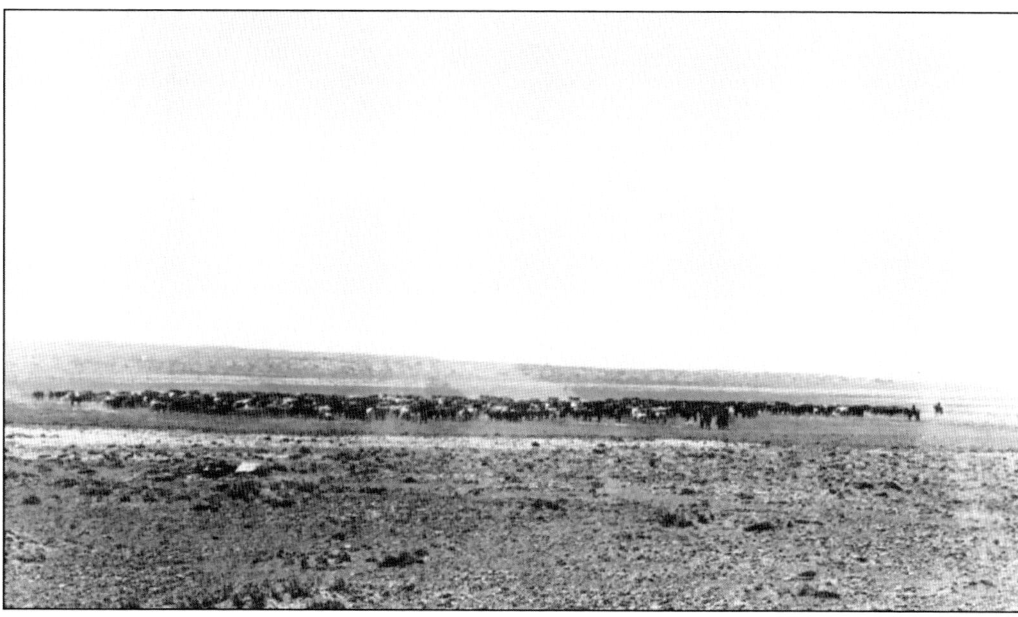

When the Hash Knife cowboys arrived at Obed Meadow, they found sheep grazing there. The situation immediately caused an age-old concern that there would not be adequate range for both types of livestock. Sheepherders and cattlemen traditionally did not get along, but Aztec manager Henry Warren worked with both sides to keep the peace. (Navajo County Historical Society.)

The headquarters at Obed were believed to have been constructed in 1890, based on this drawing identified as Camp Kinsley. Henry and Edward Kinsley tried to assign the moniker to the headquarters but it never stuck. Henry Warren is credited with designing the adobe brick building, described by Burt Mossman as "a good place, big rooms." Rooms on the bottom floor included a kitchen and dining room.

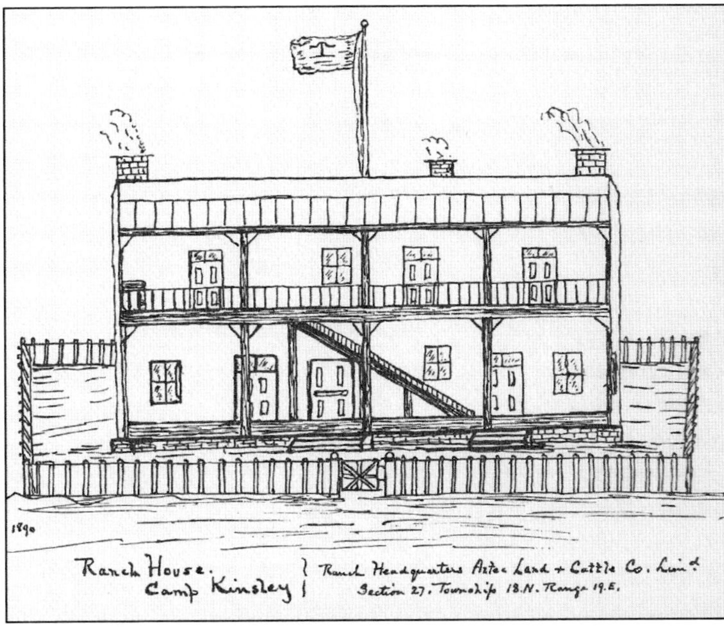

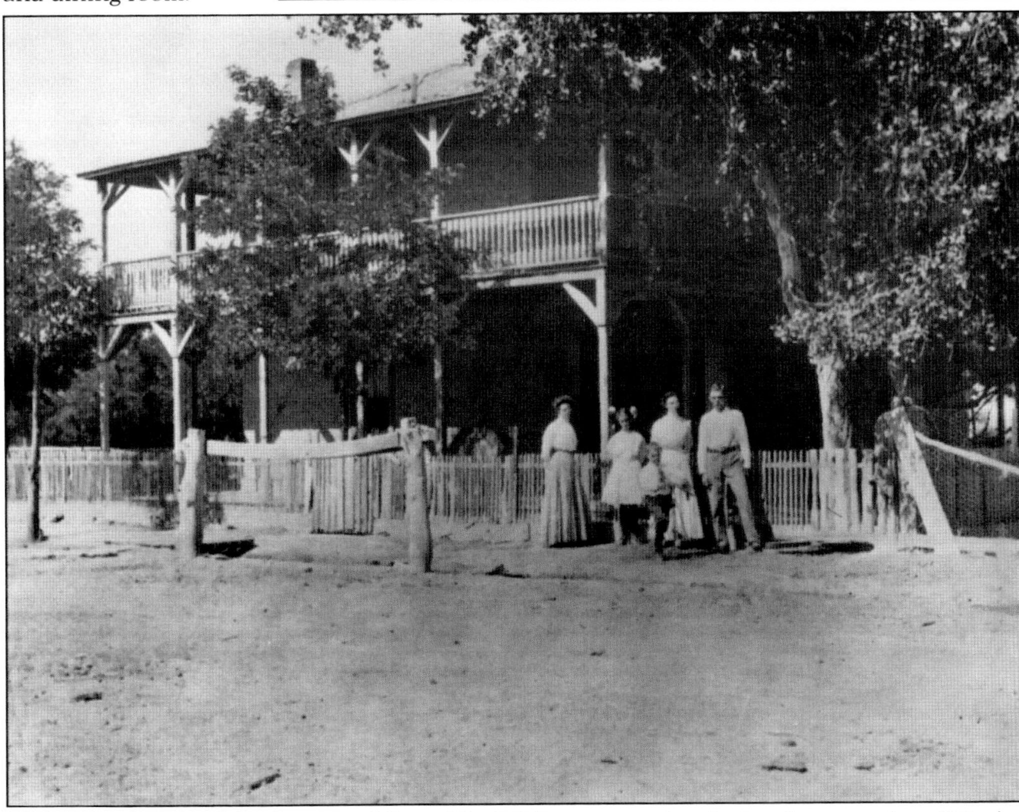

Mossman's room was on the second floor. The Wallaces moved to the headquarters from Winslow soon after their daughter Ruth was born. Mossman said the family—Frank, Cora, Emmet, Frances, Margery, and Ruth—lived in one of the large rooms downstairs. Some of the family may be pictured here in front of the headquarters.

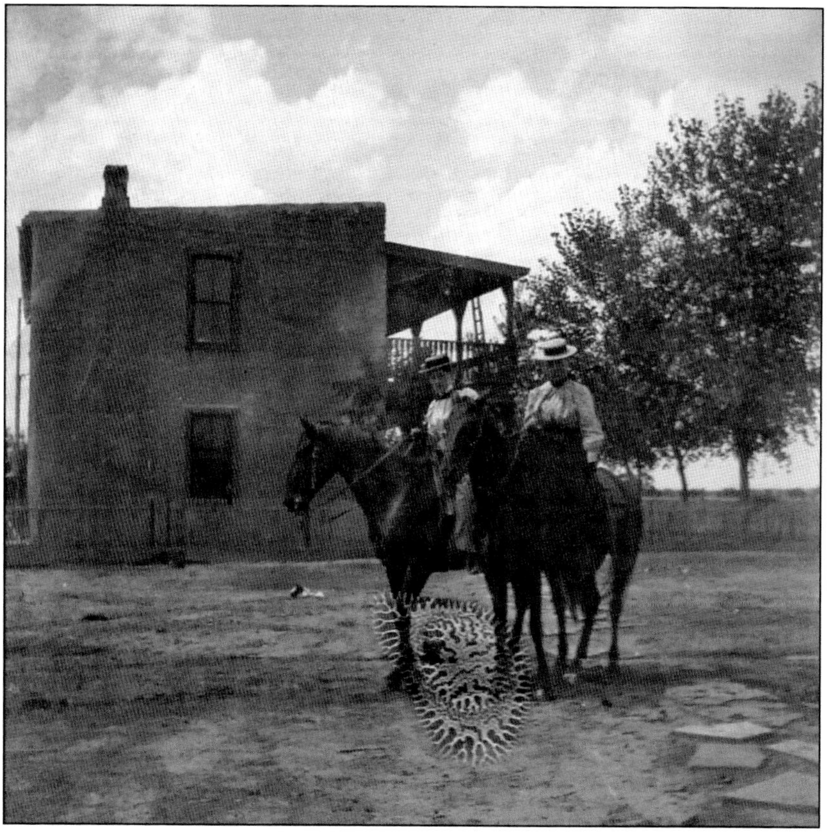

Cora Wallace (right) and a friend pose on horseback by the headquarters. Ruth Wallace would later remember, "Mama did the cooking for the cowboys and took care of them as her own." Ruth also recalled that Burt Mossman "very seldom left his room. His job was strictly to keep the vast records of the [Aztec] Cattle Company, and no doubt [this] took lots of his time."

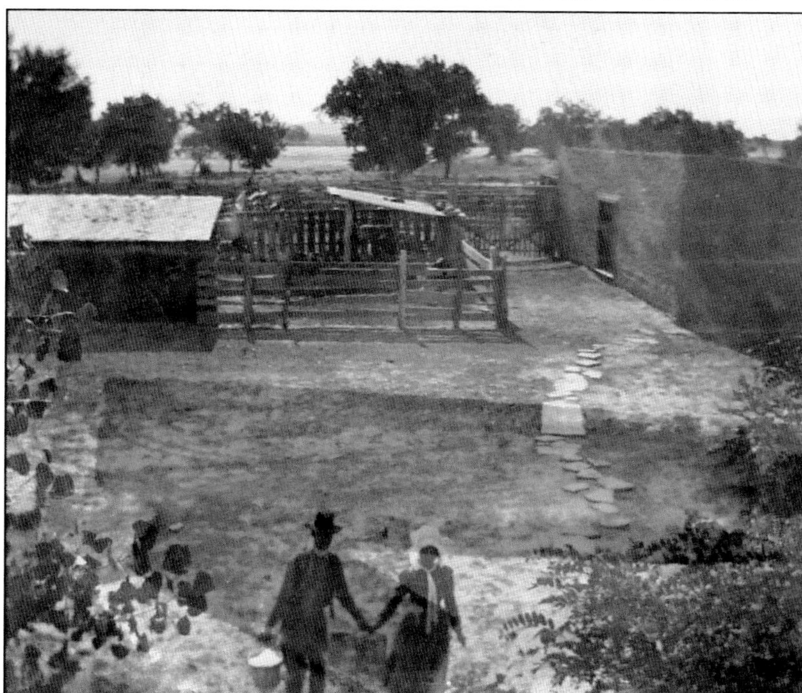

As remote as the headquarters appeared, there were several ranches between Obed and Holbrook. Here, George Hennessey and neighbor Annie Despain are seen carrying buckets from the headquarter's outbuildings in about 1899.

Approximately 30 cowboys, such as the unidentified man here, worked for the Hash Knife when George Hennessey was hired. Some of them still used nicknames, but fewer did so out of a need to hide from the law. A few questionable characters certainly worked amongst the group, but overall the Hash Knife's notorious reputation was receding.

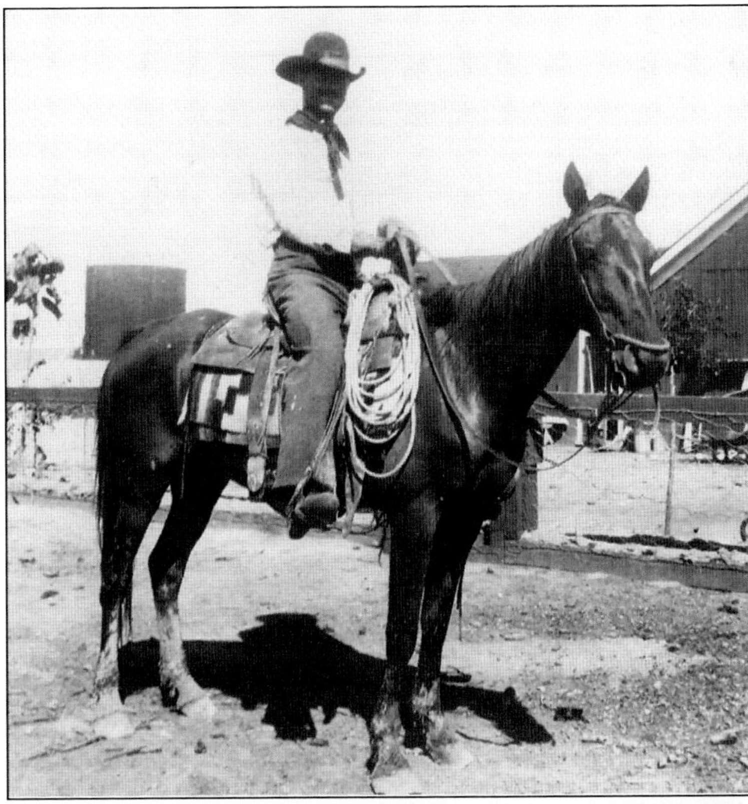

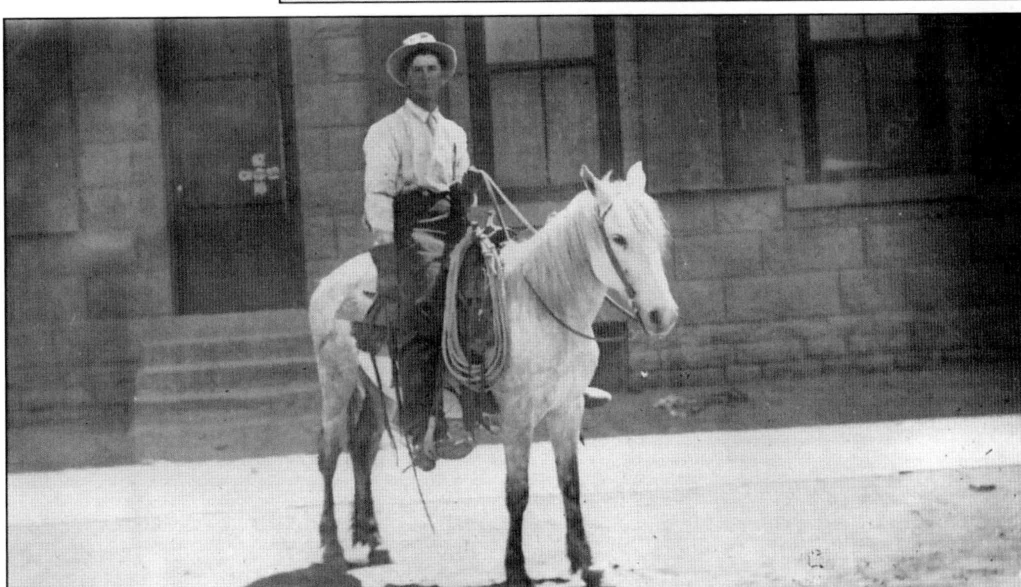

Another cowboy, probably from the Hash Knife, is seen here near Holbrook's downtown. Hennessey remembered that when the boys went drinking in town, they gave their six-shooters to Sheriff Joe Woods. "You had to carry a gun," Hennessey explained. "We were gathering some of these wild cows and sometimes you had to shoot one to keep it from hooking your horse."

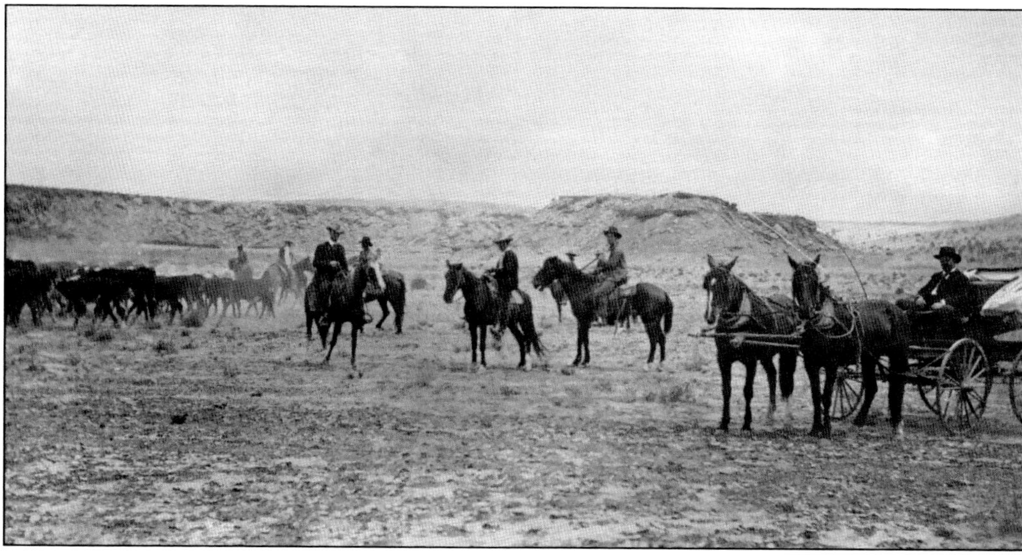

Aztec officials occasionally visited the Arizona range, largely unaware that a few bad guys still lingered among their employees. "The boy who was riding 'rough string' [supplying cowboys with fresh horses] was from Texas and I knew him there," George Hennessey remembered. "He also knew that I knew there was a thousand dollar reward for him back in Texas. I always got good horses."

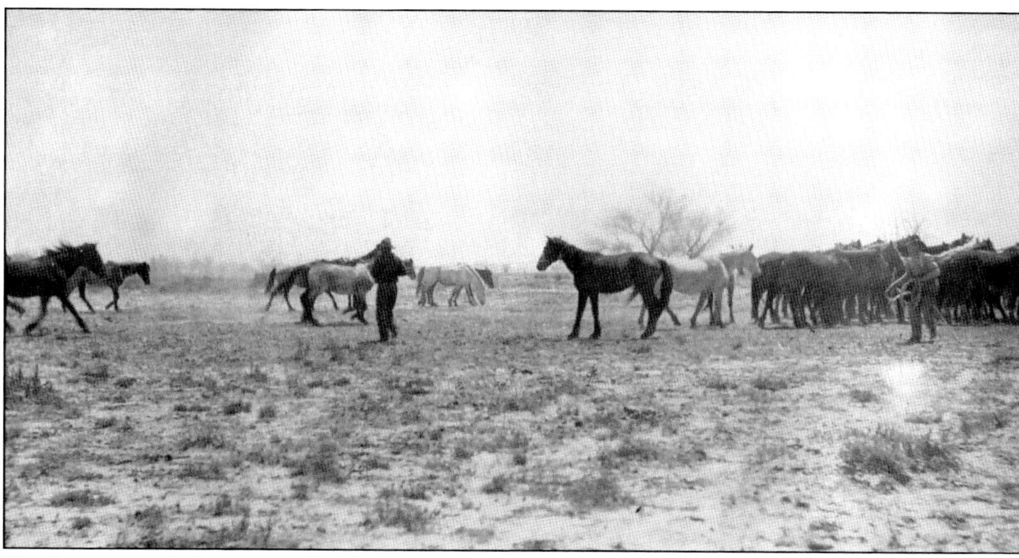

Cowboys wrangle horses on the Aztec range. "I consider it a damn good outfit," Hennessey said. "They were all good cowboys and good men. The ones I knew made something for themselves, ran businesses or held public office." Fellow cowboy Homer "Uncle Dick" Grigsby shared Hennessey's sentiment: "There were good cowboys, good horses, and long hours."

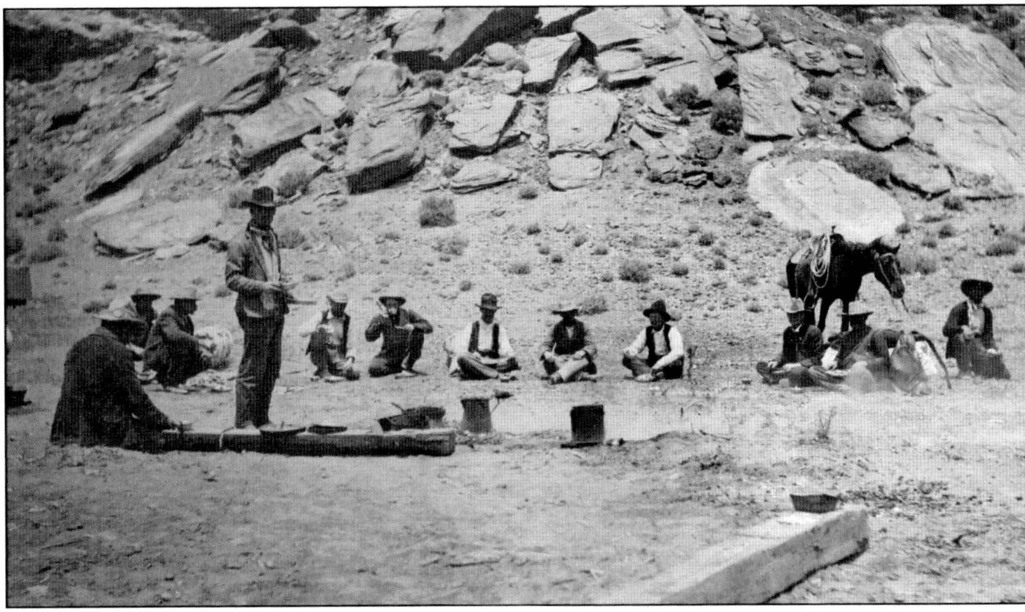

A popular postcard depicted cowboys dining on the range. "We enjoyed the life very much," said Hennessey. "There was no responsibility, only to just work. You had to be a pretty good cowboy to hold your job with the Hash Knife. Knowing how to work cattle is something you can't learn from a book. That comes from experience, working with good cattlemen and being willing to learn."

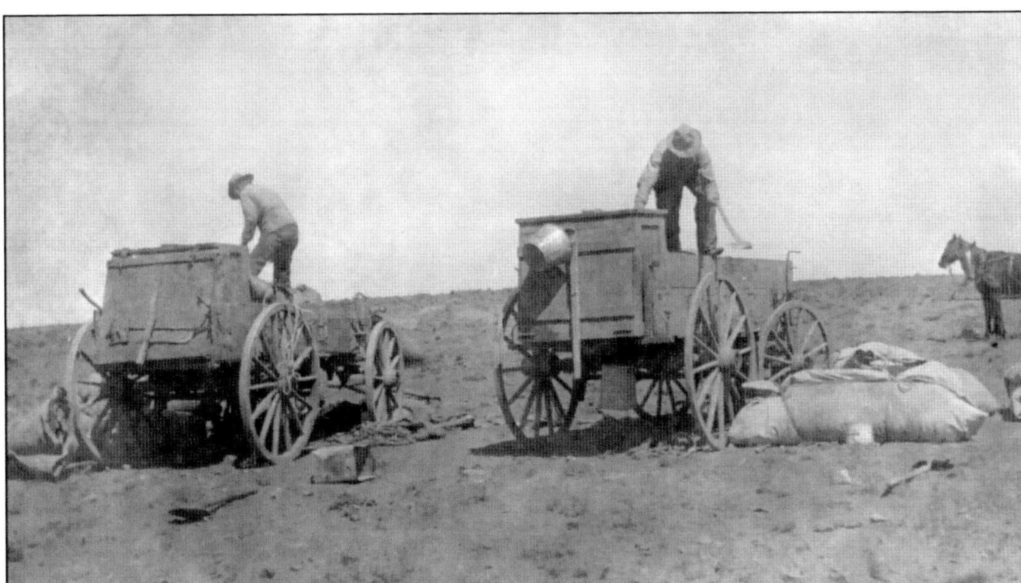

Two wagons, an "East Wagon" and a "West Wagon," oversaw the expansive Hash Knife range. "They generally had about eight to ten cowboys, but they had lots of outside men during round-up season," Hennessey remembered. "I've seen as many as 20 or 25 men with the wagon." Each cowboy was provided with three circle horses, three cutting horses, and two night mounts.

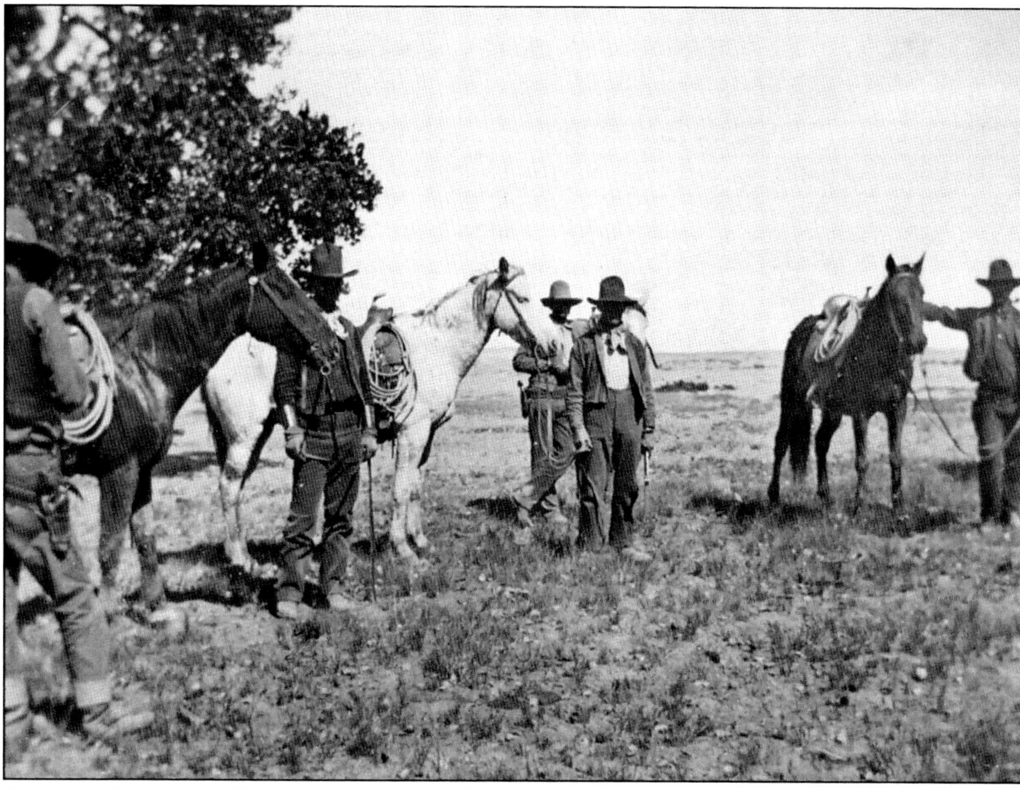

Hash Knife cowboys (from left to right) William Hogin, George Hennessey, Frank Wallace, Cap Bagnall, and Tom South pause for a photograph while working the range. During their leisure time, Hennessey remembered, "Our most fun was to get on a horse and get throwed off!"

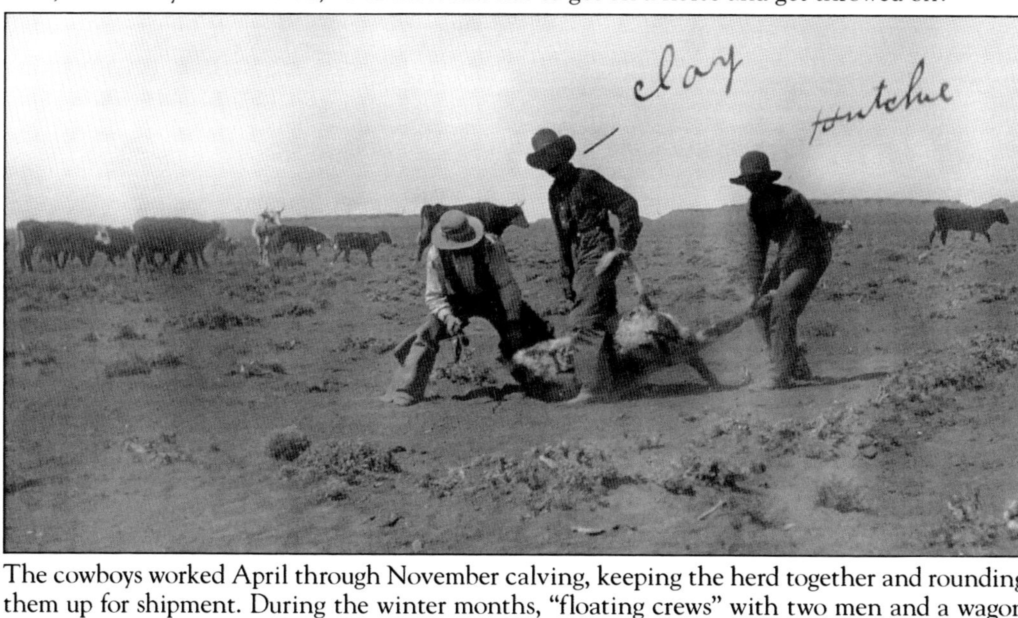

The cowboys worked April through November calving, keeping the herd together and rounding them up for shipment. During the winter months, "floating crews" with two men and a wagon spent their time looking after the cattle and branding. Here, "Clay" and "Hutchie" hold a calf as a third unidentified cowboy prepares to brand it.

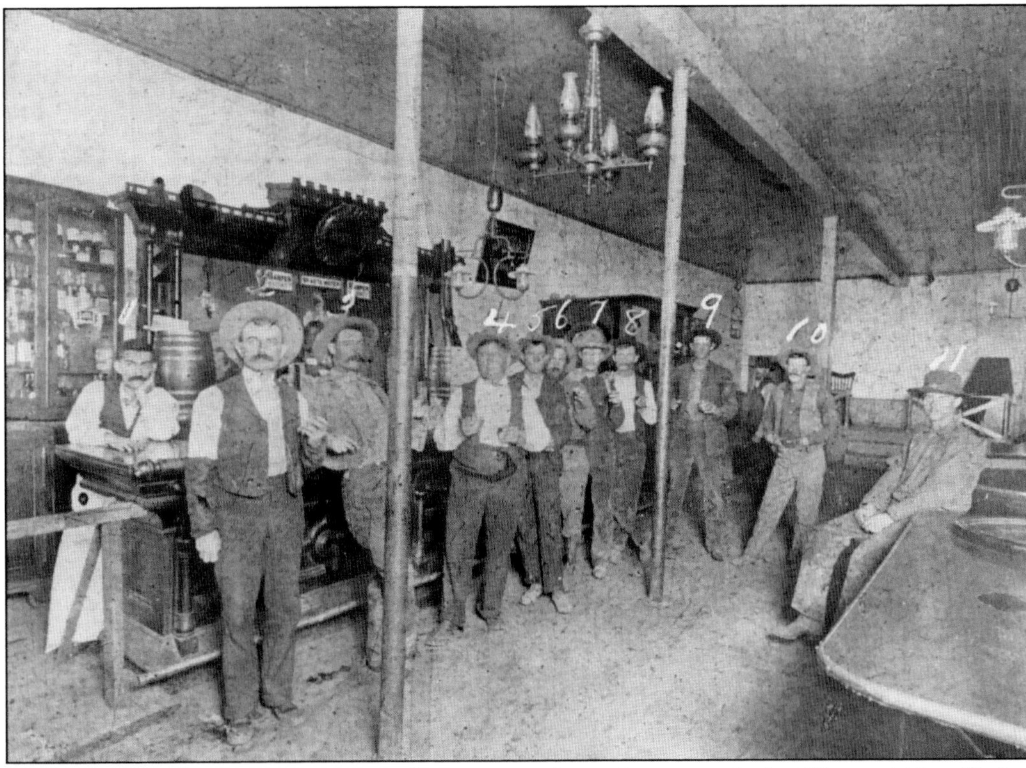

Hash Knife cowboys partake in refreshments at a favored watering hole. Often misidentified as the Bucket of Blood in Holbrook, this tavern is most likely the Fashion Saloon in Winslow. The men (from left to right) are bartender Mike Oyster (or Billie Burke), Lucien Creswell, Bill Balcom, Frank Black, Cap Bagnal, Tom Williams, George Hennessey, Ed Bargman, Doug Johnson, Frank Dane, and Johnny Hoffman.

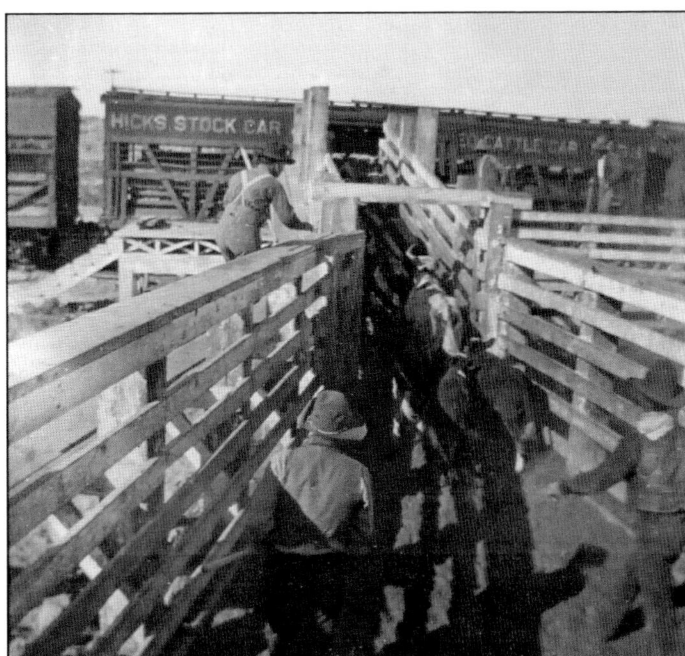

In 1899, the Aztec Land and Cattle Company ordered their men to start shipping cattle out of Arizona. Older steers were sent to Kansas, followed by the mother cows and their calves. Here, Bill Hogan (front left) and George Hennessey (front right) are loading cattle on the train at Winslow. Hennessey guessed that 25,000 head were shipped in 1899. The man on the fence is unidentified.

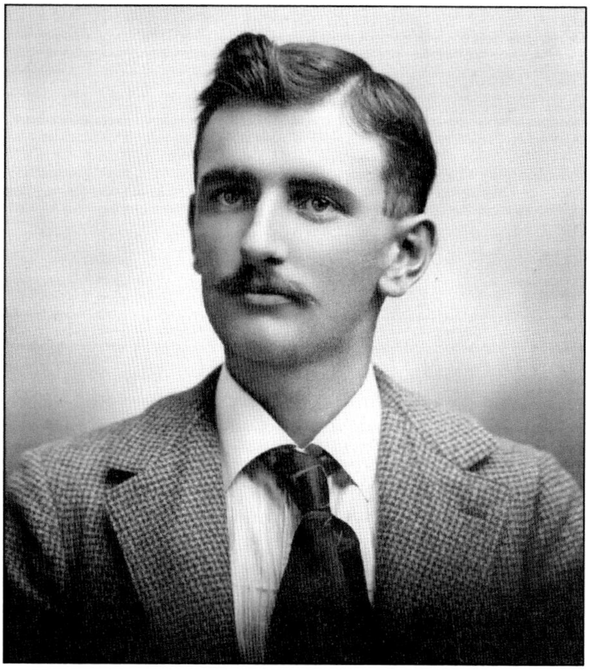

Cowboy Wynn Howe was a friend of Frank Wallace and George Hennessey. He may have worked for the Hash Knife near Winslow, or possibly later near Wallace's OW Ranch in Apache County. Howe later moved to Denver, where this portrait was taken. He died there in 1964.

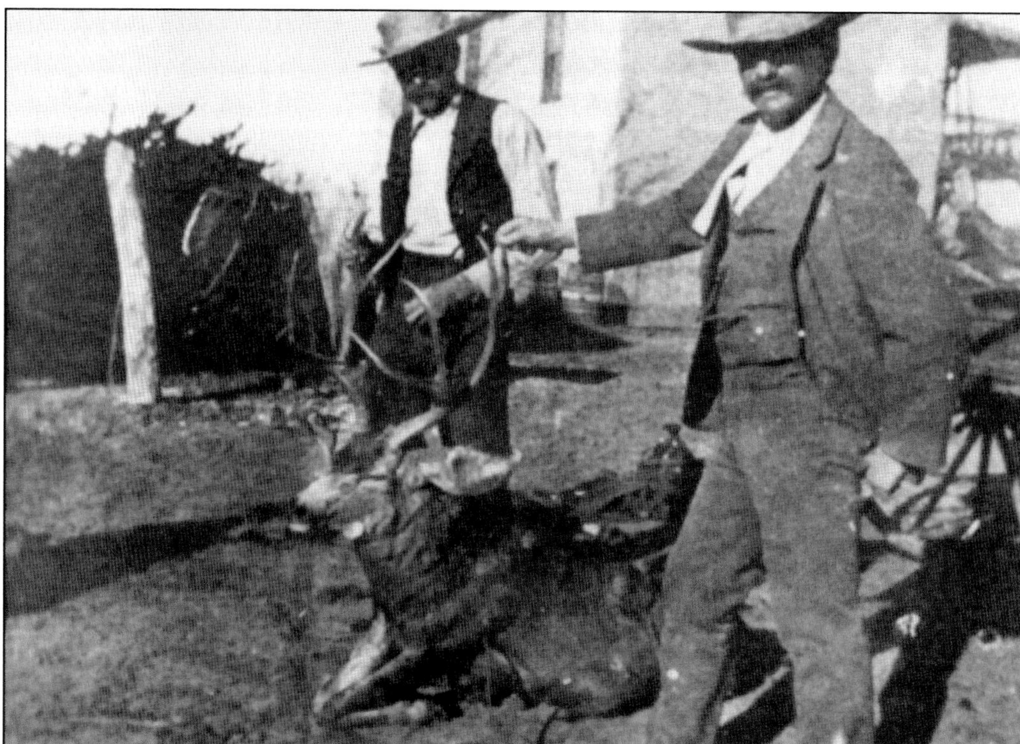

Wallace and Burt Mossman show off a fresh kill at the headquarters at Obed around 1900. Other residents of the ranch at that time were Hash Knife cowboys Moses Tate, Red Holcomb, James Donohoe, John Hoffman, Alonzo King, Robert Ricketts, Charles Moss, and Pete Pemberton. When another Wallace child, Bertha, was born later that year, Mossman named her.

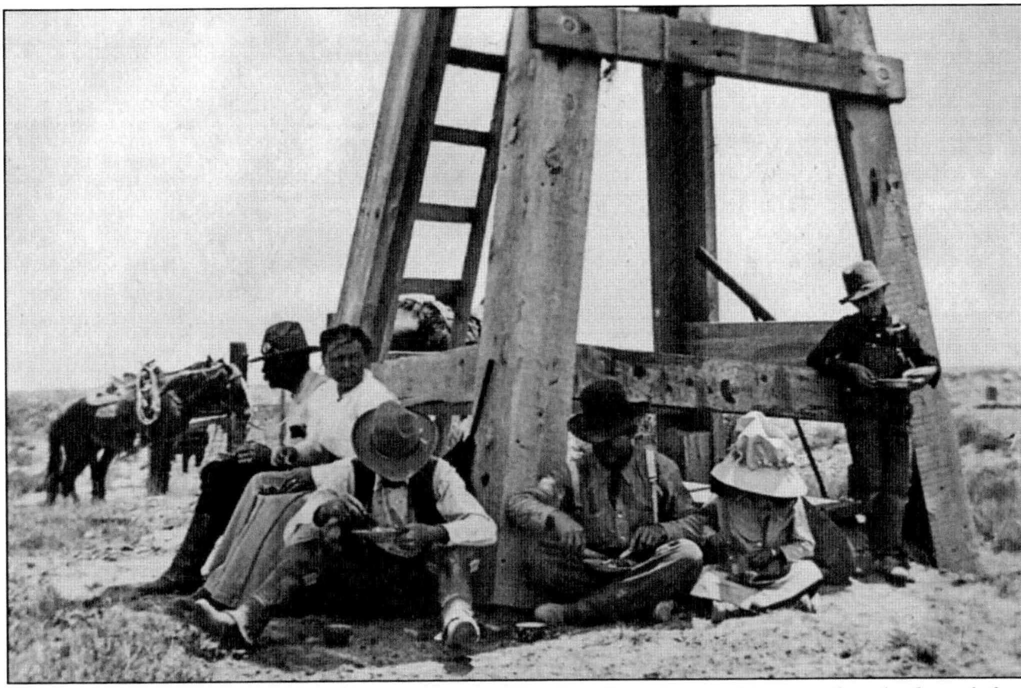

Working the range at the headquarters was a family affair. Pictured here at lunch, from left to right, are Frank and Cora Wallace, George Hennessey, an unidentified man, one of the Wallace girls, and Emmet Wallace. The older Wallace children were sometimes sent to bring fresh horses to the men on the range; on this occasion Cora may have accompanied them with fresh eats.

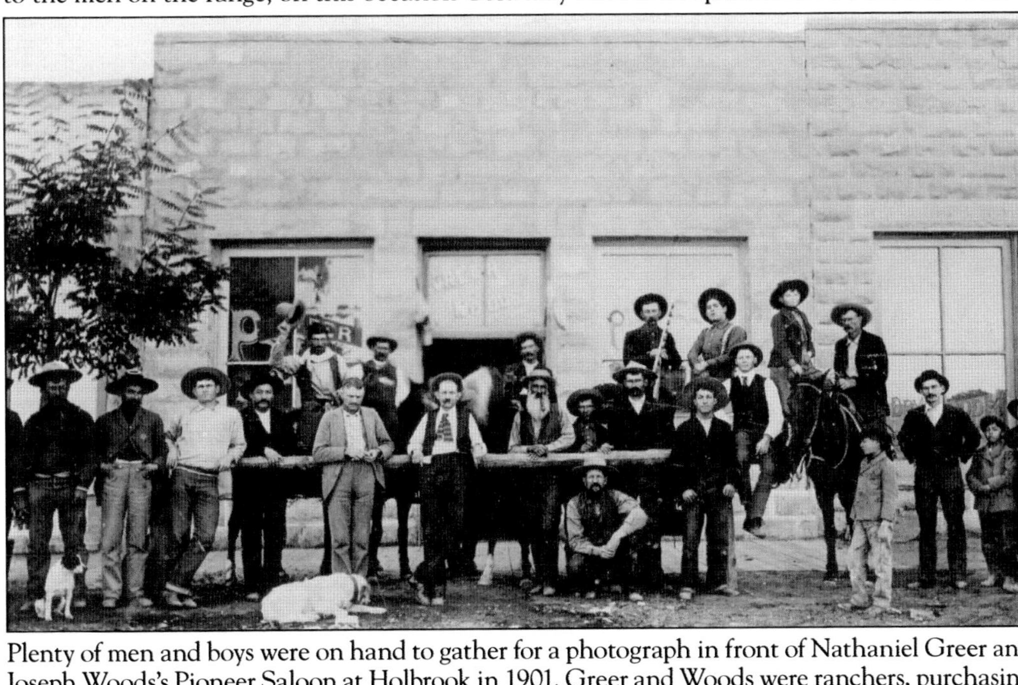

Plenty of men and boys were on hand to gather for a photograph in front of Nathaniel Greer and Joseph Woods's Pioneer Saloon at Holbrook in 1901. Greer and Woods were ranchers, purchasing the saloon in 1890. Both were friends with a number of Hash Knife cowboys. In this image, George Hennessey is leaning in the doorway of the saloon.

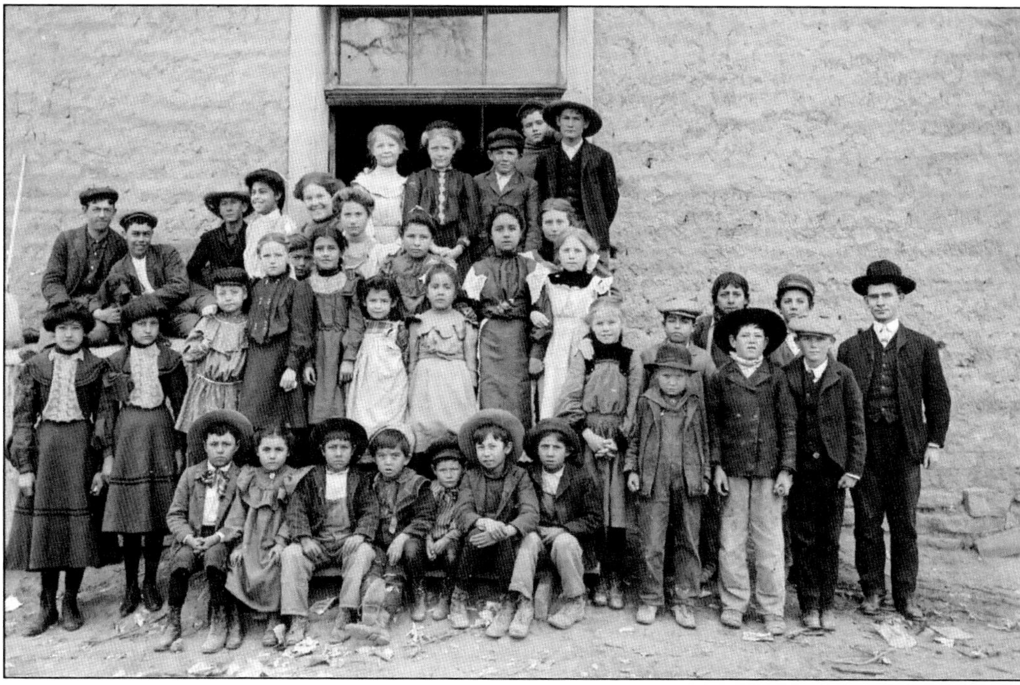

The Wallace children attended school at Joseph City. In this c. 1903 image, Ruth and Margery are third and fourth from the left in the second row. Emmet is on the far left in the third row. Frances is in the top row, second from the left. The other children are unidentified.

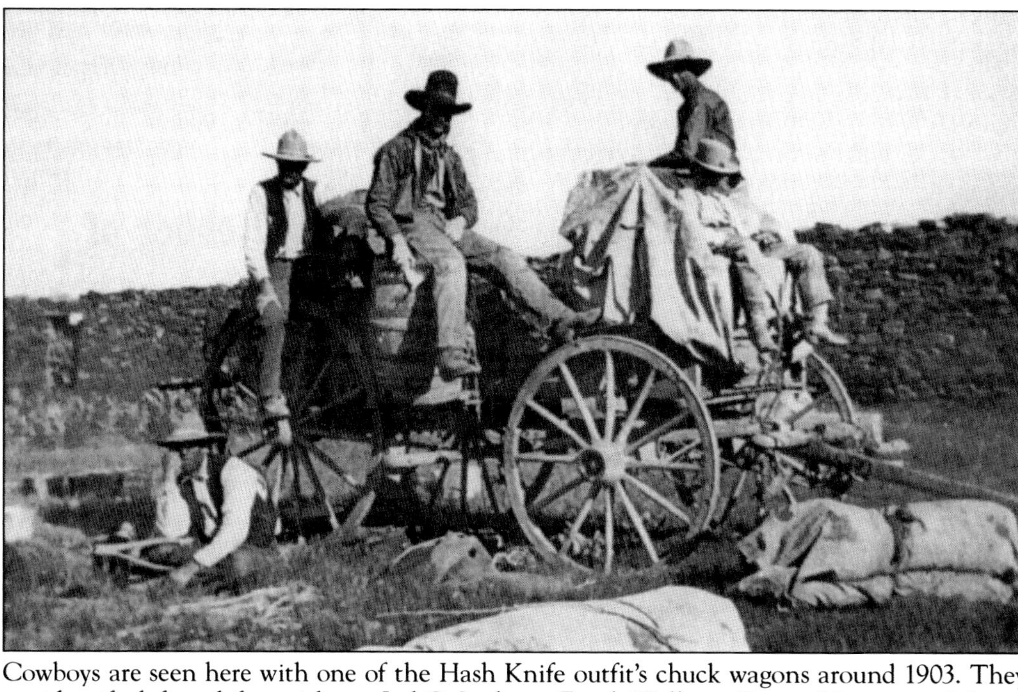

Cowboys are seen here with one of the Hash Knife outfit's chuck wagons around 1903. They are identified, from left to right, as Jud G. Lathrop, Frank Wallace, George Hennessey, Johnny Hoffman, and Emmet Wallace. The men were still living at the Hash Knife headquarters after Burt Mossman resigned, with the exception of Lathrop, who resided in Holbrook.

Six

After the Aztec

Buying the Hash Knife brand was just one of many purchases Babbitt Brothers made as they built up their cattle empire. Likewise, the Aztec Land and Cattle Company continued trading and selling rangeland. There was little else for Frank Wallace to do beyond caretaking for the Hash Knife headquarters, so in 1900 he purchased cattle from neighboring rancher Will C. Barnes. At the end of the year, George Hennessey quit to work as foreman for the Wabash Cattle Company before starting his own ranch in 1903. He later joked that his first "headquarters" was a bedroll under a tree.

In 1904, the Wallace's returned to Holbrook where their last daughter, Minnie, was born. Wallace bought ranchland at Adamana, located 25 miles east of Holbrook. The first family home there was a large tent. "We were flooded out so we moved to higher ground about seven miles east," Ruth Wallace remembered. "Our father and the men he employed as cowboys built a frame house large enough to hold all of us."

Ruth remembered life at the ranch. "The adjoining ranchers would go on round-ups twice a year with one chuck wagon and one cook. Each ranch had their own cowboys and string of horses. They would be gone weeks at a time. Sometimes our father would take two of us with him to take care of the horses. It was a lonely time as we missed home. Usually me and Margery went with them." Over the next decade, Wallace built his ranch up and formed partnerships with son Emmet, cattleman Nathan Bly, George Hennessey, and former Hash Knife cowboy Jim Donohoe.

In March 1917, Holbrook was finally incorporated. W.R. Scorse acted as mayor, pending the first official election the coming May. To his own utter surprise, the first elected mayor was George Hennessey. The following year, Wallace purchased the old ranch that was owned by the Blevins family during the Blevins-Tewksbury range war of 1887. The ranch was now known as the OW.

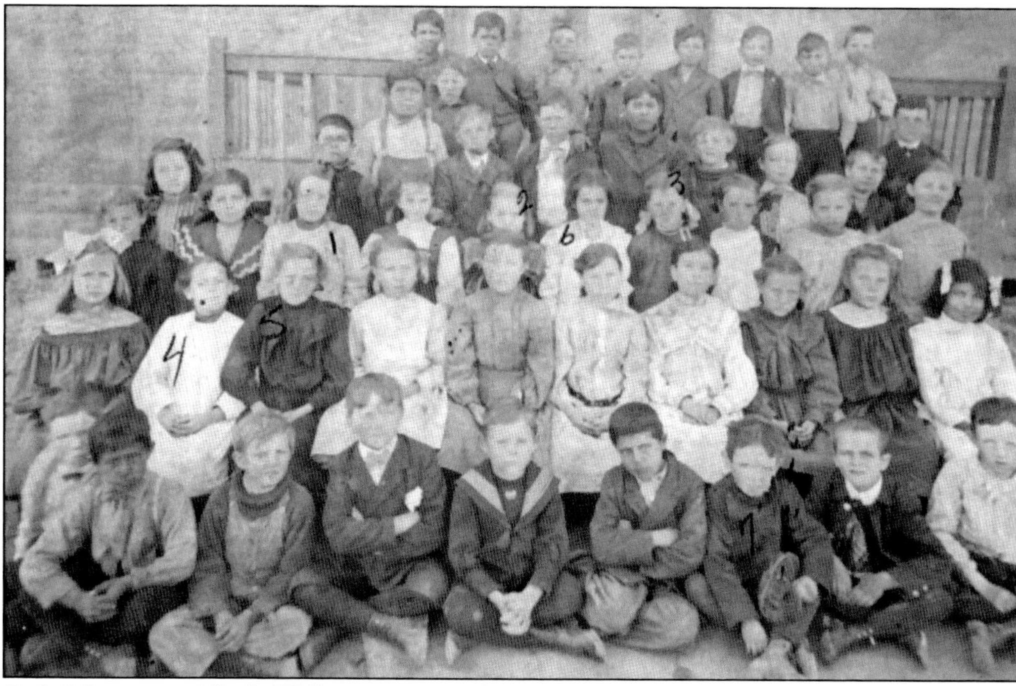

Only Margery and Ruth Wallace appear to have been in school when this c. 1904 image was taken at Winslow. The numbers identify some of the students here as 1. Mildred Sutton, 2. Ruth Wallace, 3. "Toots" Wyrick, 4. Lela Sutton, 5. Margery Wallace, 6. Ruth Dunklin, and 7. Leon Sutton. Soon after this photograph was taken, the Wallaces returned to Holbrook.

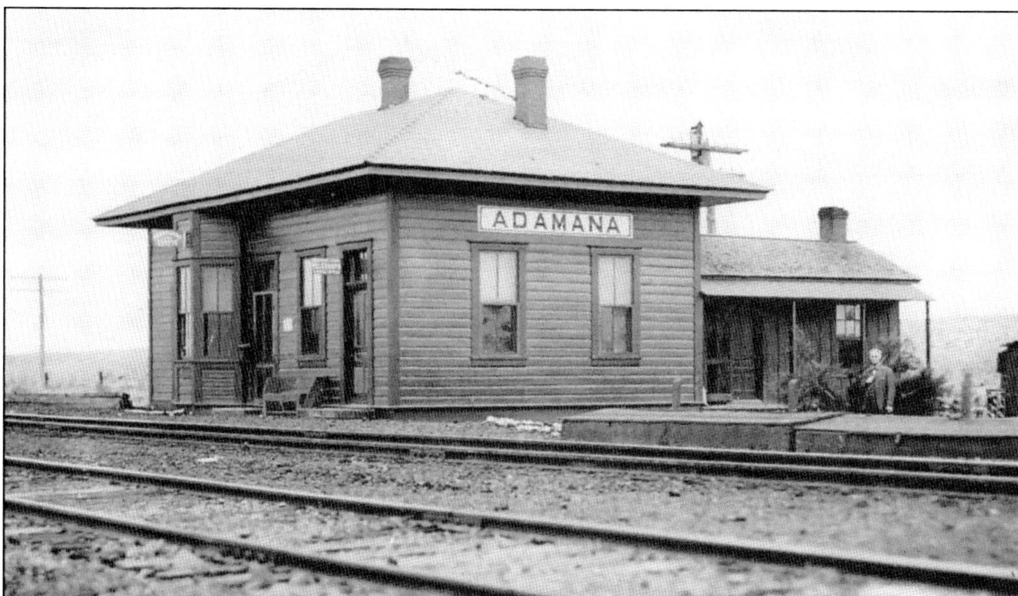

In 1897, the Santa Fe Railroad purchased the Atlanta & Pacific Railroad that ran by Adamana. Ruth later remembered, "Special trains stopped here to take tourists to see the petrified forests." She also described Adamana as "a desolate place [where] we depended on the windmills for water." (Navajo County Historical Society.)

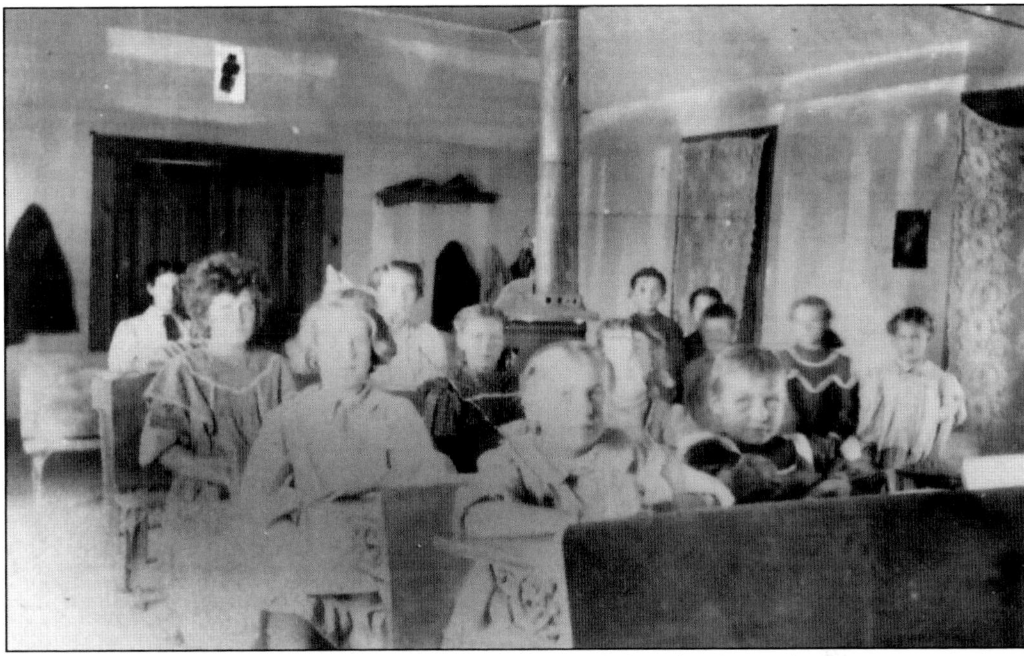

Ruth Wallace (on the right in the front desk) described the school at Adamana as "a one room building with desks and a pot belly stove to keep us warm. There were about 10 to 12 children and one teacher that taught all grades from first to eight . . . We walked two miles down the Santa Fe Railroad tracks to school."

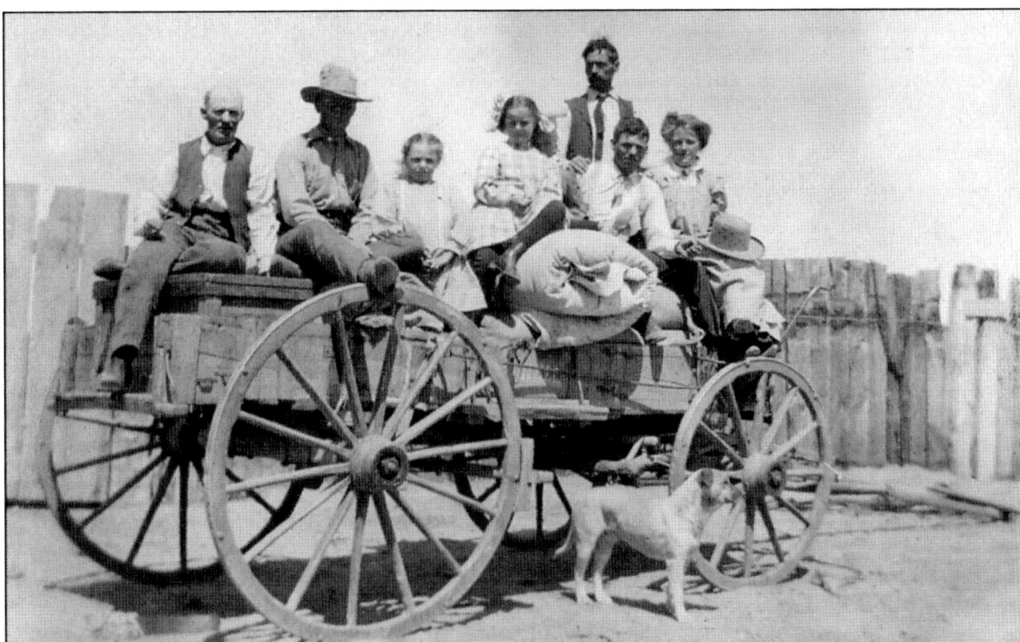

Although life could be lonely at Adamana, the Wallaces often received visitors in the way of friends from Winslow and Holbrook, as well as neighboring ranchers. Frances Wallace, on the far right, poses with a group in this wagon at the family ranch around 1905.

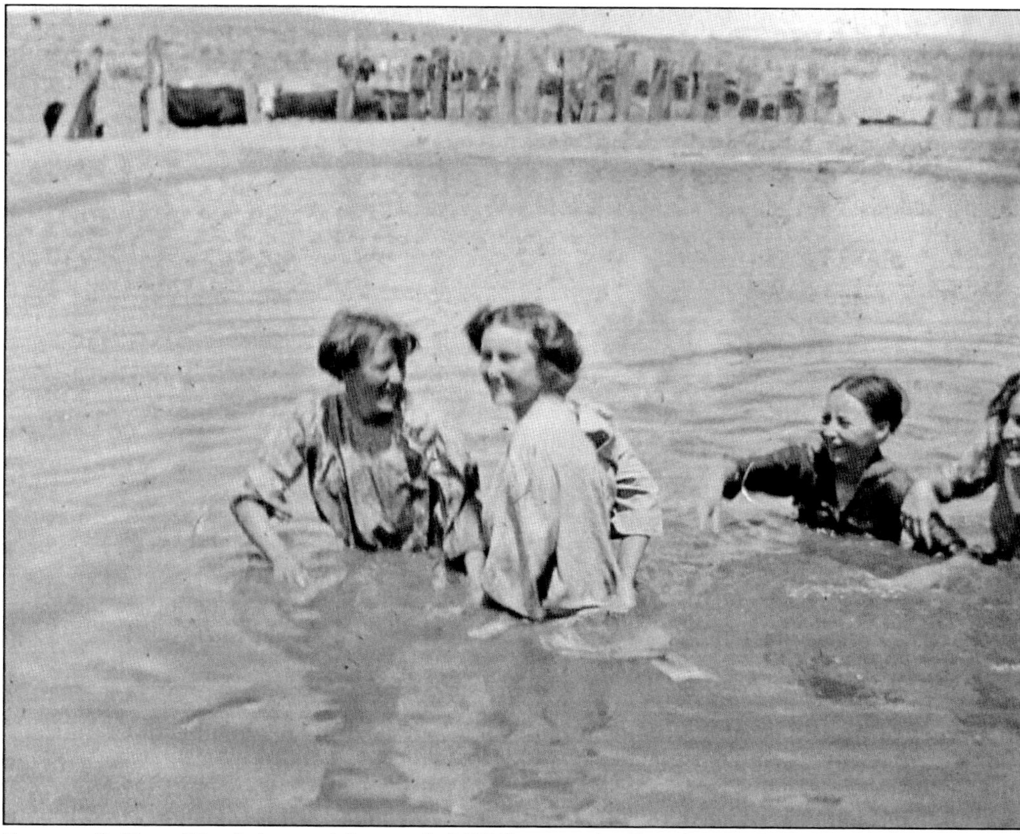

Frances (left) and Ruth (second from right) Wallace cool off in the stock tank with friends. Ruth remembered supplying her father with fresh horses on the range. "It was our job to get the horses to them at certain times so they could change as they rode from early in the morning to late in the day. When we got home, Mama would have a hard time getting us clean."

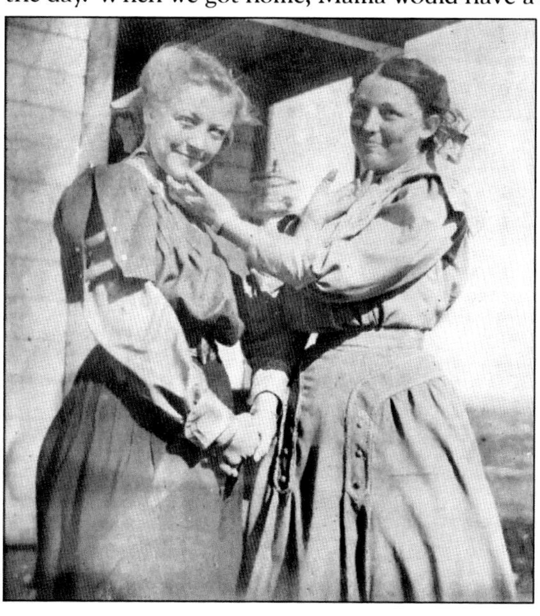

Frances (pictured here on the left) made many lifelong friends in Holbrook, Winslow, Joseph City, and even Adamana. Those who signed her autograph album included former Hash Knife cowboys James Donohoe and Barney Stiles; Stiles's son Jot; Amelia Despain, who lived one ranch over from the headquarters at Obed; and Homer "Uncle Dick" Grigsby.

By 1907, George Hennessey had made enough money to pay off the family mortgage in Texas. Following a visit to "Aunt Nettie," Hennessey came back through New Mexico, where he bought and sold a ranch at more profit. This image, taken in December 1905, is identified as "Aunt Nettie and family," but their exact relationship to Hennessey is unclear.

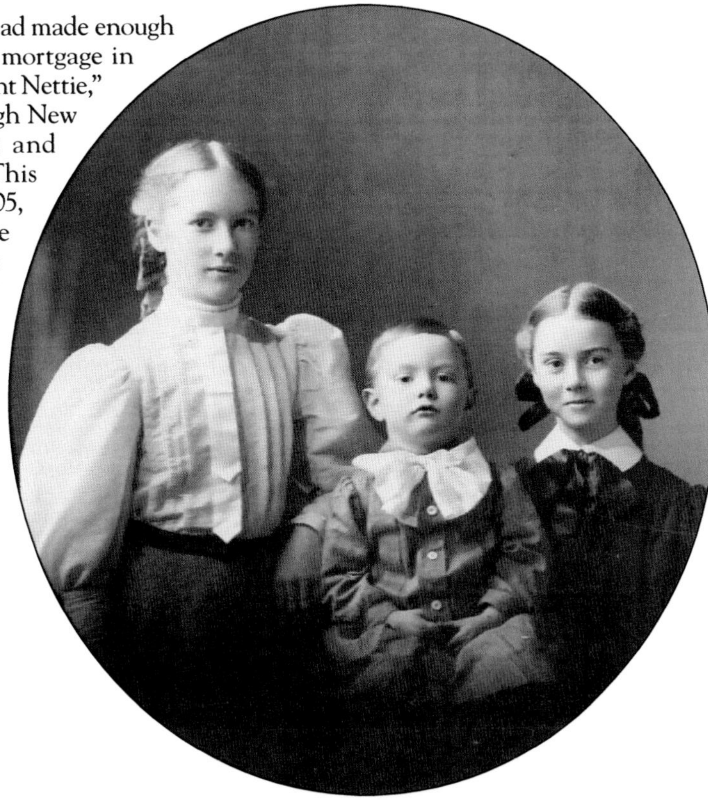

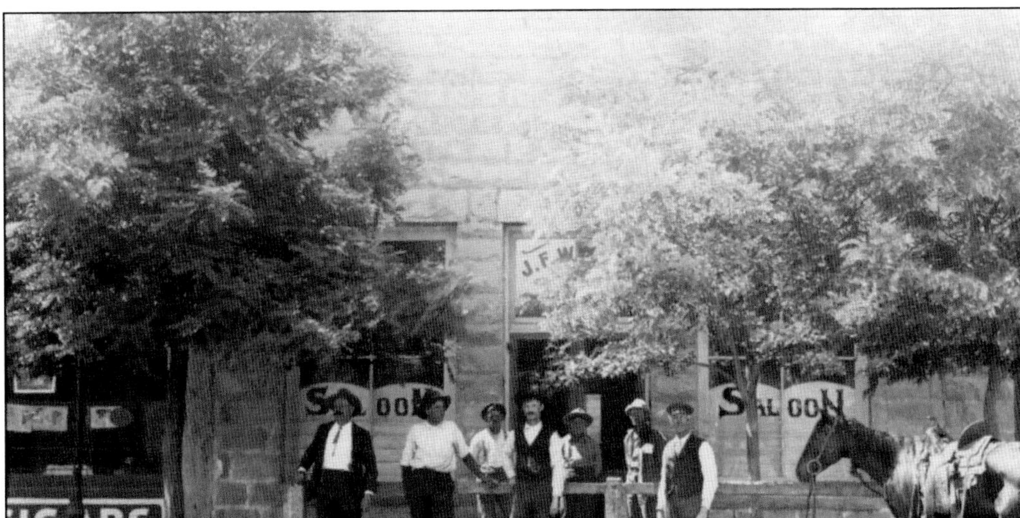

In 1908, on an apparent whim, George Hennessey ran the Bucket of Blood saloon in Holbrook for about a year. In this image he is posing with friends in front of Joseph Woods's place. Deputy Sheriff Allen is on the far left. Hennessey is in the center with the black vest. Henry Scorse is on the far right.

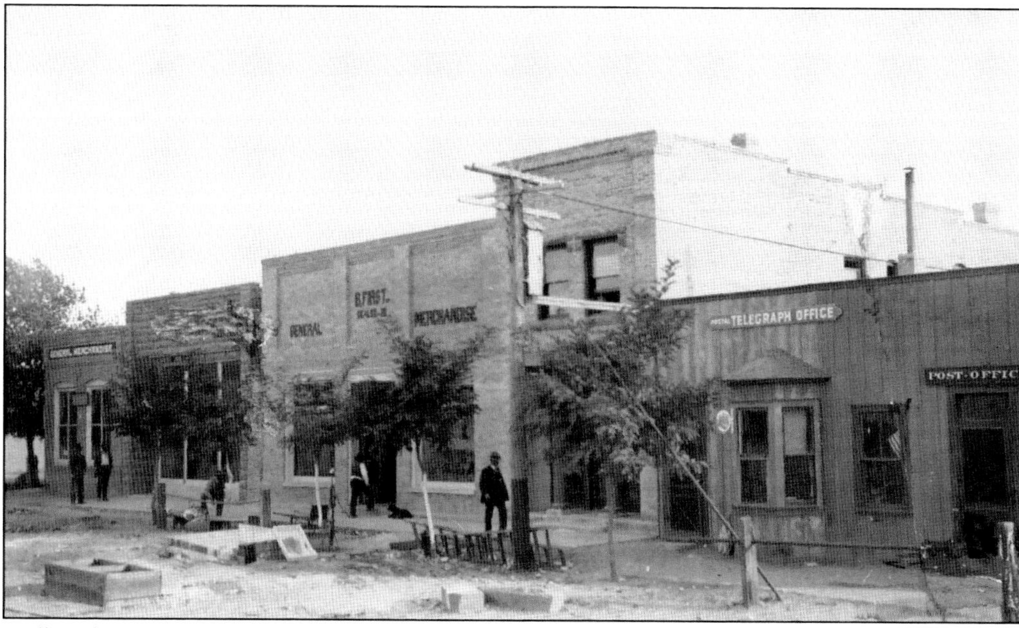

Holbrook, pictured here in 1909, was about 25 miles from Adamana. Cora Wallace must have missed going to town regularly, but "Mama always had a large kettle of beans on the stove and lots of home-cooked bread," Ruth Wallace recalled. "She cured the meat, made soap from scraps of pork so we had plenty." (Navajo County Historical Society.)

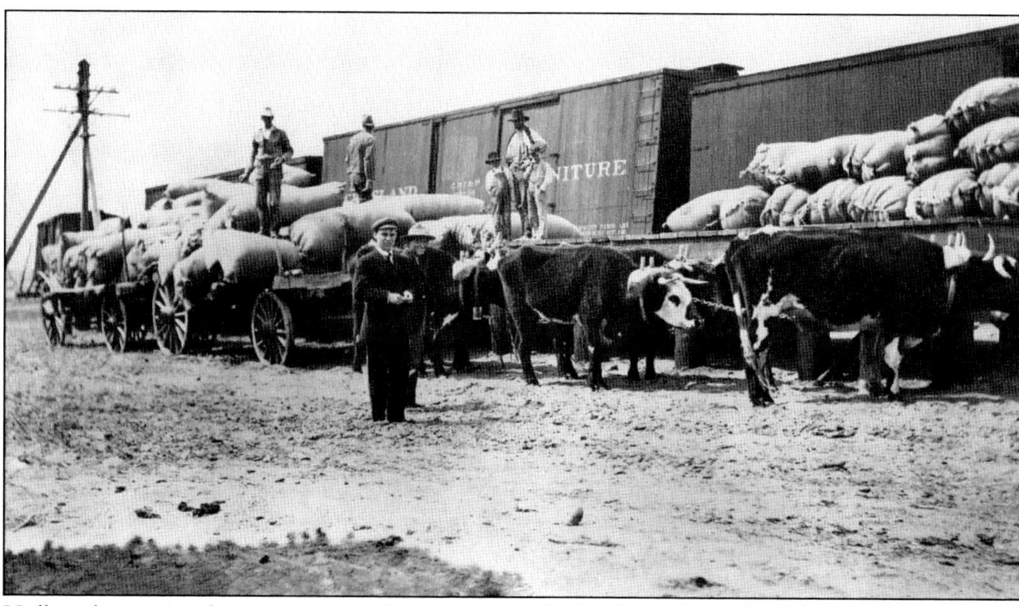

Holbrook remained an important shipping point for both cattle and wool. Ruth remembered, "The cattle buyers would come each year to make a bid for cattle. The steers were shipped twice yearly to Kansas City and what the market was on arrival was what we received. In those days the prices were very low."

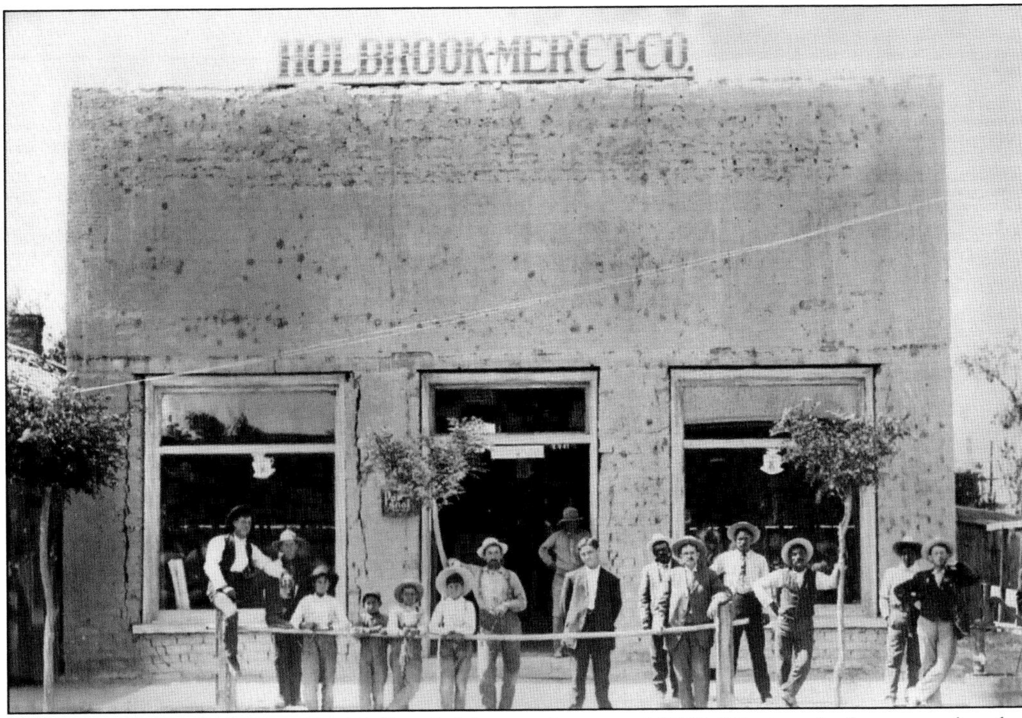

Townsfolk gather in front of the Holbrook Mercantile around 1910. "During the lean months, they depended on the local merchants in Holbrook to finance them," said Ruth. "With the high interest we paid, there would be little left by the time my parents got theirs. It was likely they sold their souls to the Company store. Having no money was a fact of life and the mothers made do."

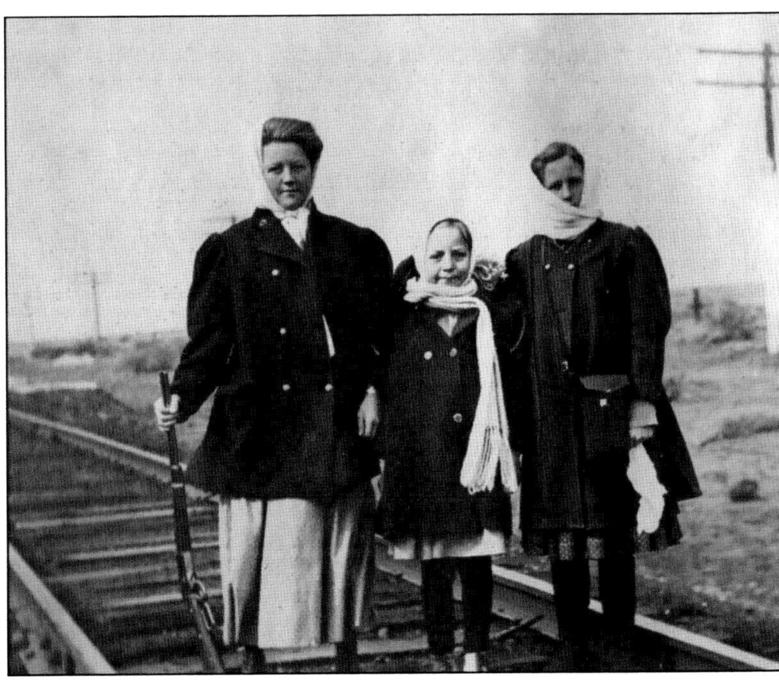

Frances, Ruth, and Margery Wallace pause for a picture along the railroad tracks at Adamana. The girls appear to be wearing store-bought coats, but their dresses were almost certainly homemade. Cora managed to do well for her large family. "We always managed to have plenty to eat and clothing to wear," said Ruth.

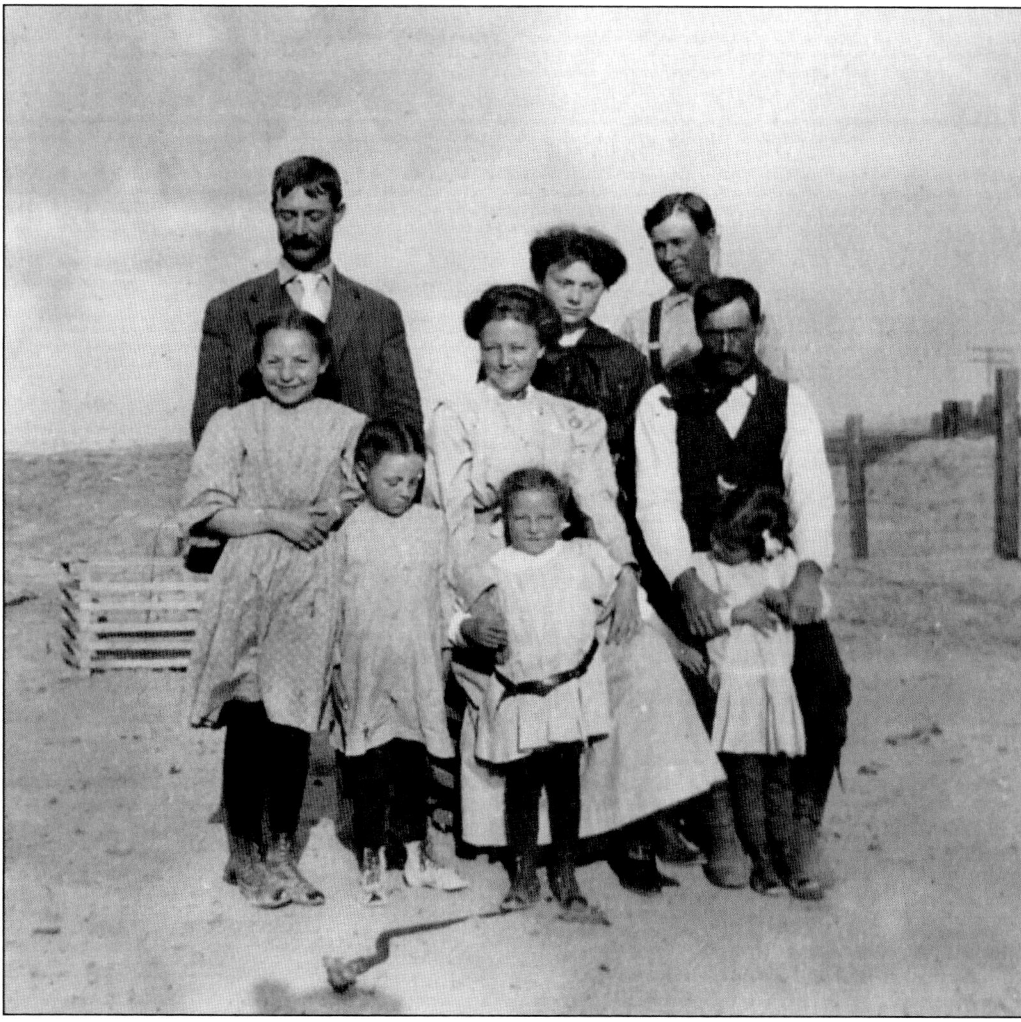

In this photograph, taken at Adamana, Ruth, Ann, and Minnie Wallace are in front, from left to right. The fourth child on the right is unidentified. In the back are, from left to right, George Hennessey, Frances Wallace (seated), and three unidentified family friends. Hennessey, ever a jokester, appears to be tickling a giggly Ruth.

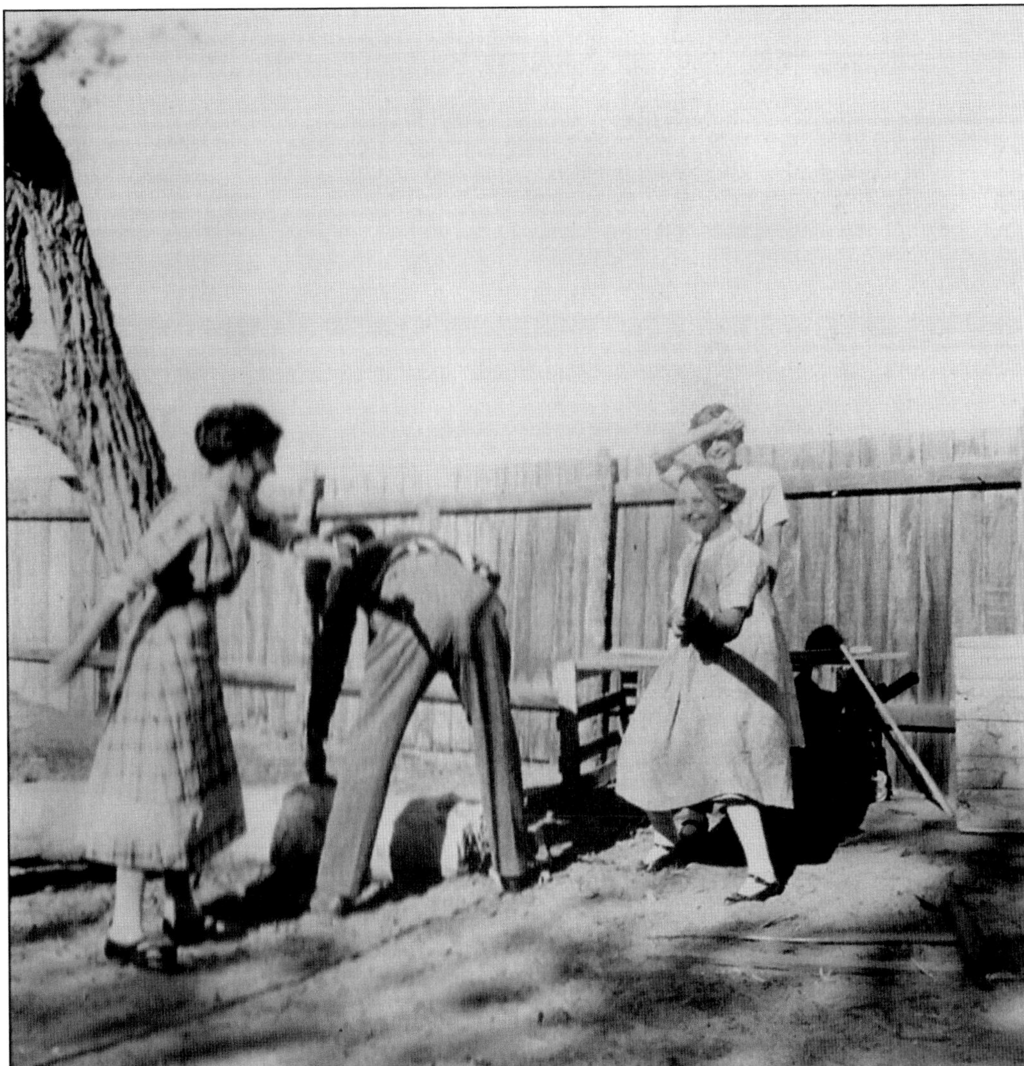

Even as he pursued his own business endeavors, George Hennessey visited the Wallace family often at Adamana. Friendly horseplay seems to be the name of the game in this image: Margery Wallace is bending Hennessey over while her sister Ruth pretends to be taking a board to his backside. The third girl on the far right may be one of the younger Wallace girls, Bertha.

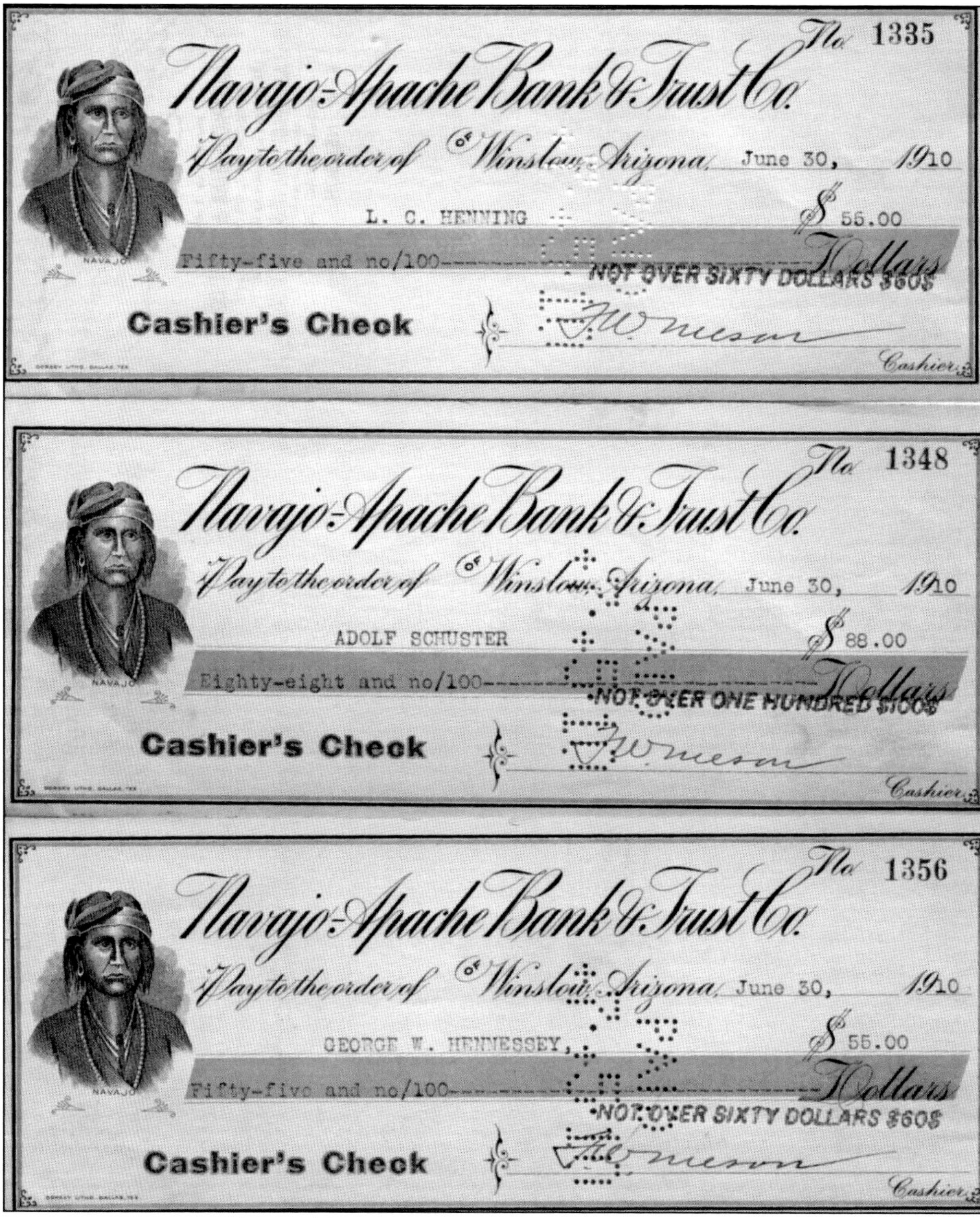

George Hennessey may have sold his portion of the Long H back to Frank Wallace in 1910 because he wanted to purchase George Sharp's ranch north of Holbrook. Profits came not just from his cattle, but also side jobs. These checks, possibly dividends, are made out to Hennessey, Lloyd C. Henning, and Adolf Schuster, all prominent businessmen of Holbrook.

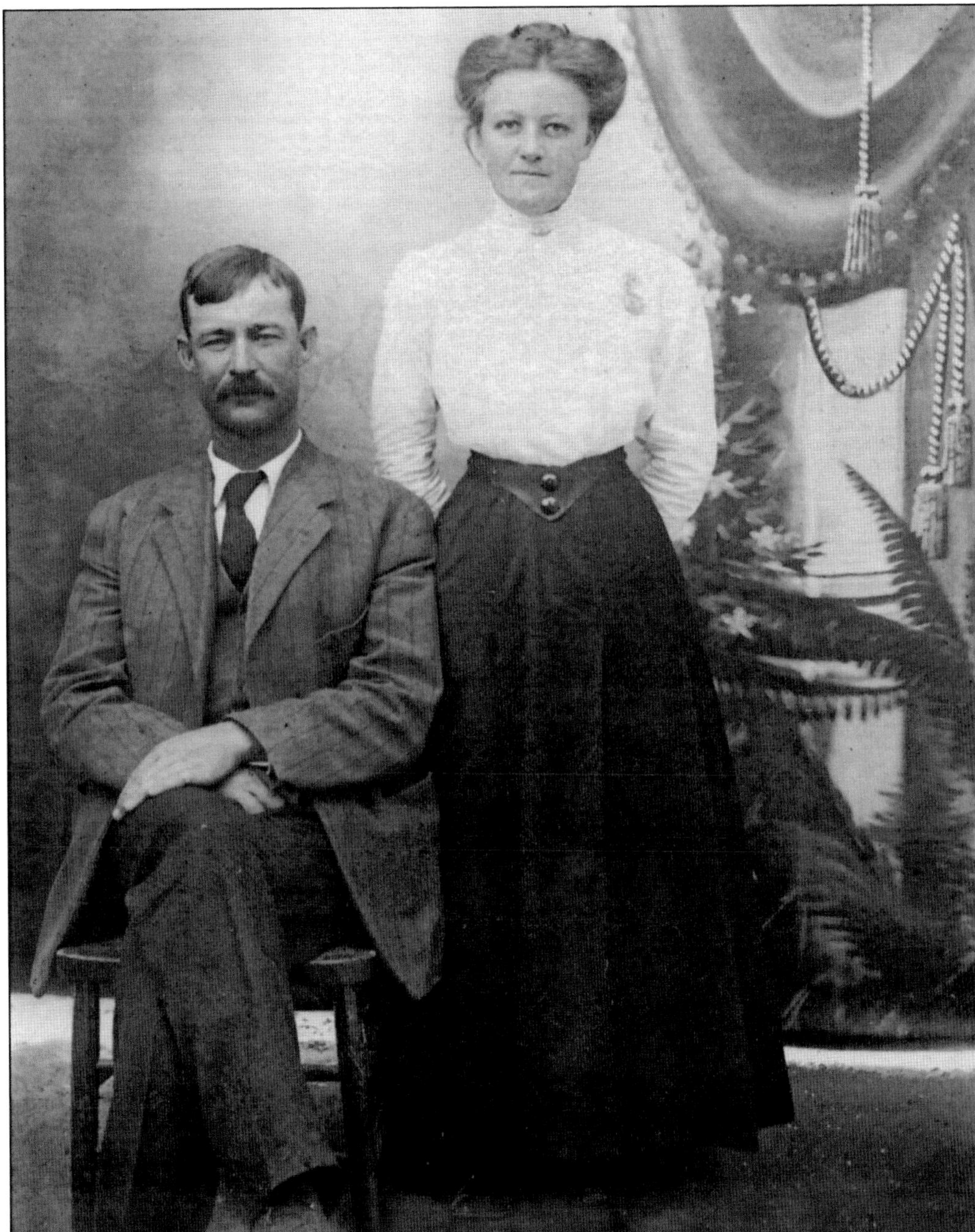

In April 1911, George Hennessey married Frank Wallace's daughter Frances. Frances was 20 years old at the time; Hennessey was 31. The wedding took place at the Wallace home in Adamana and was well attended by friends and neighbors. The event even made local newspapers, which described the ceremony and reception as quite the grand affair. The newlyweds would later move to Holbrook.

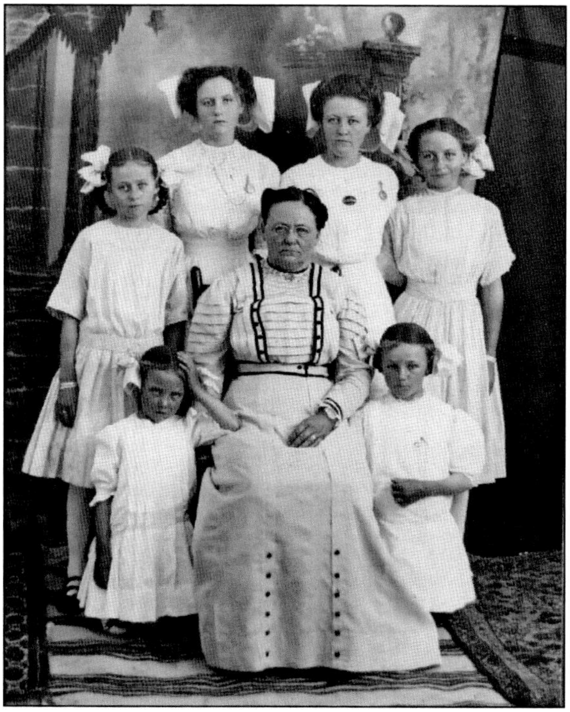

Cora Wallace painstakingly made each of her daughters a new dress for Frances's marriage to George Hennessey. The occasion was celebrated with this photograph, taken a short time after the wedding. The girls are, from left to right, Minnie, Bertha, Margery, Frances, Ruth, and Ann.

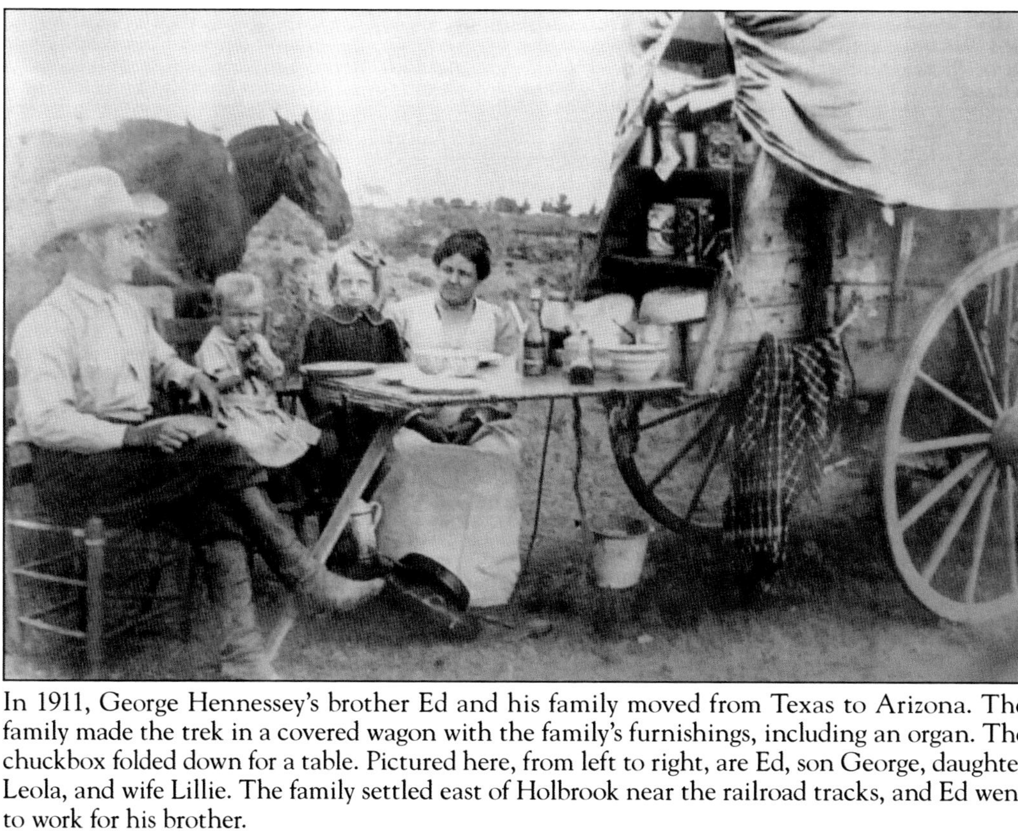

In 1911, George Hennessey's brother Ed and his family moved from Texas to Arizona. The family made the trek in a covered wagon with the family's furnishings, including an organ. The chuckbox folded down for a table. Pictured here, from left to right, are Ed, son George, daughter Leola, and wife Lillie. The family settled east of Holbrook near the railroad tracks, and Ed went to work for his brother.

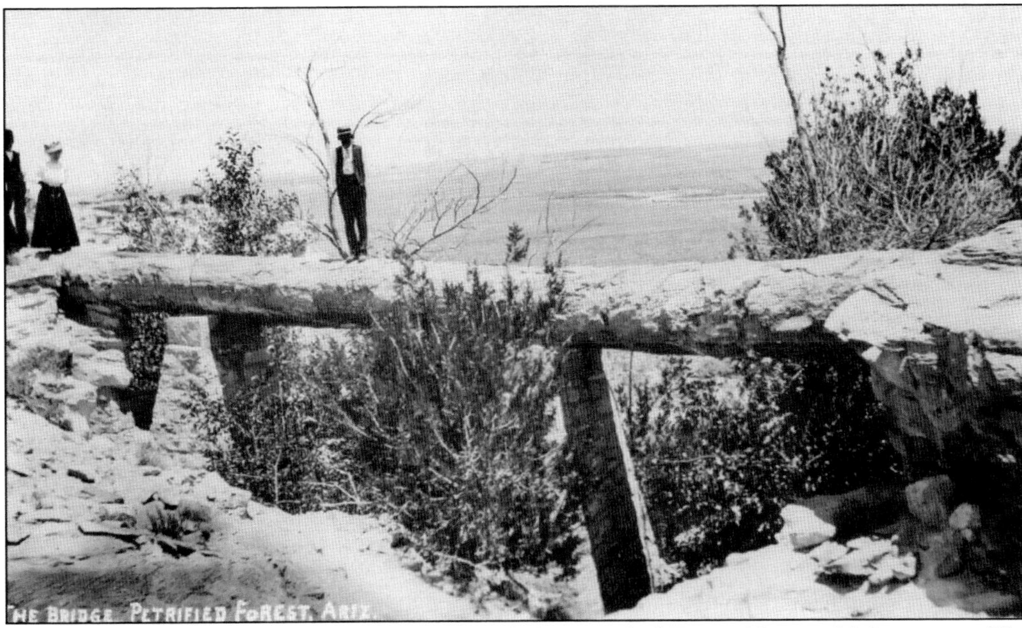

In 1906, Pres. Theodore Roosevelt designated the Petrified Forest National Monument. The landmark butted up against George Hennessey's spread and spanned north to Hennessey Butte, which is named for him. Family lore tells of the many times Hennessey's cattle were found wandering in front of the steps leading to the visitor's center. Park rangers would ride out and find him to ask if he would come get his cows.

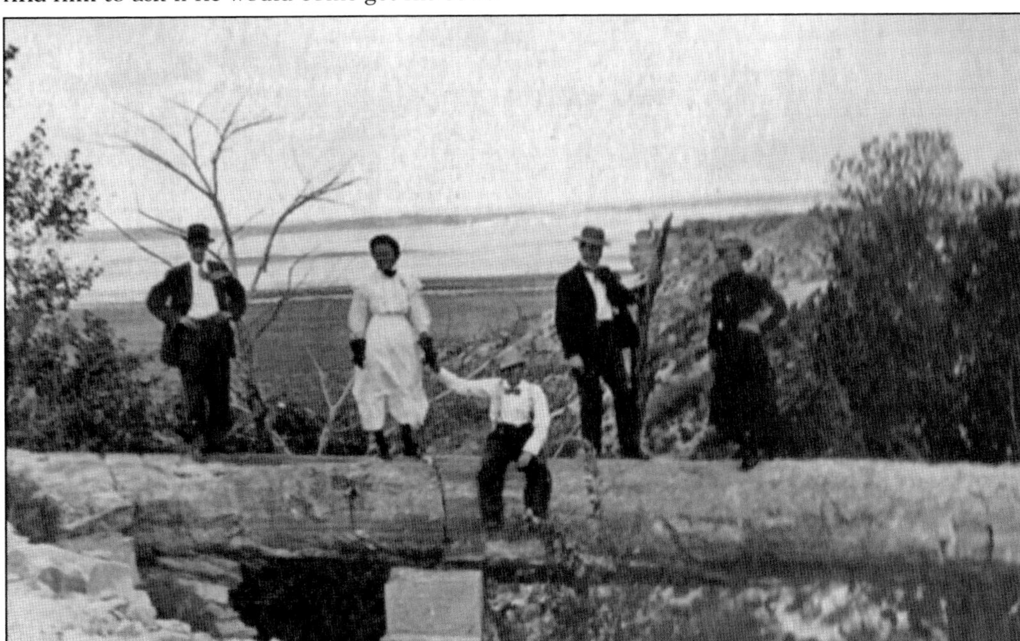

Although the Petrified Forest is protected today, locals still considered it a playground of sorts. George and Frances Hennessey (far left) gathered with friends on the popular petrified bridge when this image was snapped shortly after their marriage. These days, visitors must stick to designated trails, and access to the bridge is forbidden.

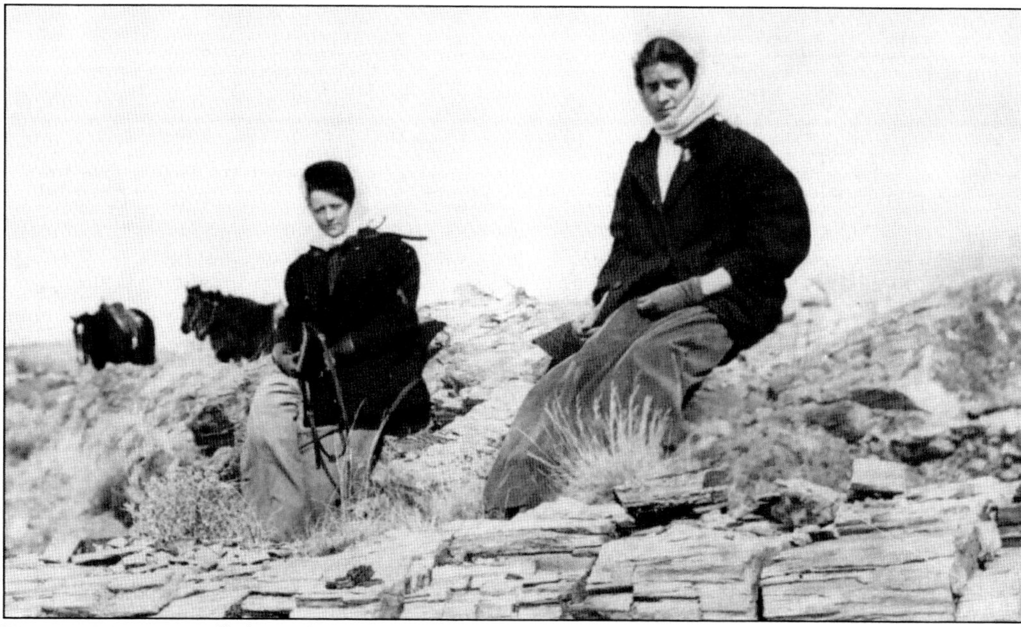

Frances Hennessey (left, with an unidentified woman) took frequent rides around the Petrified Forest with family and friends. This image appears to be a winter excursion since the ladies are dressed warmly. Although the train from Adamana took visitors to the park, horseback seems to be the more favored mode of transportation. The ladies may have been taking lunch to cowboys on the range, or simply enjoying the day.

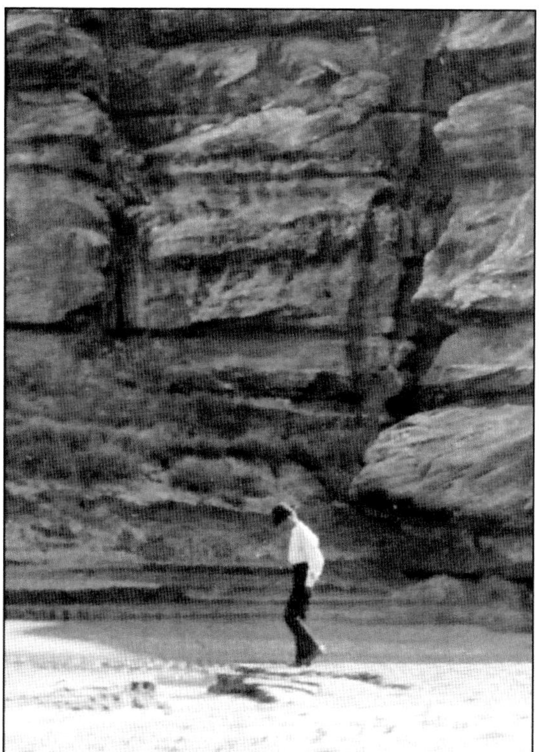

George Hennessey takes a contemplative stroll along the Little Colorado River during a picnic outing. There was a lot to think about: his ranch was prospering as he continued doing business with local cattlemen that included his old friends from the Hash Knife. He had also just married, and was planning to move back to Holbrook and start a family.

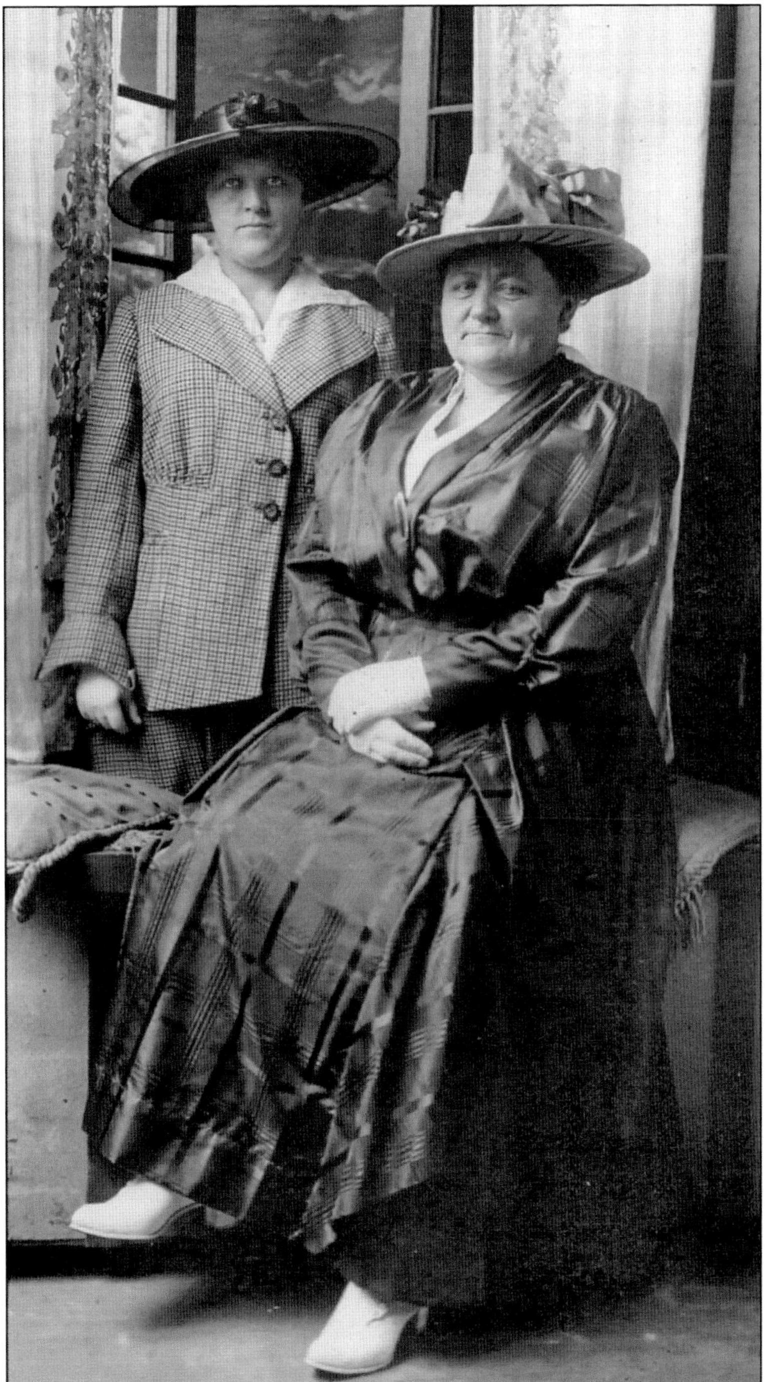

In time, Frank Wallace's ranch at Adamana began prospering. The money enabled Cora and her children to purchase "store-bought" clothing, buy better furnishings, take vacations, and enjoy the finer things in life. Here, Frances and Cora show off their new suits at the local photographer's, probably at Holbrook. Family members recalled that Cora had gone to finishing school as a girl and always dressed like a lady.

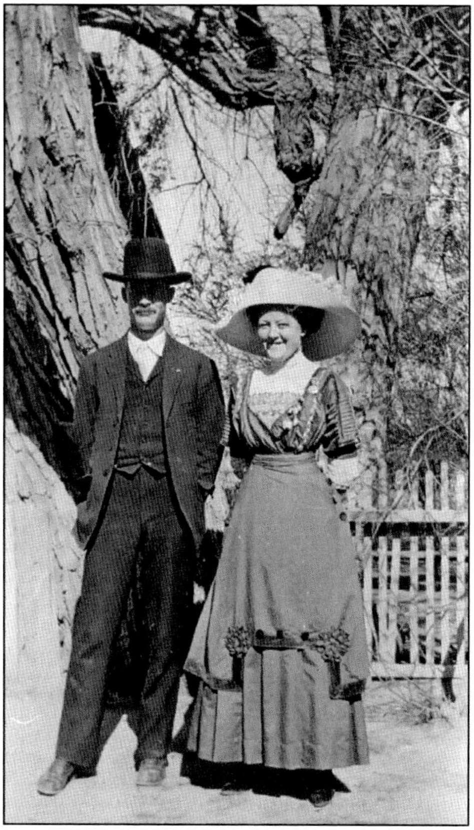

In 1912, George and Frances Hennessey were able to purchase property in Holbrook on which to build their own home. The couple, pictured here, now dressed as city folk and enjoyed the upper social circles of Holbrook. "She did love to be pampered," said Frances's granddaughter Suzanne Peterson. Likewise, George enjoyed spoiling his new wife as much as he could, even as he continued running cattle.

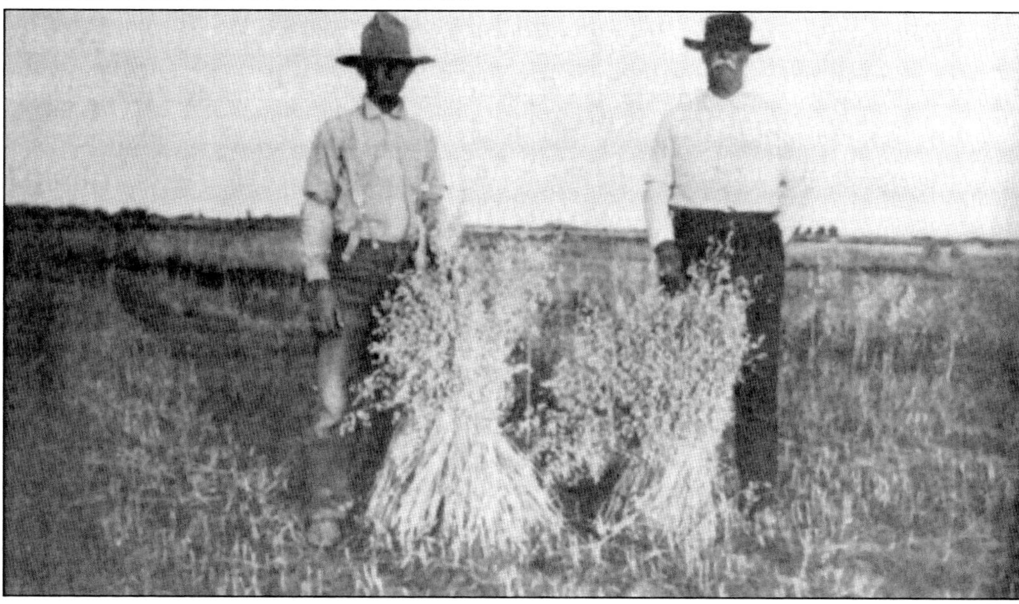

Frank Wallace and Hennessey now had little regret over leaving the Aztec Land and Cattle Company. The company tried farming in 1905 but eventually realized that desert soil and alkali water was hardly conducive to growing crops. The new endeavor must have been terribly disappointing to longtime Aztec manager Henry Warren, pictured here on the left in 1912.

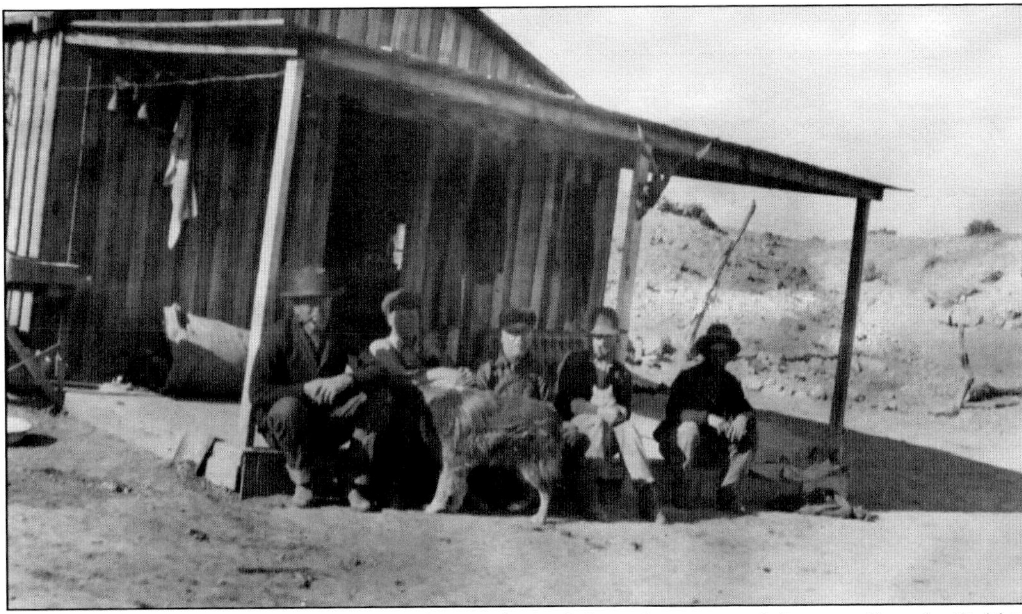

In contrast to the failing Aztec farms, the Hash Knife brand continued doing well under Babbitt Brothers. Barney Stiles eventually sold out his interest in the outfit, but Charles Wyrick of Winslow became a Babbitt Brothers partner in 1914. In this image, taken shortly after Wyrick became part owner, unidentified cowboys enjoy a little rest with their dog at one of the Hash Knife line camps. (Old Trails Museum.)

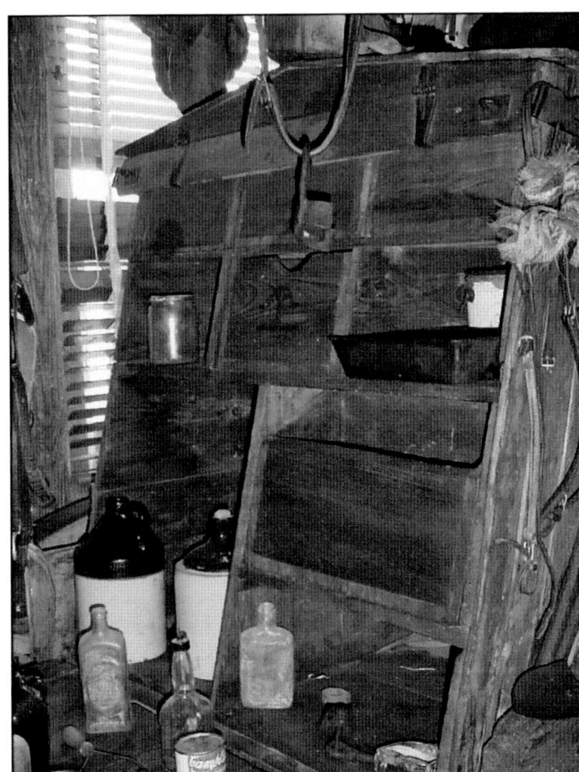

When he left the Hash Knife, George Hennessey procured a chuck wagon from the Aztec Land and Cattle Company for his own use. The wagon would prove useful at his new ranch. After years of use, the body did occasionally require maintenance, including the rebuilding of the chuckbox on the back. Hennessey applied the Hash Knife brand to the box in fond commemoration of the outfit.

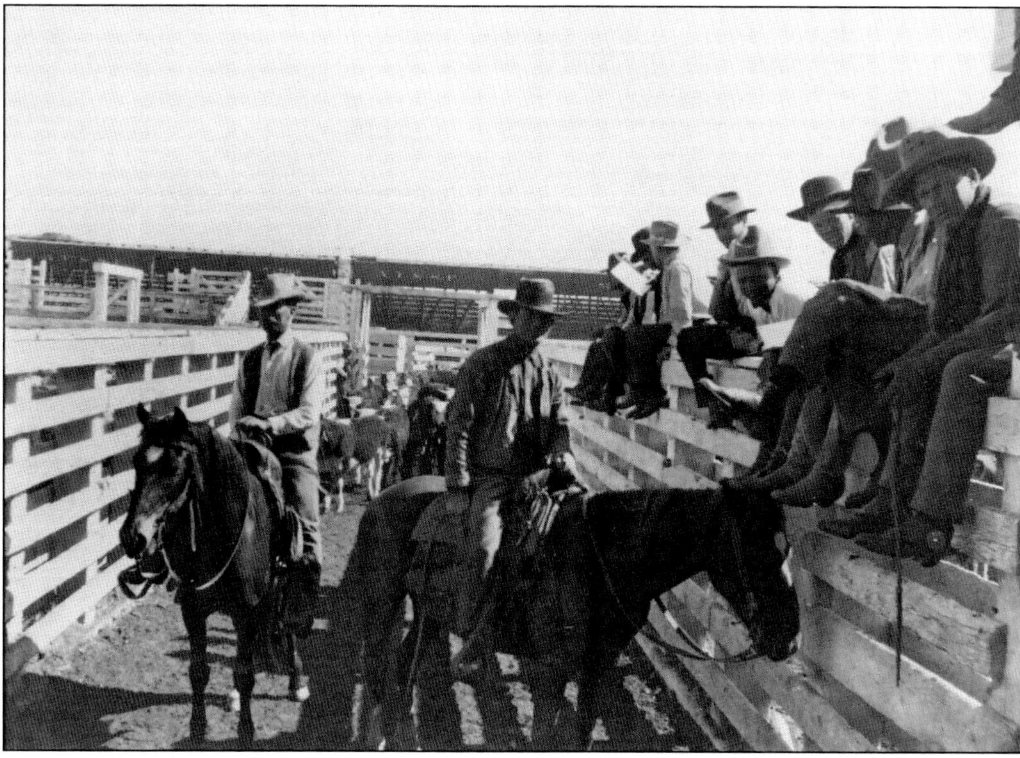

A group of unidentified hands gather at the stockyards near Holbrook. Some of the men hold ledgers and clipboards, identifying them as cattle inspectors, or possibly buyers. Ruth Wallace remembered, "It was tough times for cattlemen in those days. Our father used to say if they had one good year out of seven, we would be lucky."

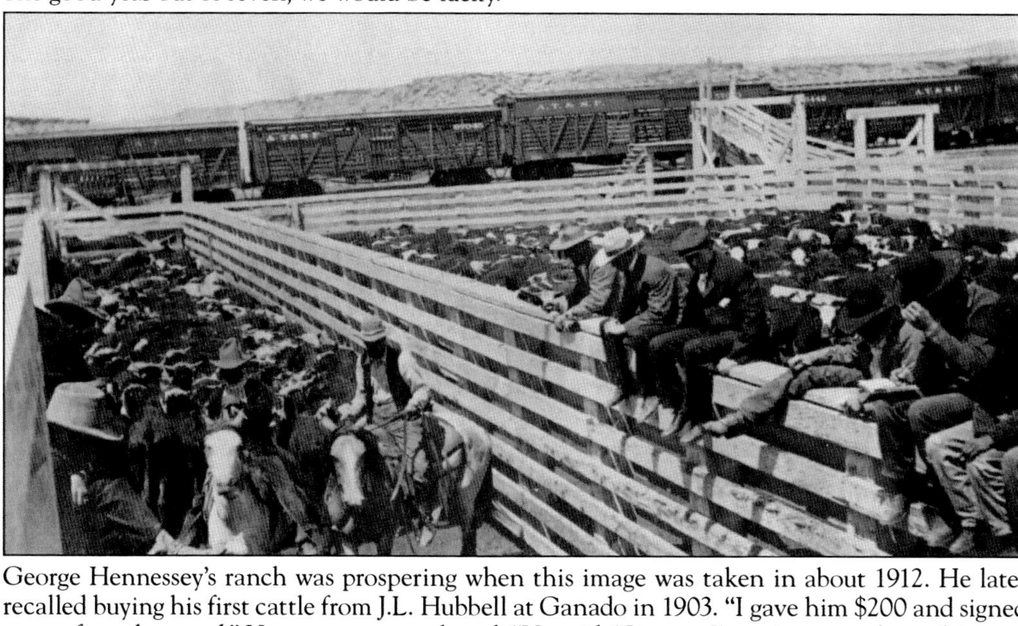

George Hennessey's ranch was prospering when this image was taken in about 1912. He later recalled buying his first cattle from J.L. Hubbell at Ganado in 1903. "I gave him $200 and signed a note for a thousand," Hennessey remembered. "He said, 'George, I'm going to endorse this note and take it to the First National Bank at Albuquerque. You'd better meet it.' And I did, too."

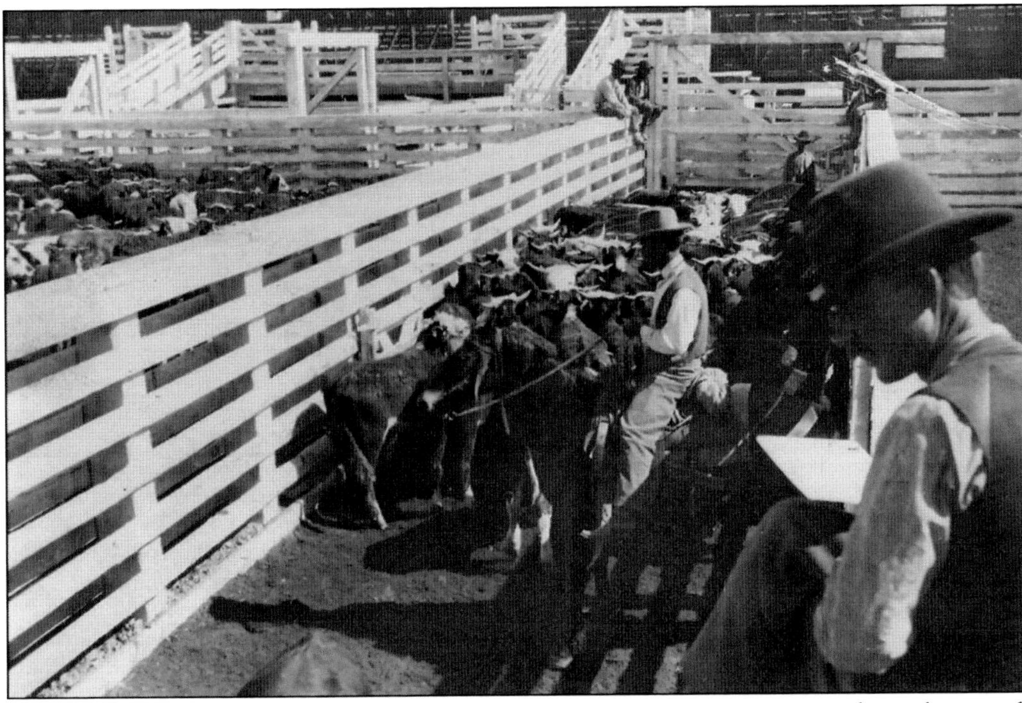

Hennessey was a charter member of the Arizona Cattle Grower's Association and was also a cattle inspector for several years. He often worked with his old friends from the Hash Knife. Hennessey is on the right in this image. The man on horseback is former Hash Knife cowboy James Donohoe, who partnered with Frank Wallace and lived with the family at Adamana.

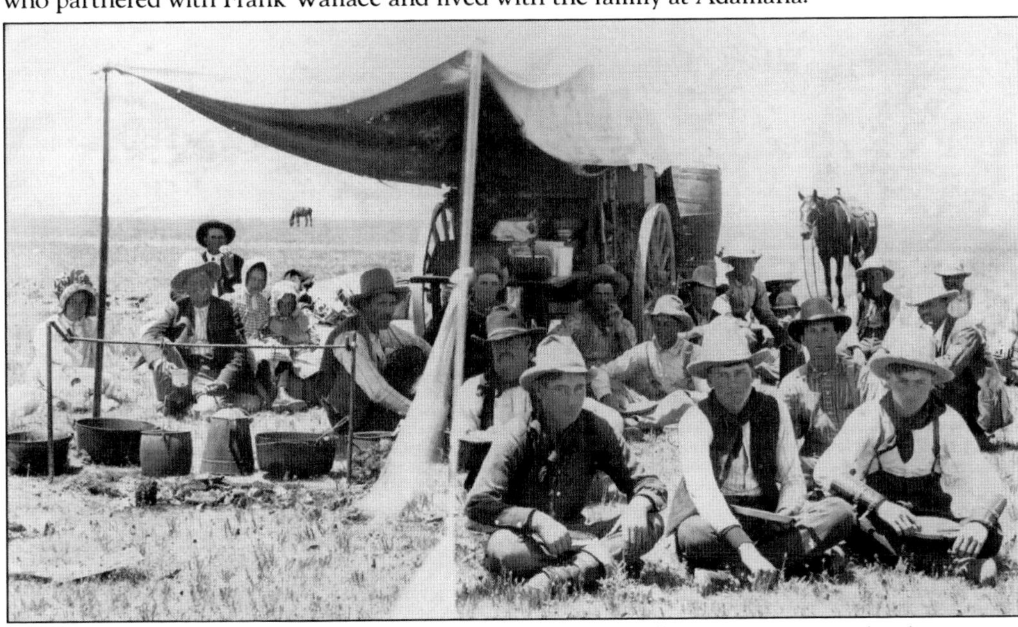

Other ranches were established on former Aztec Land and Cattle Company land over time. They included the XIT, a branch of the famous Texas outfit. Like the Hash Knife, the XIT had also expanded to Arizona and purchased some Aztec land south of Winslow. Pictured here are cowboys from the outfit, dining at the chuck wagon. (Old Trails Museum.)

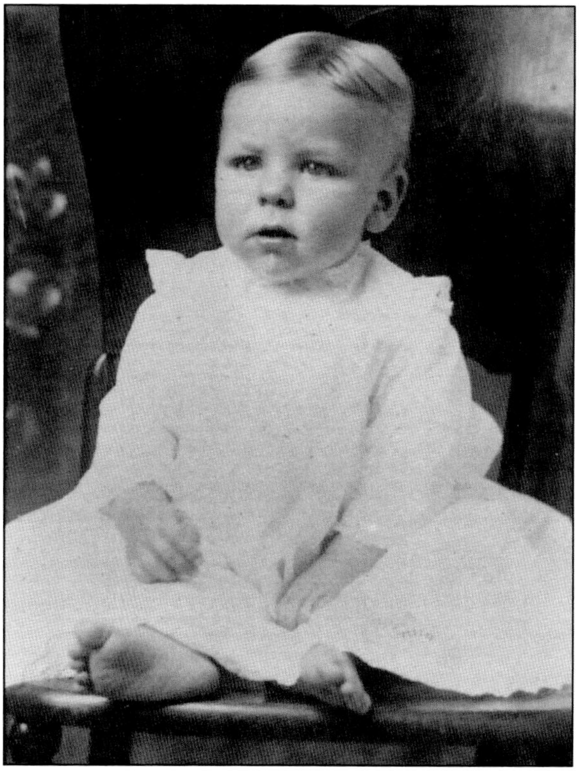

The Wallaces were still living at Adamana when their youngest child, Jack, was born in 1912. He was most likely named for Frank's half-brother, who remained close to the family and had died earlier that year. Soon after Jack was born, the family left Adamana and relocated to their new home in Holbrook.

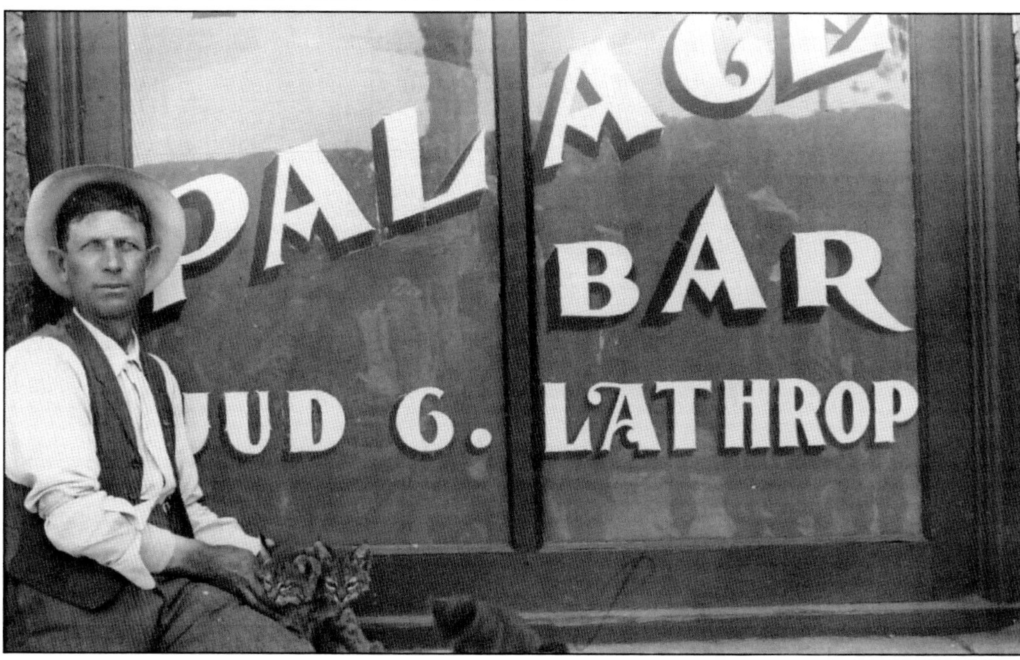

By 1913, the infamous "Bucket of Blood" in Holbrook was called the Palace Bar and owned by former Hash Knife cowboy Jud G. Lathrop, seen here with two lynx cubs and a kitten. The Palace must have been so named for only a short time, as it is never mentioned in Holbrook history. Lathrop, who lost one leg as a young man, later moved to Winslow and died in 1948.

In 1914, Margery Wallace (left, with sister Frances) married James Donohoe at Holbrook. Just a year later, she succumbed to scarlet fever at the tender age of 18. Ruth Wallace remembered, "Margery had a sweet voice and she would sing songs to me and tell me what they were about . . . She was a frail child." Donohoe remarried a short time later, but divorced and eventually moved to California.

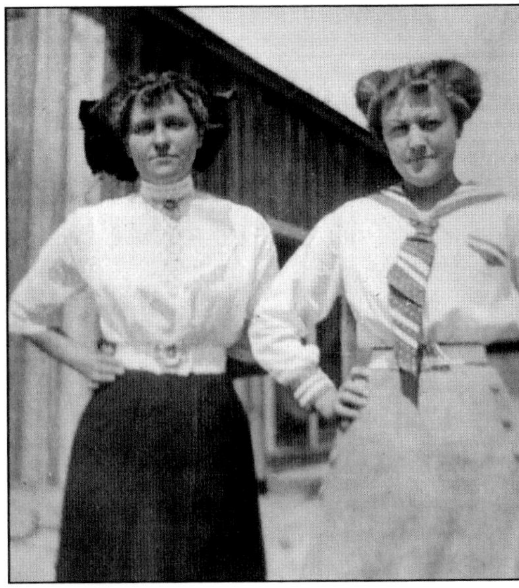

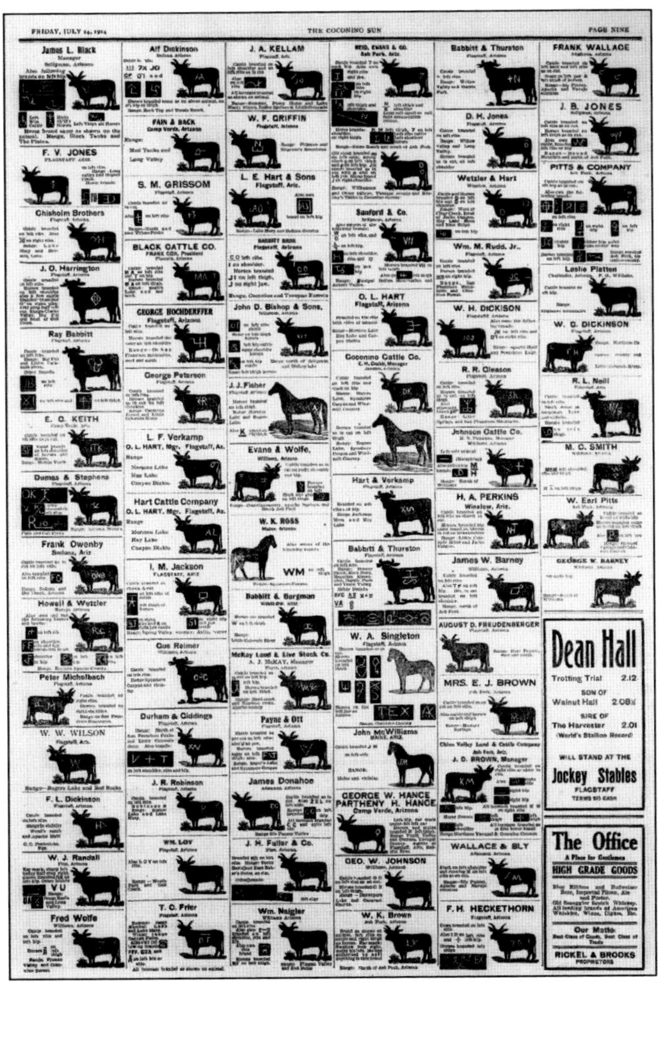

FRIDAY, JULY 24, 1914 THE COCONINO SUN PAGE NINE

James L. Black

Alf Dickinson

J. A. KELLAM

Babbitt & Thurston

FRANK WALLACE

FAIR & BACK

W. F. GRIFFIN

D. H. Jones

J. B. JONES

F. V. JONES

S. M. GRISSOM

L. E. Hart & Sons

Wetzler & Hart

PITTS & COMPANY

Chisholm Brothers

Sanford & Co.

BLACK CATTLE CO.

Wm. M. Rudd, Jr.

J. O. Harrington

Leslie Platten

O. L. HART

GEORGE HOCHDERFFER

John D. Bishop & Sons

W. H. DICKISON

W. D. DICKINSON

Ray Babbitt

George Peterson

Coconino Cattle Co.

R. R. Gleason

R. L. Neill

J. J. Fisher

E. O. KEITH

L. F. Verkamp

Johnson Cattle Co.

M. C. SMITH

Evans & Wolfe

Dumas & Stephens

Hart & Verkamp

H. A. PERKINS

W. Earl Pitts

Hart Cattle Company

W. K. ROSS

Frank Owenby

Babbitt & Thurston

James W. Barney

GEORGE W. BARNEY

I. M. Jackson

Babbitt & Bergman

Howell & Wetzler

AUGUST D. FREUDENBERGER

W. A. Singleton

Dean Hall

Gus Reimer

McKay Land & Live Stock Co.

MRS. E. J. BROWN

Peter Michelbach

W. W. WILSON

Durham & Giddings

Payne & Ott

John McWilliams

J. R. Robinson

James Donohoe

GEORGE W. HANCE

PARTHENY H. HANCE

F. L. Dickinson

WALLACE & BLY

WM. LOY

J. H. Fuller & Co.

W. J. Randall

GEO. W. JOHNSON

The Office

HIGH GRADE GOODS

T. C. Frier

Wm. Neigler

W. K. Brown

F. H. HECKETHORN

Fred Wolfe

RICKEL & BROOKS

A 1914 newspaper shows some of the brands from northern Arizona. Included here are the brands of Babbit Brothers including those of Ray Babbitt, Babbitt and Thurston, and Babbitt and Bargman's Hash Knife. Brands for James Donohoe, Frank Wallace, and Wallace and Bly are also visible. Wallace had gone into business with Nathan Bly back in 1907. Later, Frank's son Emmet was also made a partner.

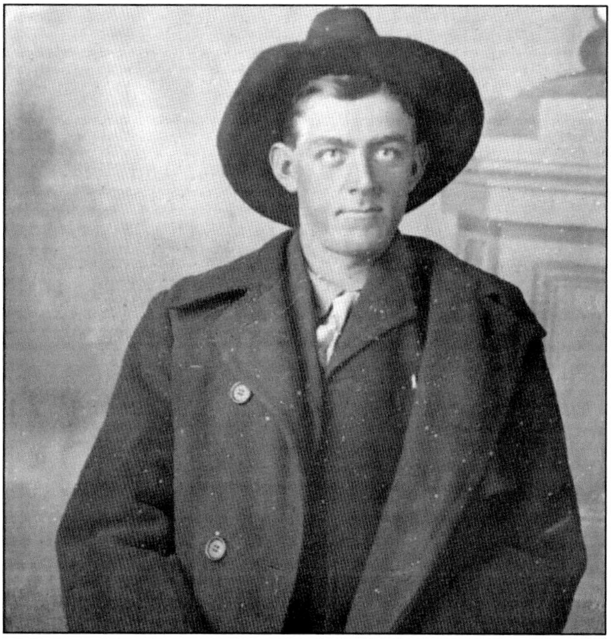

Emmet Wallace started his own ranch after marrying Amy Smith in 1914. Amy figured he decided to marry her after learning of her first aid skills when his sister, Minnie, was bit by a rattlesnake. "The rattlesnake incident proved I would make a good ranch wife," Amy said. The newlyweds' first child, Robert, was born at the Wallace home in Holbrook in 1916.

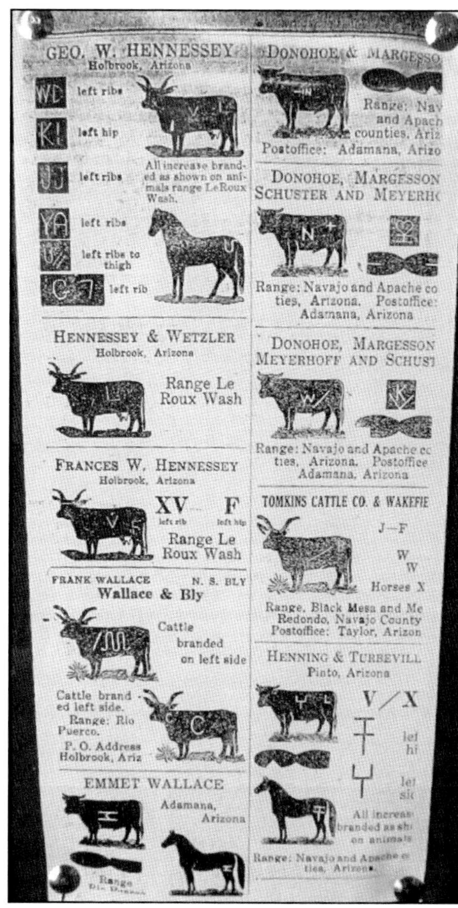

GEO. W. HENNESSEY
Holbrook, Arizona

left ribs
left hip
left ribs
All increase branded as shown on animals range LeRoux Wash.
left ribs
left ribs to thigh
left rib

HENNESSEY & WETZLER
Holbrook, Arizona
Range Le Roux Wash

FRANCES W. HENNESSEY
Holbrook, Arizona
XV left rib
F left hip
Range Le Roux Wash

FRANK WALLACE N. S. BLY
Wallace & Bly
Cattle branded on left side
Cattle branded left side.
Range: Rio Puerco.
P. O. Address Holbrook, Ariz

EMMET WALLACE
Adamana, Arizona

DONOHOE & MARGESSO
Range: Nav and Apach counties, Ariz
Postoffice: Adamana, Arizo

DONOHOE, MARGESSON SCHUSTER AND MEYERHO
Range: Navajo and Apache co ties, Arizona. Postoffice: Adamana, Arizona

DONOHOE, MARGESSON MEYERHOFF AND SCHUST
Range: Navajo and Apache co ties, Arizona. Postoffice Adamana, Arizona

TOMKINS CATTLE CO. & WAKEFIE
J—F
W W
Horses X
Range, Black Mesa and Me Redondo, Navajo County
Postoffice: Taylor, Arizon

HENNING & TURBEVILL
Pinto, Arizona
V / X
All increase branded as sh on animals
Range: Navajo and Apache co ties, Arizona

More family brands (with the exception on Tomkins & Wakefield and Henning & Turbeville) are shown in this news clipping, on display at the Navajo County Historical Society. The date is likely 1915, since that is the year Emmet Wallace established his own ranch. It is interesting to note that even Frances Wallace Hennessey had her own brand.

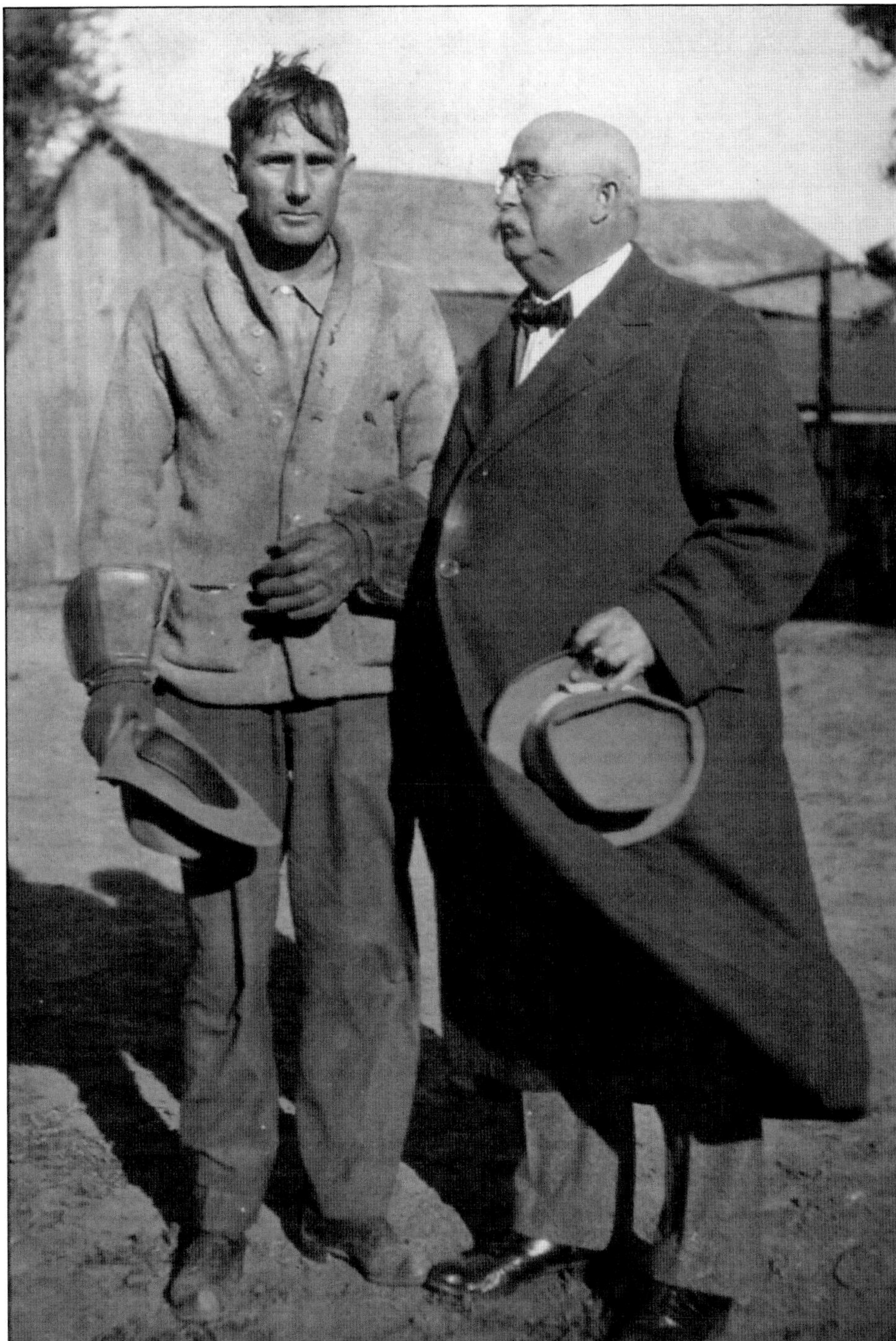

George Wylie Paul Hunt was Arizona's first state governor, serving an amazing seven terms. The self-proclaimed "Old Walrus" is seen here on a campaign visit to Holbrook in 1916. Shortly afterward, Hunt was temporarily ousted from office following what he claimed was a fraudulent election. Hunt poses with Indian trader William Williams. Photographs of the governor posing with "the common man" were distributed for publicity purposes.

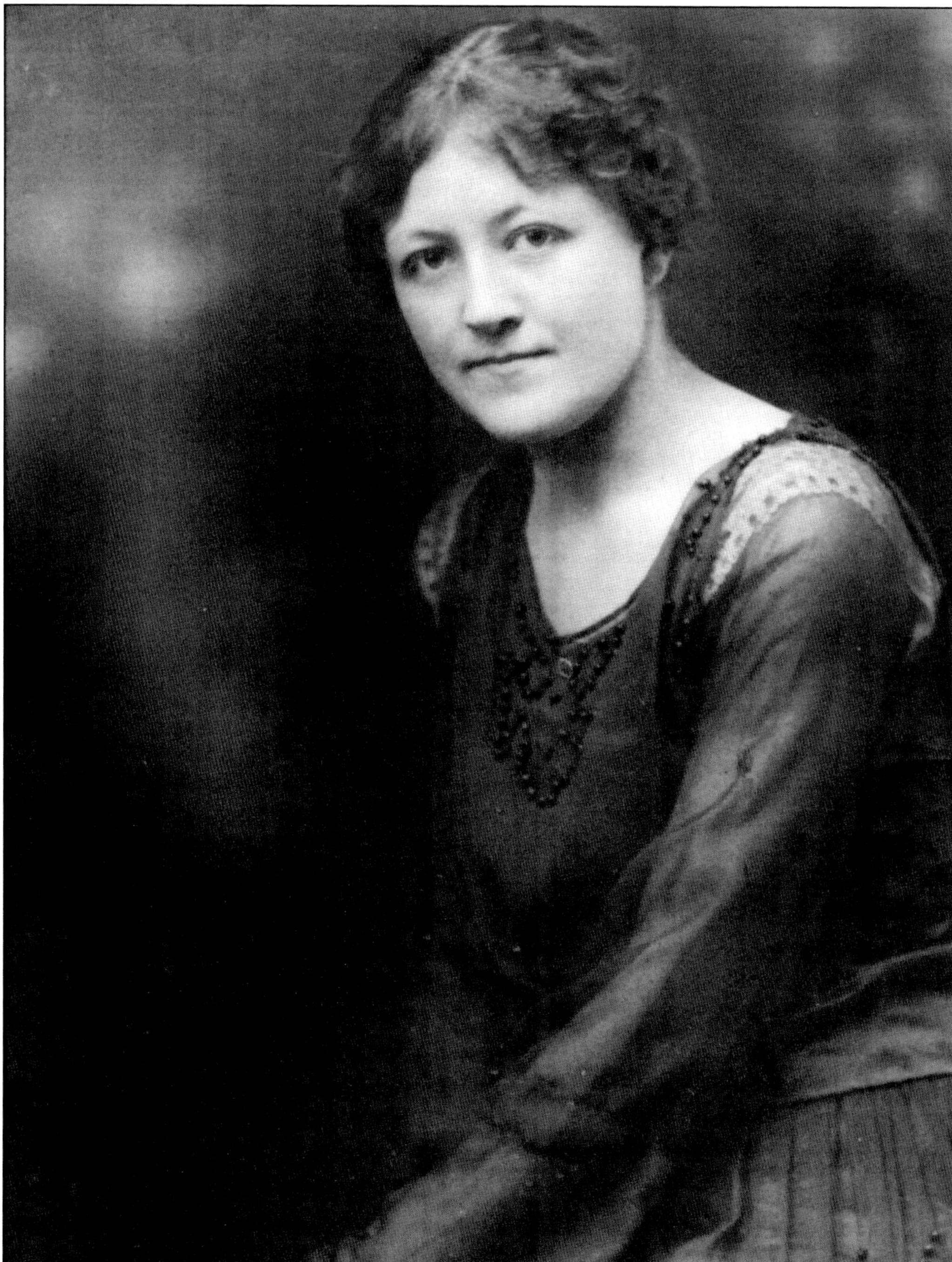

Frances Hennessey jumped to the top of social circles when her husband was elected mayor of Holbrook in 1917—on a write-in ticket. Hennessey was at his ranch when his friends, including Frank Wallace, paid him a visit. "A bunch of fellows came riding out from Holbrook," he later remembered. "My father-in-law said, 'You're the mayor of Holbrook.' I said, 'Hell, I'm not running.' He said, 'Well, you're elected anyhow.'" Hennessey later said the story of his friends hog-tying him and taking him back to Holbrook to be sworn in was not really true.

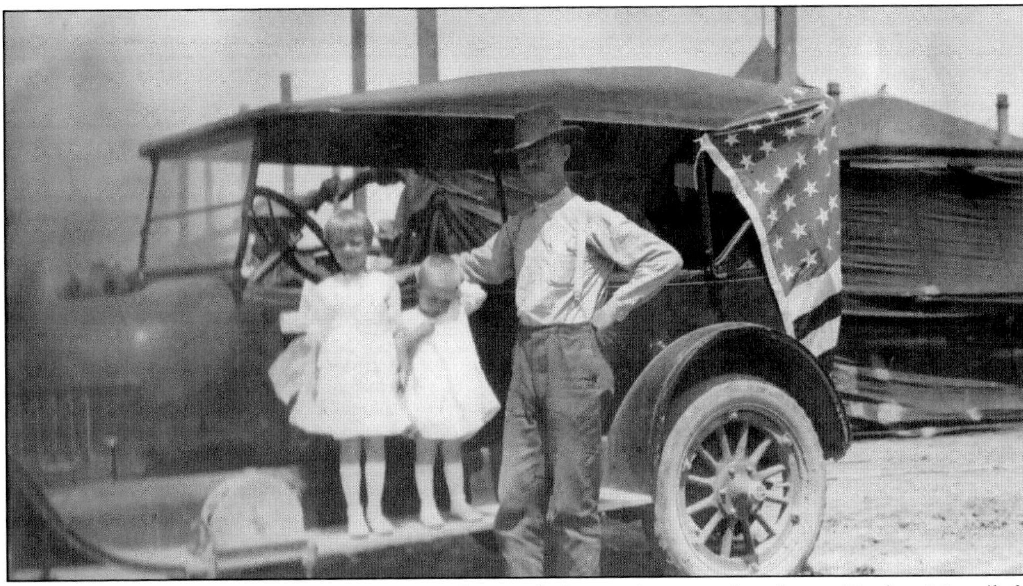

George Hennessey, pictured here, was a doting father to his two daughters. Evelyn Mae (left) was born 1913 in Holbrook, and Omah "Betty" Elizabeth (right), was born 1916 in California. According to Betty's daughter, Suzanne Peterson, George had sent Frances to the coast in hopes she would feel better. A nurse was sent along, too, which turned out to be a good idea.

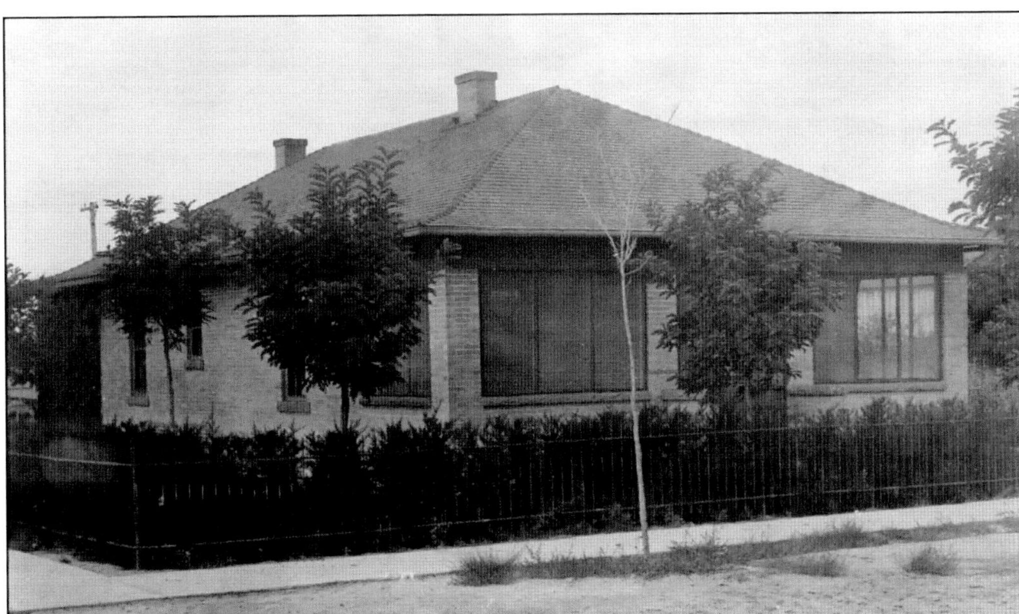

George Hennessey's home with Frances was at the corner of Arizona Street and North Second Street in Holbrook. The couple was living there by the time Evelyn was born. When this photograph was taken around 1918, the house was amongst the nicest in town. The structure still serves as a residence today.

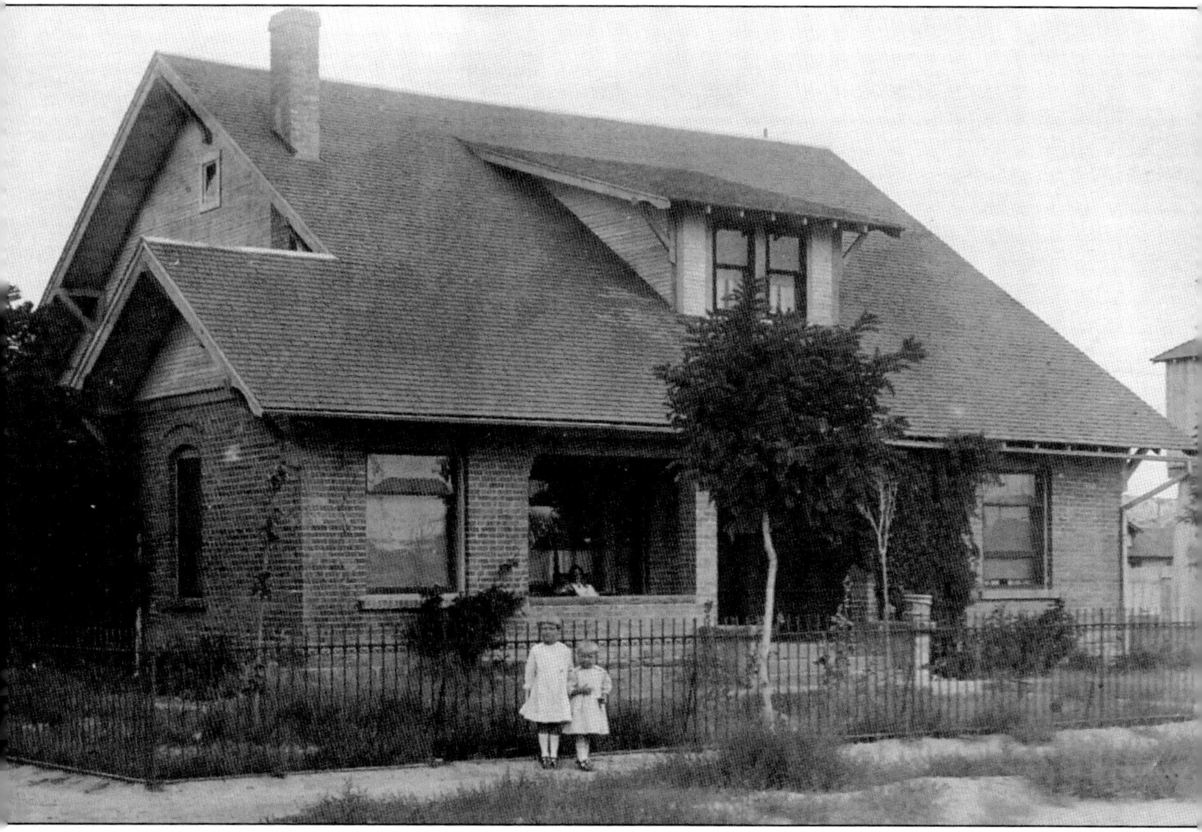

Cora Wallace purchased property across the street from the Hennesseys in 1913. Frank built her a lavish new house, and the family—Frank, Cora, Bertha, Ann, Minnie, and Jack—moved from Adamana. Evelyn and Betty Hennessey were photographed in front of the house around 1918. By 1920, the Wallaces were alternately spending time at their newly purchased OW Ranch near Young. Today, the former Wallace home is still among the nicest in Holbrook.

Seven

The OW Ranch and the End of an Era

In 1917, Frank Wallace and Nathan Bly purchased the OW Ranch, near Young, from H.J. "Jim" Ramer. At the OW, the Wallaces dined on beef, fowl, fish, and elk. Cows supplied butter, cheese, milk, and cream. Water was plentiful from Canyon Creek, and neighbors supplied potatoes. Cora Wallace fed her chickens and turkeys ample table scraps. Once, after making some wine, she threw the fermented grapes in the yard. Some turkeys ate the grapes and were soon "staggering around the yard, vainly flapping their wings."

Following the sudden death of Emmet Wallace, the family eventually moved into the house meant for him and his wife, Amy. "The Wallace family accepted me, making me one of their family," Amy remembered. Frank's friend and employee, Pat Hughes, meanwhile moved into the old family home at Adamana and was working for the Hash Knife. In 1922, Pat's son Mack also went to work for the outfit at the tender age of 12.

With the Great Depression looming on the horizon, Wallace was forced to sell the OW. The buyer, C.B. Brunson of Hollywood, California, burned down the Wallace house and constructed more a palatial home overlooking the ranch. By 1930, Frank and Cora were alternately living between Holbrook and the homes of their children. Following Cora's death, Frank sold the Holbrook house. In 1940, he was living with George and Frances Hennessey in Phoenix but often returned to Holbrook, where he would stay for months at a time.

In 1947, George Hennessey became a livestock appraiser for First National Bank of Arizona in Phoenix, which kept him out on the range. He also had an office off the lobby of the Adams Hotel. Even after retirement, Hennessey maintained contact with his many good friends from the old days. He died on January 17, 1973—the last of the hard-living, hard-working cowboys of the original Hash Knife brand.

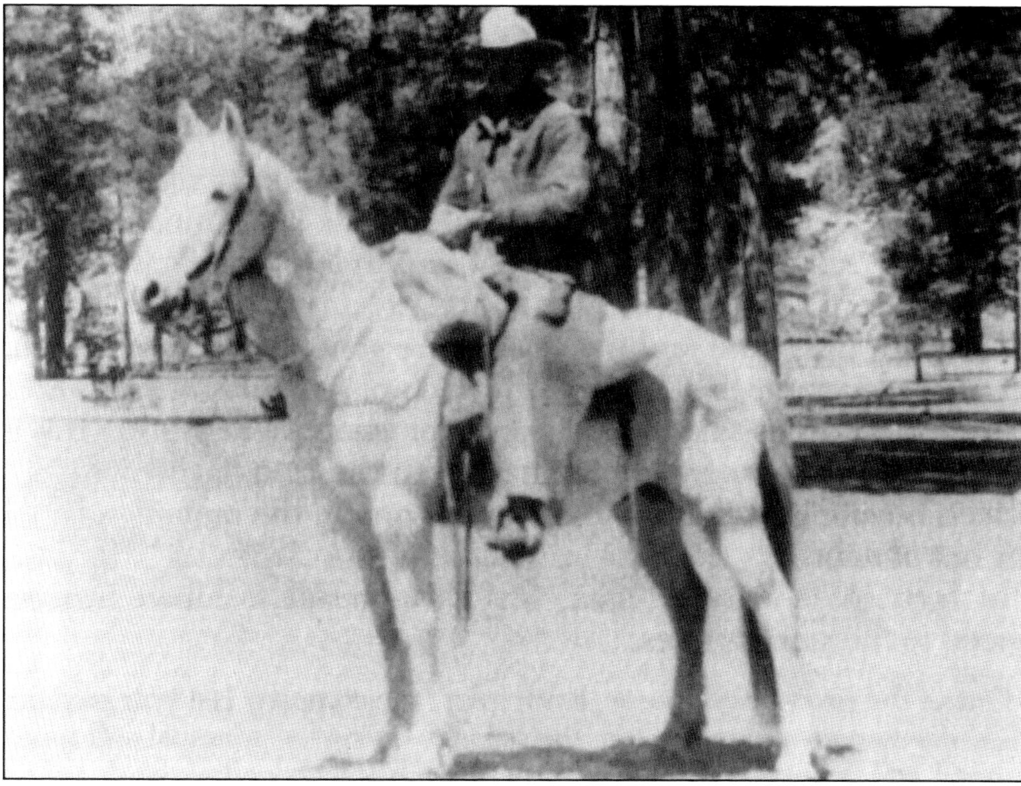

Shortly after Frank Wallace and Nathan Bly purchased the OW Ranch, Bly became ill and sold his half to Wallace. Wallace often balanced his time between the ranch and the family home at Holbrook some 74 miles away. Wallace is pictured here at Heber, a convenient stopping point between the two places. He often stayed there with his daughter Ruth and her husband, Harold Moritz.

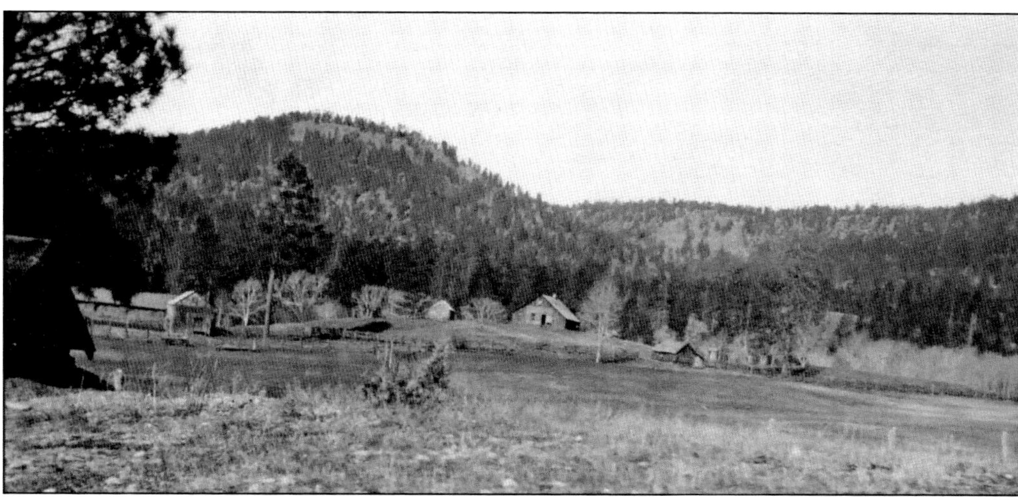

The purchase price of the OW Ranch was a whopping $150,000. Alternatively known as Canyon Creek Ranch, the spread was originally owned by Andy Cooper of the famed Blevins family. Jim Ramer bought the ranch in 1887, registering the OW brand in 1892. Over time, he expanded the ranch along Canyon Creek by purchasing additional homesteads.

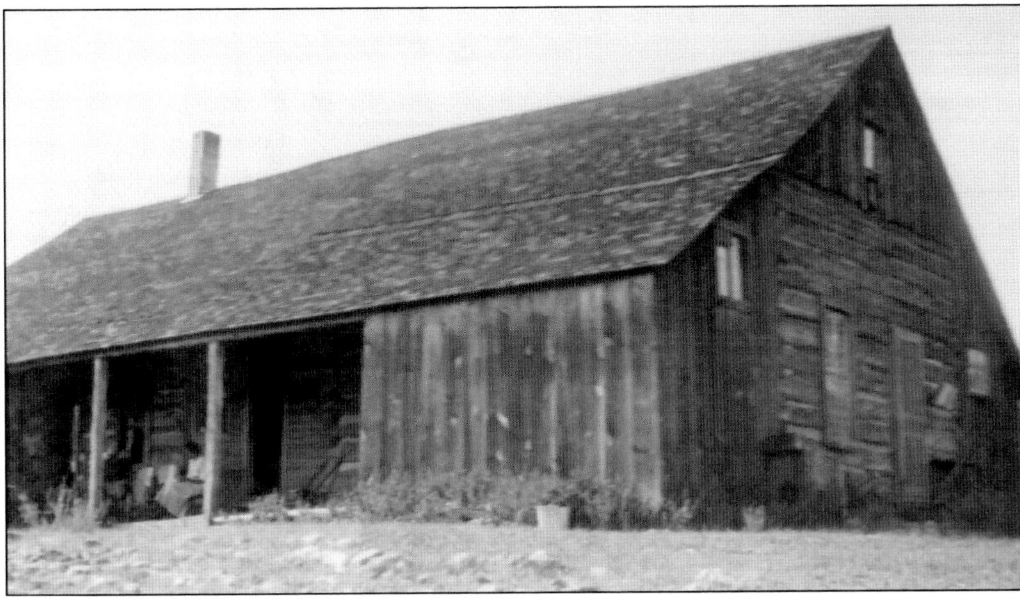

The Wallaces initially lived in the original ranch house (above). Author Norma Leonard described the place: "All the buildings were roofed with hand-hewn shingles. Light colored, freshly peeled logs formed the walls of the commissary where Indians, cowboys and other ranchers purchased flour, coffee and other commodities. Smoke frequently drifted from the chimney of the blacksmith shop as repairs were made and metal equipment manufactured for use on the ranch . . . The smokehouse to the north, where the indefatigable Mrs. Wallace carefully supervised the slaughtering of hams, always sported a rack of antlers over the door." Wallace built an additional house (below) for Emmet and Amy Wallace. "I think this OW Ranch was the most beautiful place I have ever seen," said Amy.

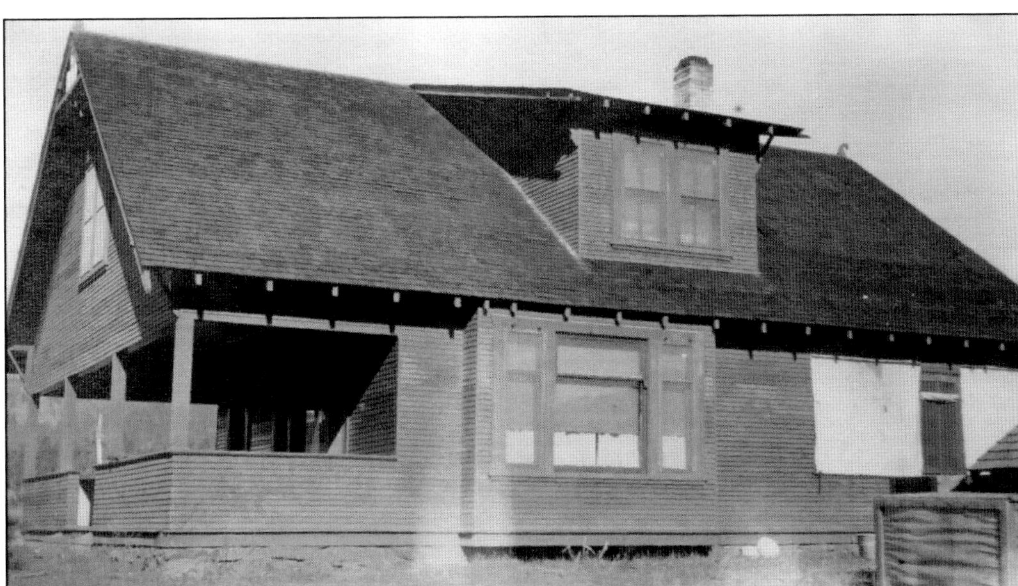

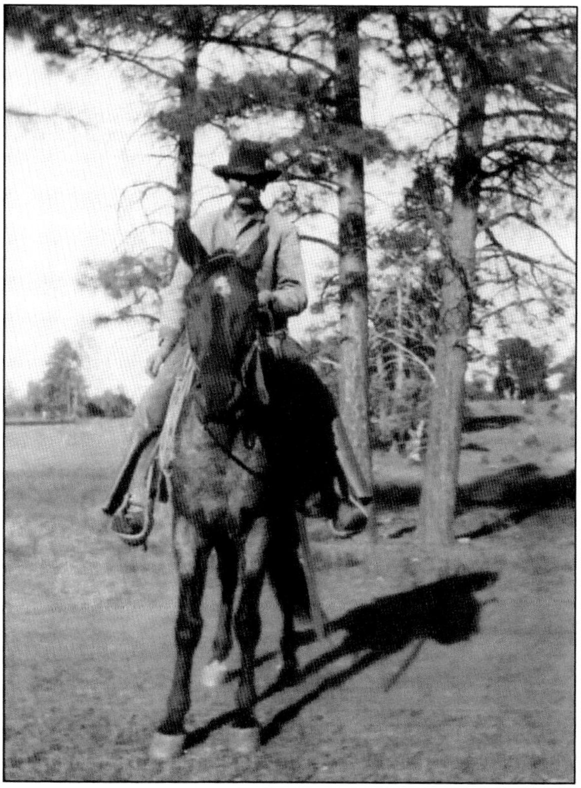

Frank Wallace poses on his horse at the OW Ranch. Amy Wallace later commented on Frank's decision to buy a car for the trips to Holbrook and back. "It was the wildest ride I ever took . . . I said 'Papa Wallace, if you would just remember that car isn't a horse, and when you come to a bush or tree unless you turn it, it is going to go right over.'"

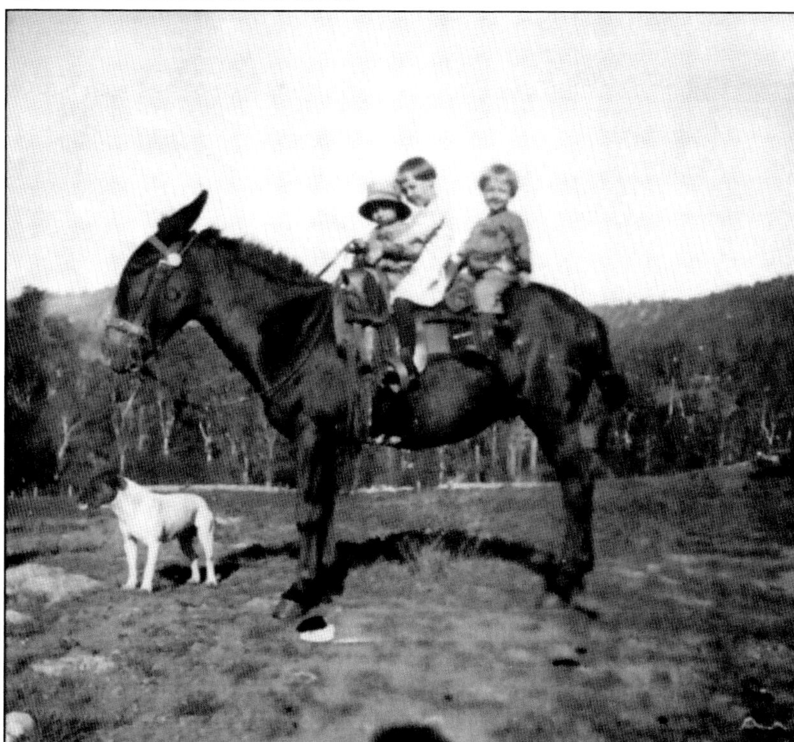

Norma Leonard described how hay was piled to the ceiling in the barn. "This provided a perfect place for a child to play," she said, "rolling from ceiling to floor without danger of being hurt." Wallace's grandchildren Harold Moritz Jr. and Evelyn and Betty Hennessey visited the OW Ranch often and had very fond memories of their time there.

Tragically, Emmet Wallace was at Adamana when he died during the 1920 influenza epidemic. He had just moved to the OW with Amy, who was visiting family in California. Emmet refused to worry her until the last minute and died before Amy could reach him. Afterward, Amy returned to California, giving birth to her second son just a month later. She named him after his father.

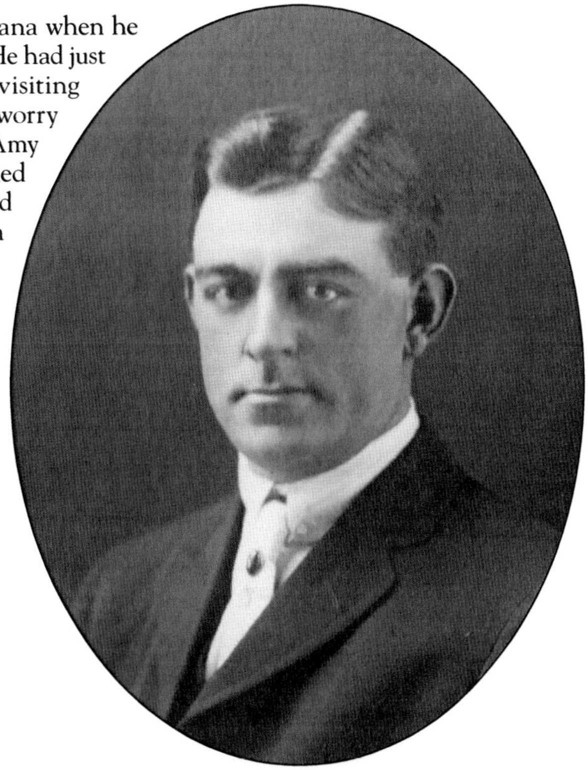

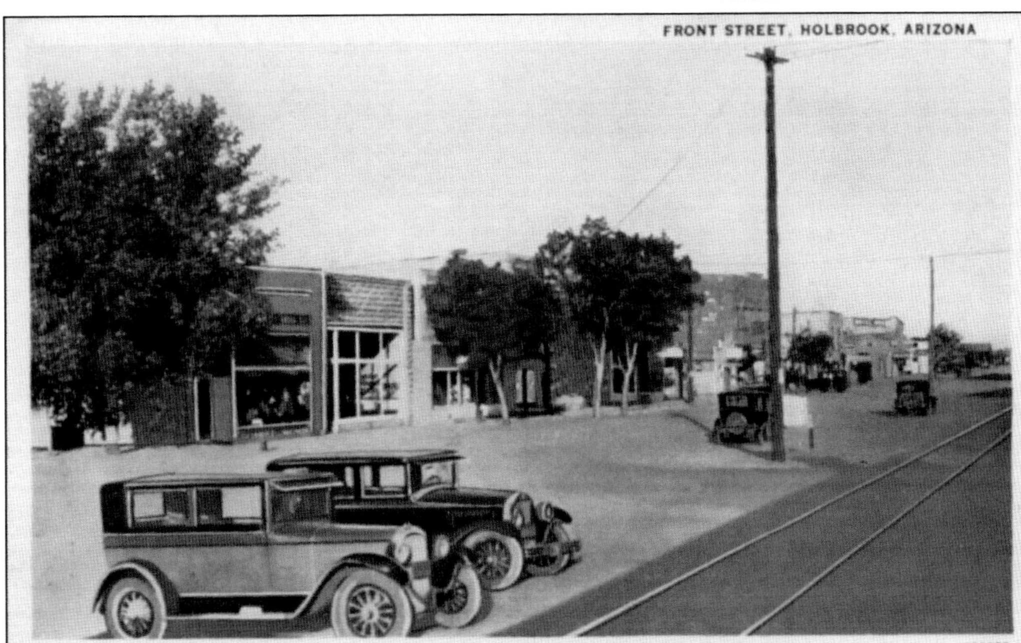

Although Arizona outlawed liquor in 1914, places like the Bucket of Blood in Holbrook stubbornly tried to stay open. Prohibition in 1920 officially put an end to all bars nationally. The downtown area appears to have taken on a cleaner, more civilized ambience when this postcard was produced. (Navajo County Historical Society.)

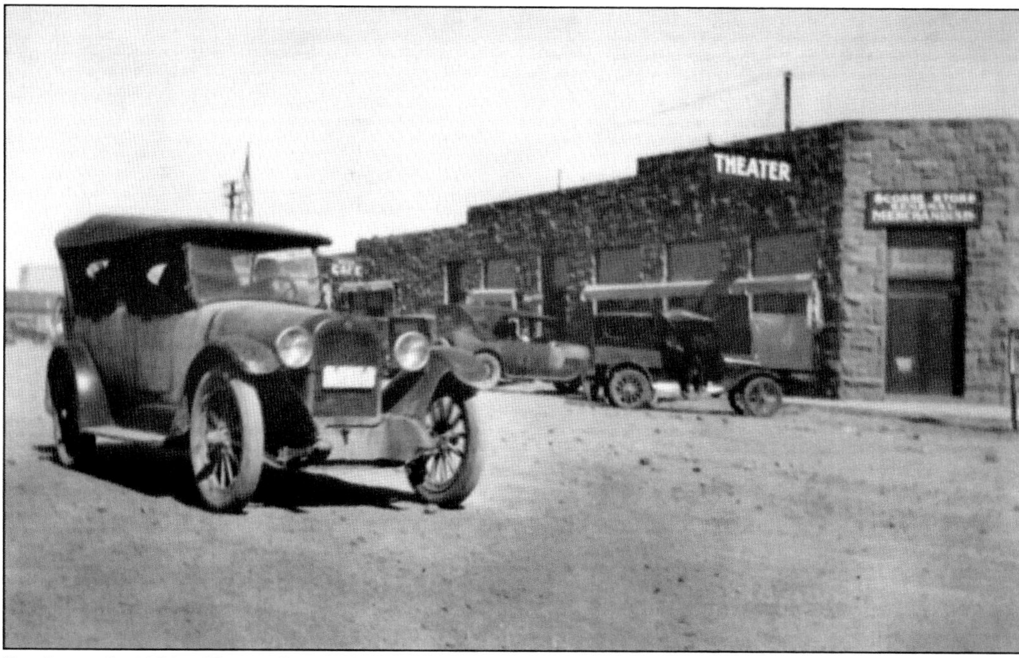

By the early 1920s, Henry Scorse Jr. was running his father's store in Holbrook. Henry Scorse Sr. is credited with constructing numerous buildings in town and attempting to dam the Little Colorado River. In 1923, however, a major flood washed out bridges, roads, railroad beds, houses, barns, and warehouses. Some floated as far as the highway bridge before being dashed to smithereens. (Navajo County Historical Society.)

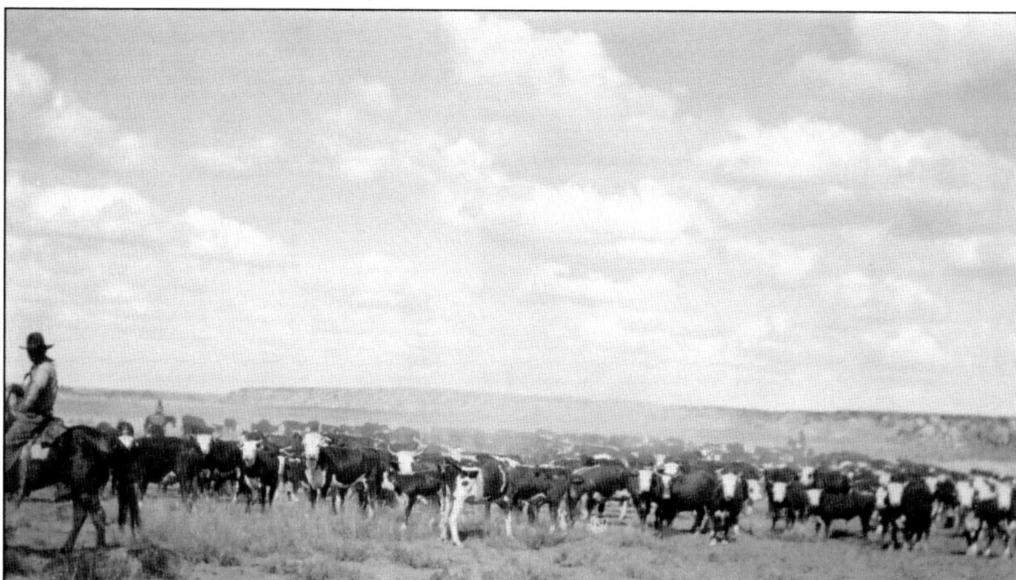

George Hennessey's ranch is pictured here in 1921. His success enabled him to buy and sell several parcels of land. By 1923 he had also formed his own Hennessey Land and Cattle Company. Hennessey also remained popular in Holbrook, where he was well known as the best square dance caller in town. Dances were assured success simply by mentioning his expected presence in the newspaper.

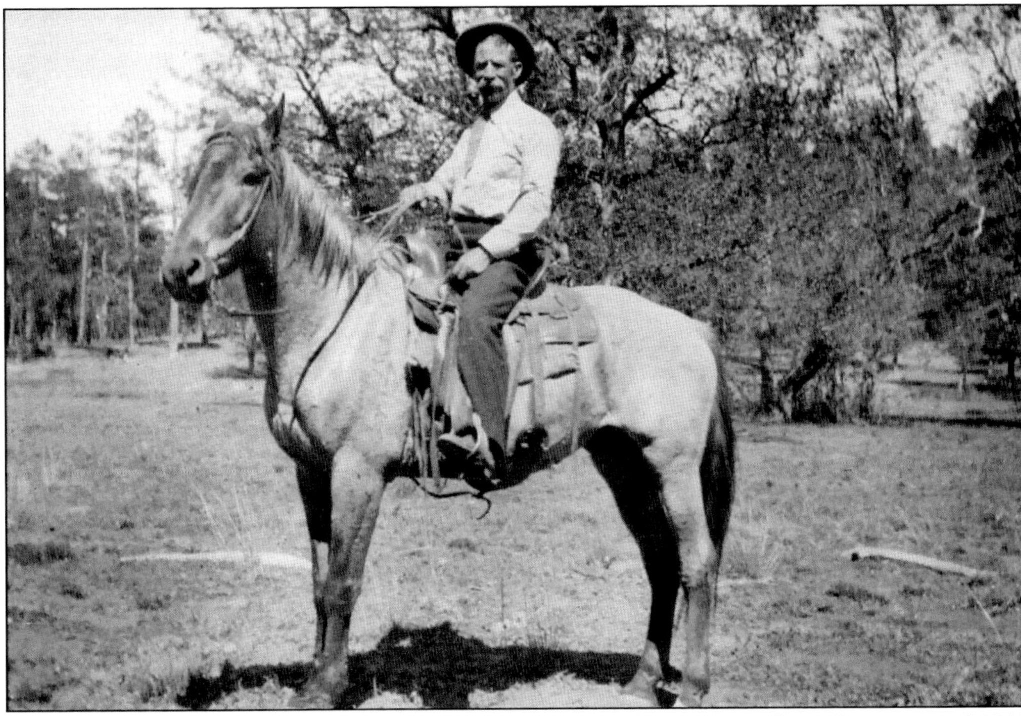

George Hennessey's father, Thomas, pictured here, moved to Arizona from Texas around 1916. He may have been working for George in 1917, along with his son Daniel. Ever the gypsy, Thomas was last listed as living with his daughter Hattie, possibly in New Mexico, in 1924. Even his place of death in 1927 remains a mystery, but he is buried in Holbrook.

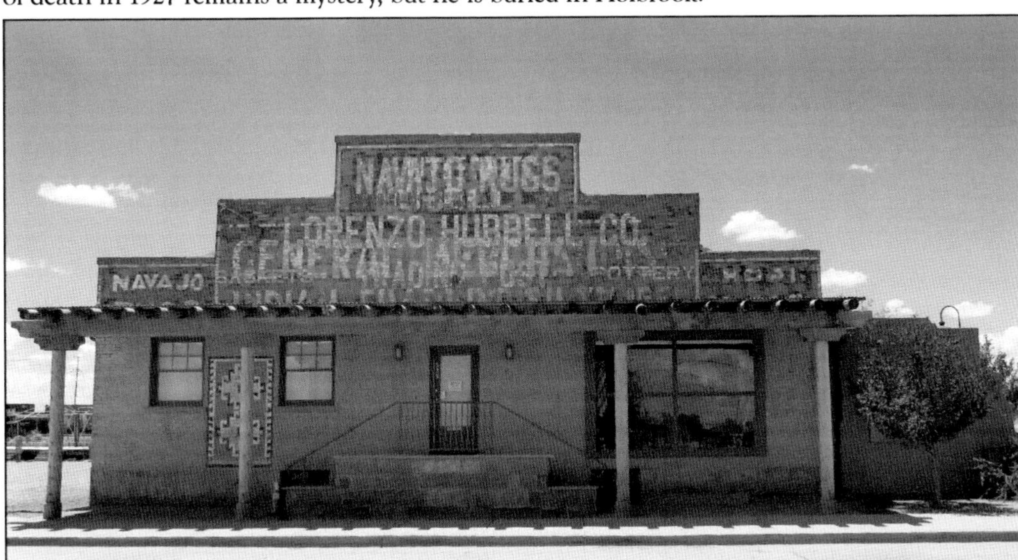

George Hennessey had long paid back J.L. Hubbell when the trading-post owner opened a new store in Winslow in 1924. The Hennessey and Wallace families did business there when they were in town. Hubbell ran the store for several years before turning management over to his brother Roman. The Winslow store finally closed in about 1953. Today, the building is owned by the city.

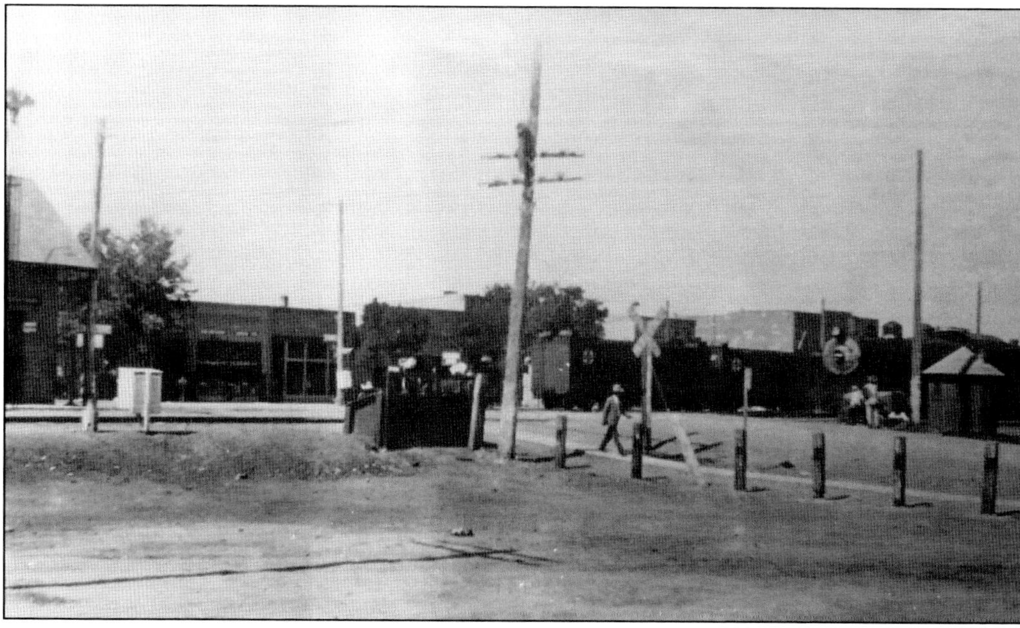

Hash Knife cowboys were scant in Holbrook by 1925. The Bucket of Blood lost its appeal after a patron "started through the swinging doors and saw two men, one lying across the other, on the floor. They had both been shot and the place was empty of living souls. The bartender had fled, fearing that he could not clear himself of the charges of murder." (Navajo County Historical Society.)

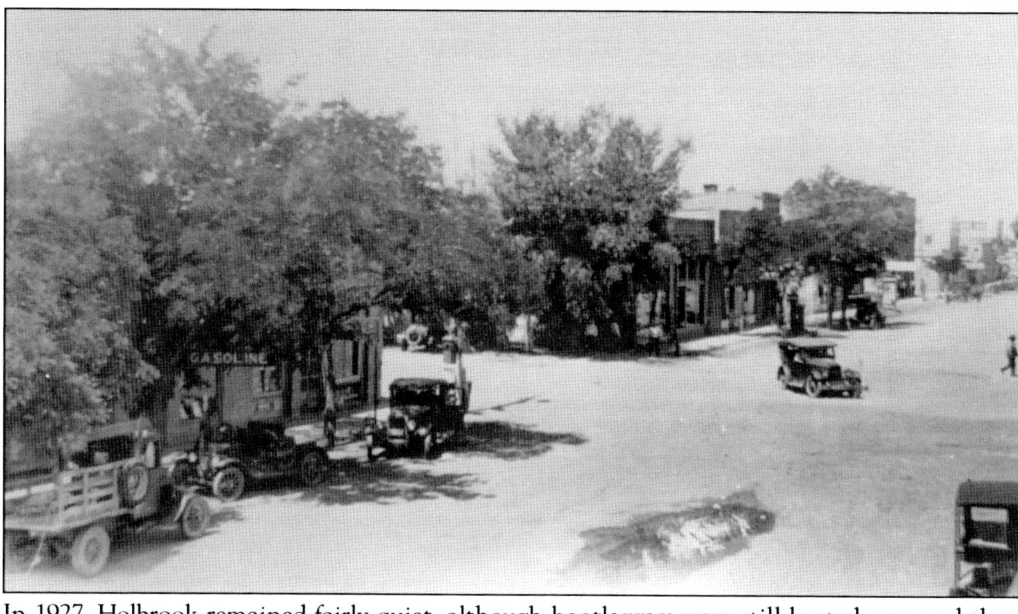

In 1927, Holbrook remained fairly quiet, although bootleggers were still busted now and then. In 1928, the local paper reported on a raid by Sheriff L.D. Divelbess, which netted around 65 gallons of moonshine. The cache was found "under the floor of the old city hall building at the west end of town." (Navajo County Historical Society.)

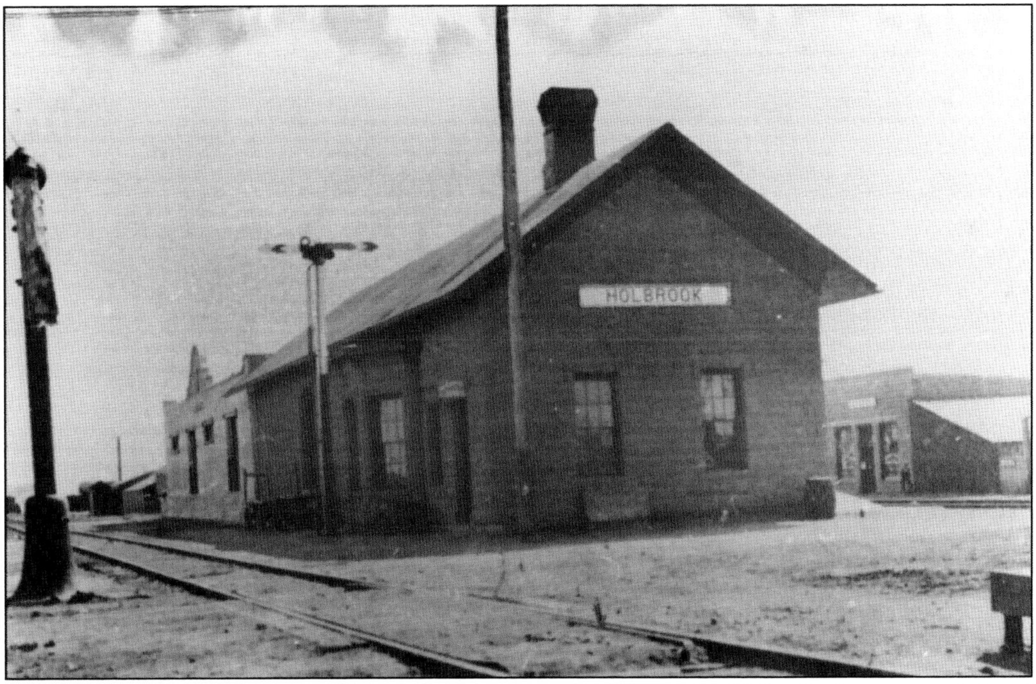

The depot at Holbrook was still a major shipping point during the 1930s. Both steam and diesel trains continued transporting passengers and shipping cattle, mail, timber, and other supplies along today's Interstate 40. (Navajo County Historical Society.)

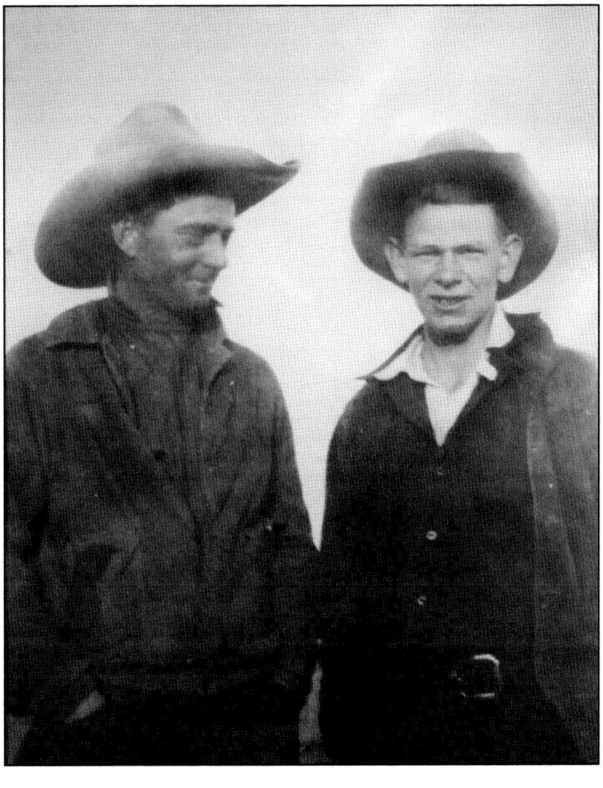

Former Hash Knife cowboys Carl Davis and Ira Hays were photographed at Winslow in 1928. Mack Hughes remembered a time in 1928 when another cowboy, Carl Bruchman, went missing. Hughes and Hays looked for him for two days before finding him dead under his horse. The animal had tripped, rolled 35 feet, and broke its neck. (Old Trails Museum.)

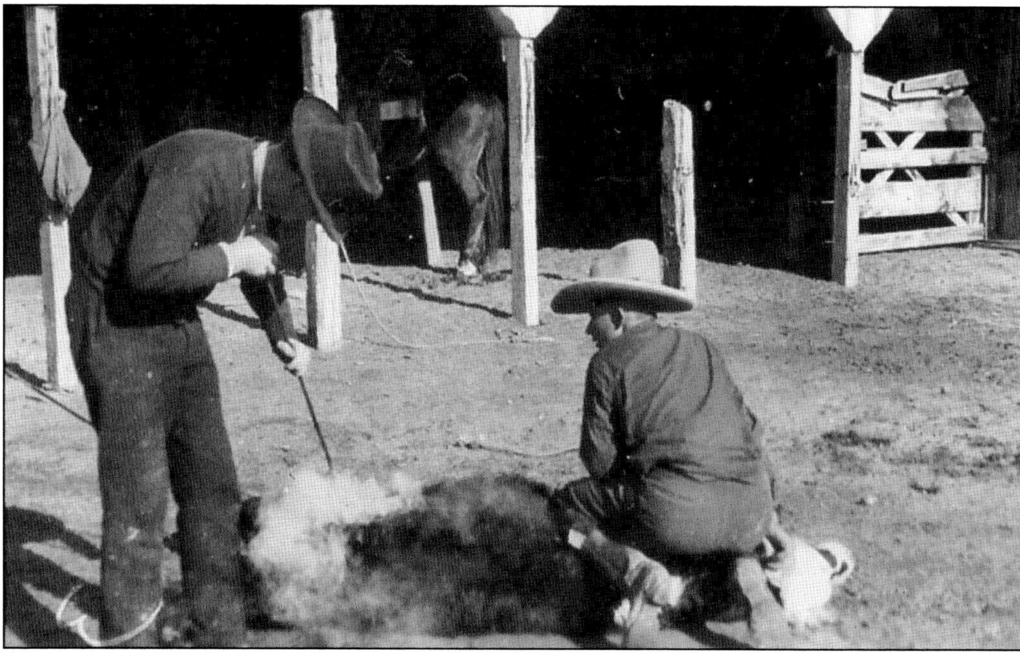

The Hennessey family photograph albums include several images of cowboys at work, including this picture of two men branding a calf. A benefit of the Hash Knife brand was that it was difficult to alter, but a good rustler—including men who worked for the outfit in the early days—could alter any brand.

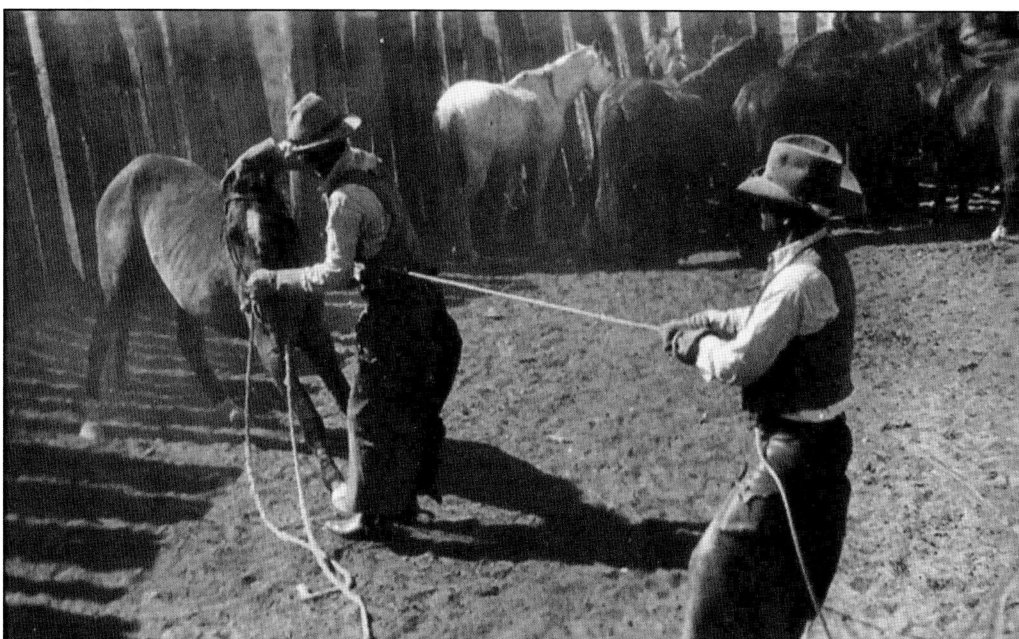

Cattle outfits always kept a large herd of horses on hand, since so many were used while herding and during round-ups. Part of the cowboy's job was to break and train wild horses or young colts. The horses were also branded. Under Babbit Brothers during the 1920s and 1930s, Hash Knife horses were marked with the Bar W brand on the left thigh.

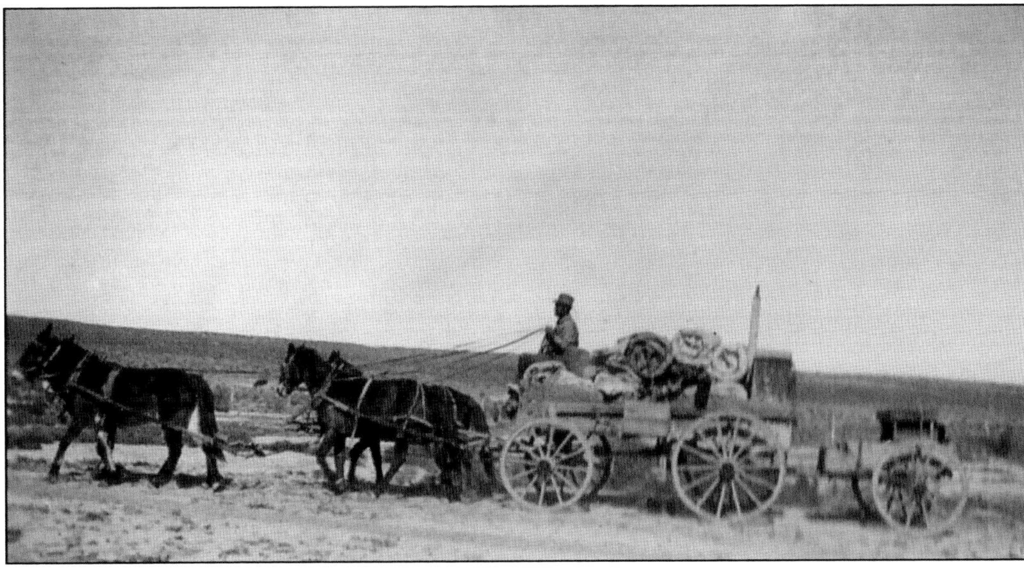

Chuck wagons were largely identifiable by the chuckbox located on the back of the wagon. They not only carried food and utensils, but also medicine, bedrolls, ammunition, extra firearms, and maybe even a bottle or two of sour mash. In camp, any available men were expected to help unload the wagon. The cook's utensils, of course, usually included the common kitchen tool for which the Hash Knife brand was named. Mack Hughes named Clair Haight, Bill Woods, and Charley Farnsworth as a few of the cooks working for the Hash Knife during the 1920s and 1930s.

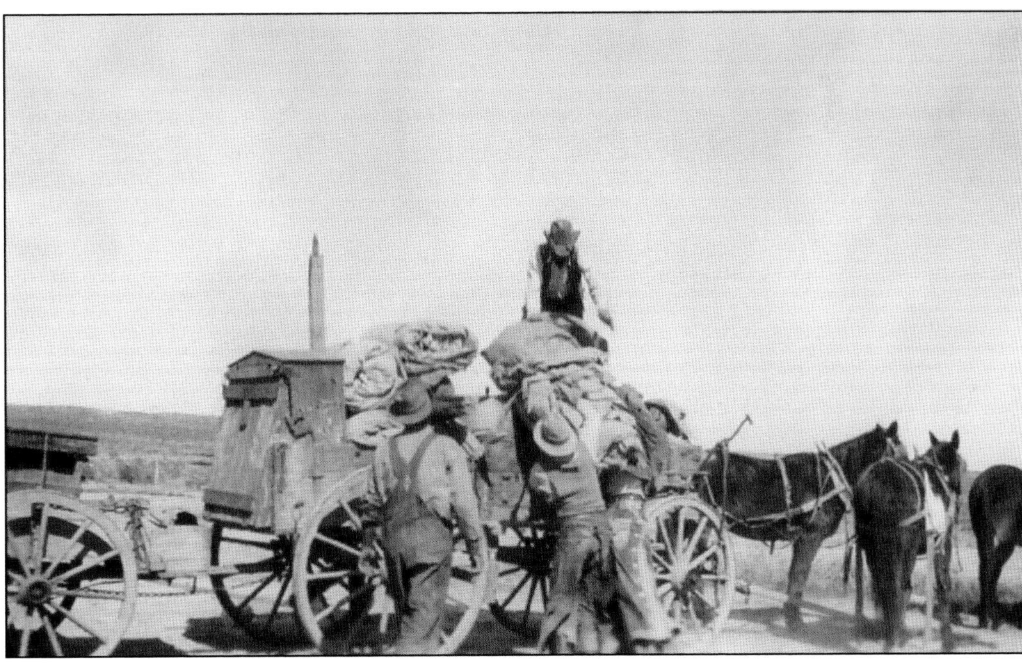

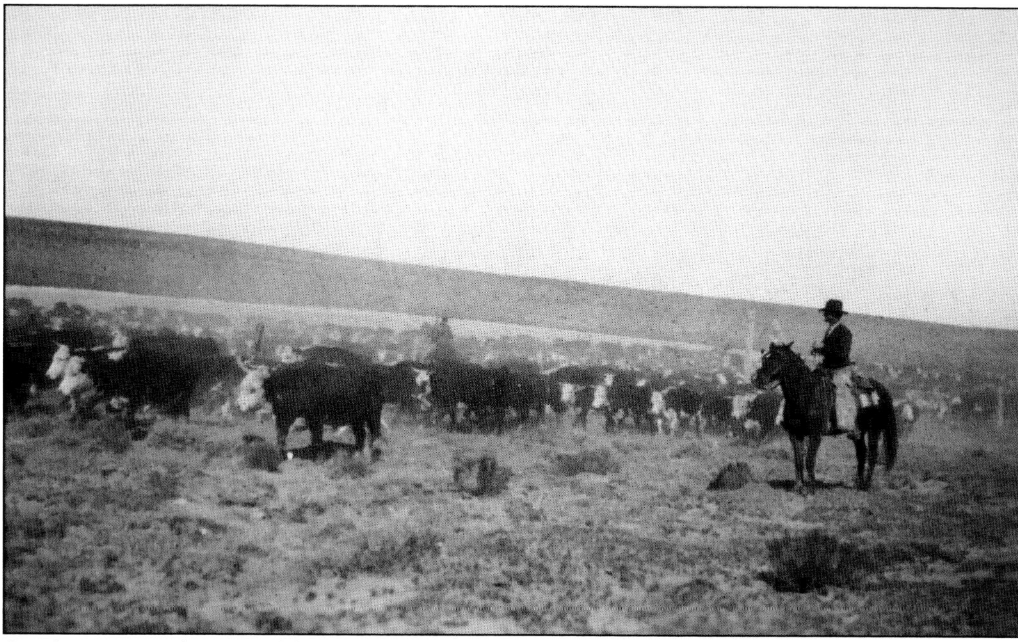

Cowboys enjoyed a special love for being outdoors and around cattle, even with the knowledge that it was hard, dangerous work. "You gotta *want* to be a cowboy, keep your eyes open and your mouth shut," Mack Hughes's father, Pat, once said of the business, "and, by Gawd, don't think you know it all the first year. Hell, I been cowboyin' all my life and I'm still learnin'."

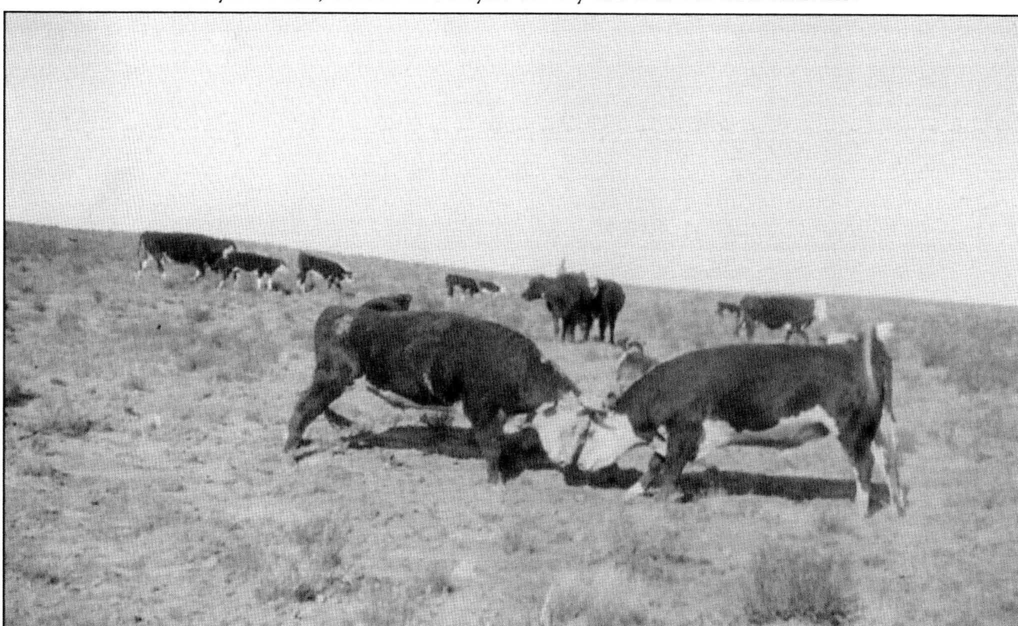

Two bulls butt heads out on the range. Bulls were apt to challenge each other, especially if one of them was new to the herd. Cowboys might pause and watch the fight, preferring a bit of entertainment in their otherwise routine workday and betting on the winner. Sometimes the tiff ended with the loser walking away, but the fight could also end in injury or death of an animal.

An unidentified cowboy ropes cattle, possibly at George Hennessey's ranch. Mack Hughes recalled Bill Shoats as a "good roper," and plenty more worked for the Hash Knife. They included Travis Windham who, back in the early days of the brand, was the winner of the first rodeo held in the United States.

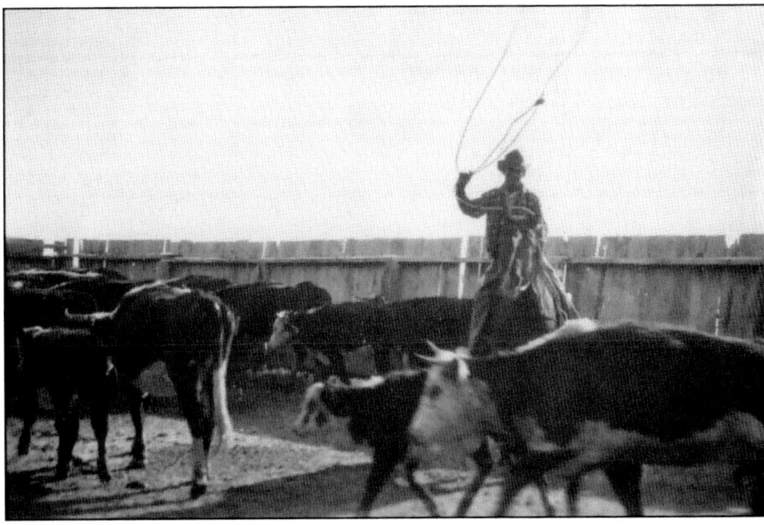

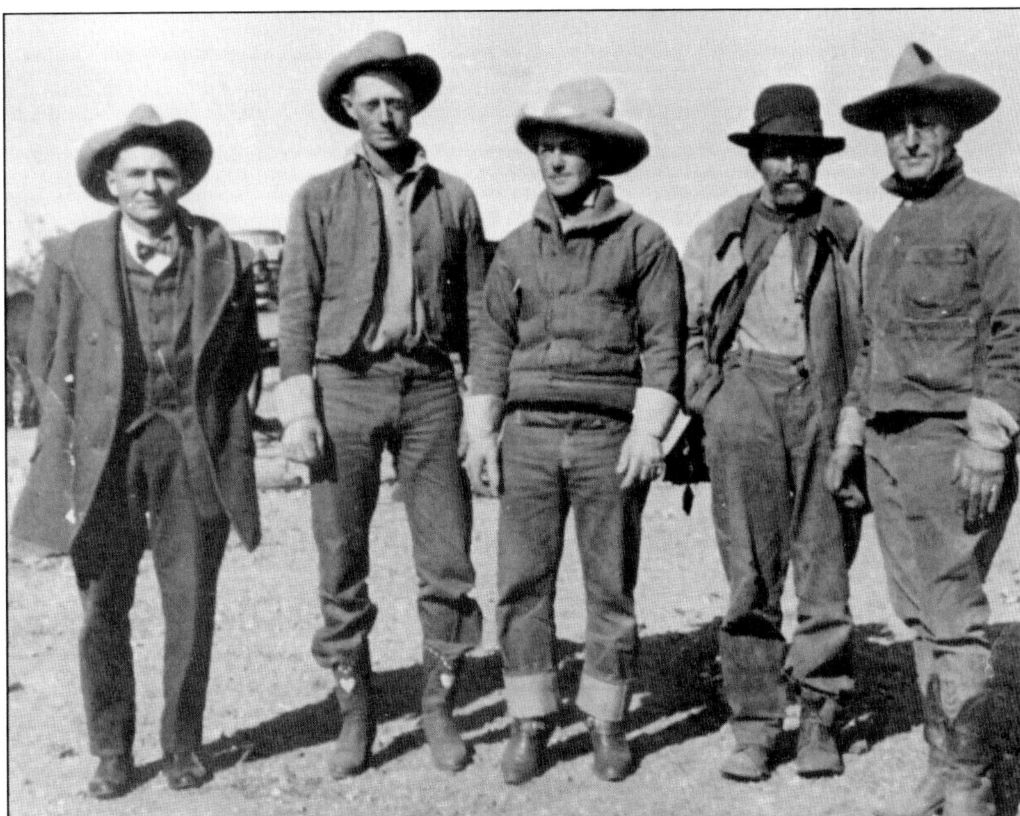

A group of mostly unidentified Hash Knife Cowboys are pictured in Holbrook in the 1930s. (Carl Davis is second from the left.) Hughes remembered several hands who had worked for the outfit in the old days, including Rufus Creswell. Hughes also recalled working with Creswell's brother, Homer. "He always rolled his bed looser than anybody," Hughes noted, "just wadded it up loose as a goose and stuff was always spilling out of it." (Navajo County Historical Society.)

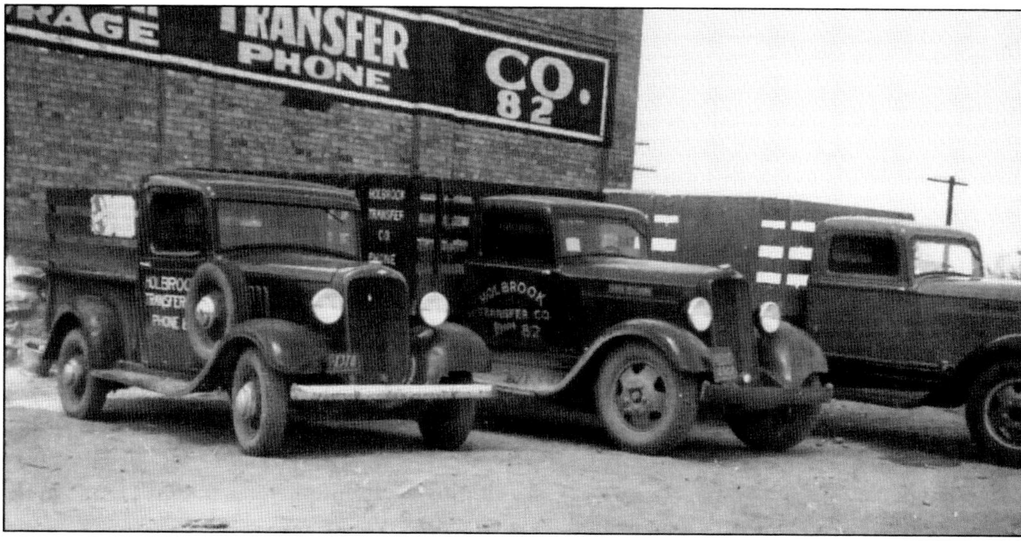

In 1932, according to George Hennessey, "My health failed me . . . I couldn't take care of my outfit so I had to sell it." Hennessey decided to try the transfer and storage business in Holbrook. The company had a nice fleet of trucks when this image was taken, but to Hennessey, "That was worse than cows, so I sold it in '34 and came [to Phoenix]."

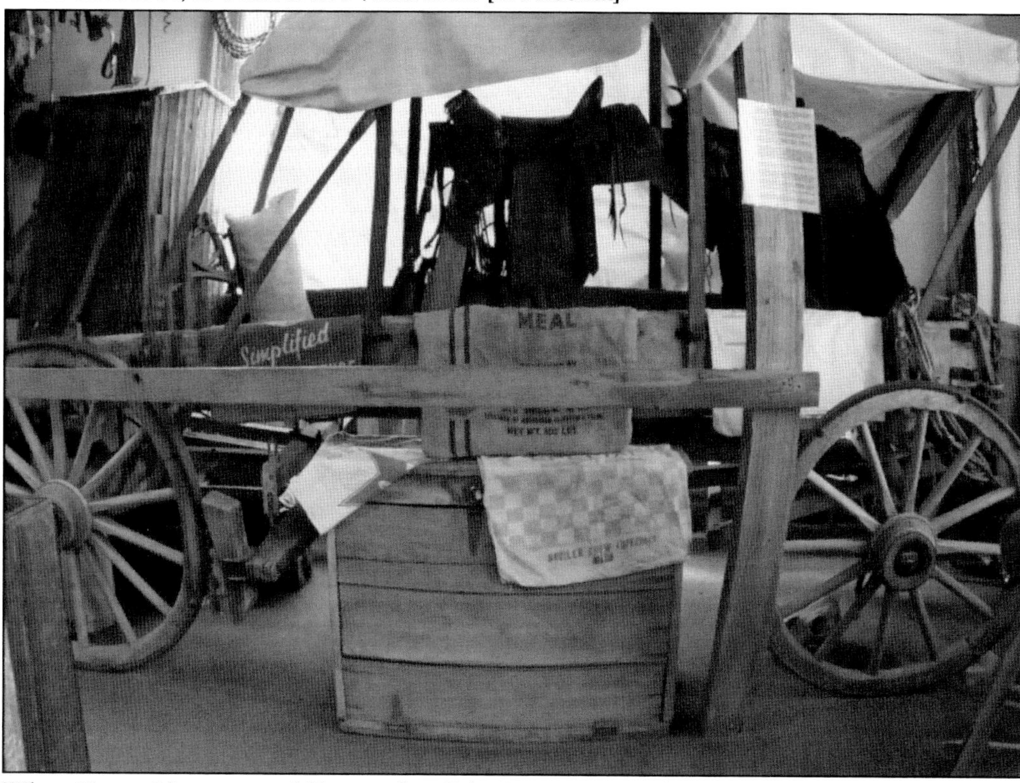

When George Hennessey sold his ranch to John Jones in 1930, the old chuck wagon from the Hash Knife went with it. C.F. Lee acquired the wagon sometime after 1944. Lee's son, Lon, later donated it to the Navajo County Historical Society. When part of Hennessey's old ranch was developed as the community of Sun Valley, the chuckbox was used at the land office to promote sales.

Frank Wallace's daughter Ann married Charles Lisitzky in 1930. Lisitzky had worked for A & B Schuster in Holbrook since 1917. In 1954, he became president of the company. After Ann died in 1959, Lisitzky married Marian Stouffer and remained close to the Wallace and Hennessey families. He died in 1990 and is buried in Holbrook.

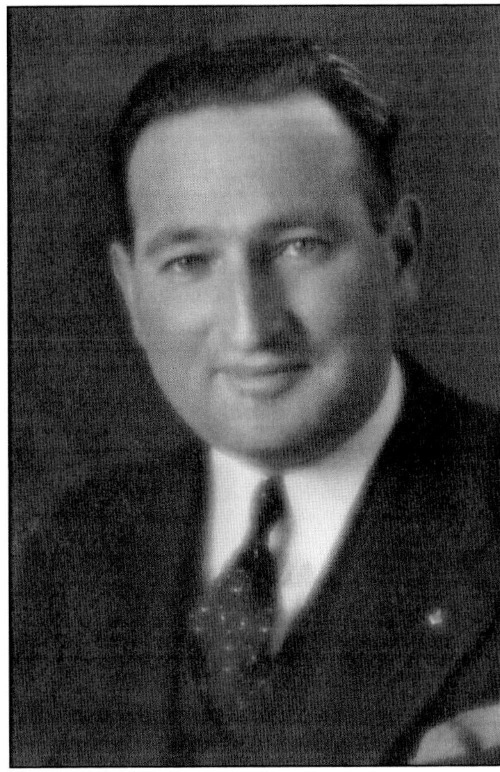

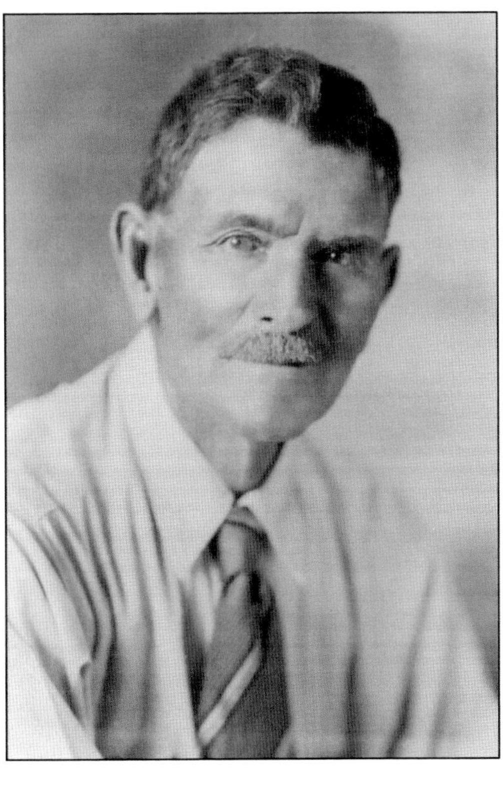

After selling the OW Ranch, Frank Wallace was "beginning to feel my age so felt it time to ease up some." His work was limited to overseeing cattle for his son Jack, as well as Burr Porter. "I stayed there for four years until I lost the sight of one eye and use of a hand," he said. "That caused me to give up cattle working."

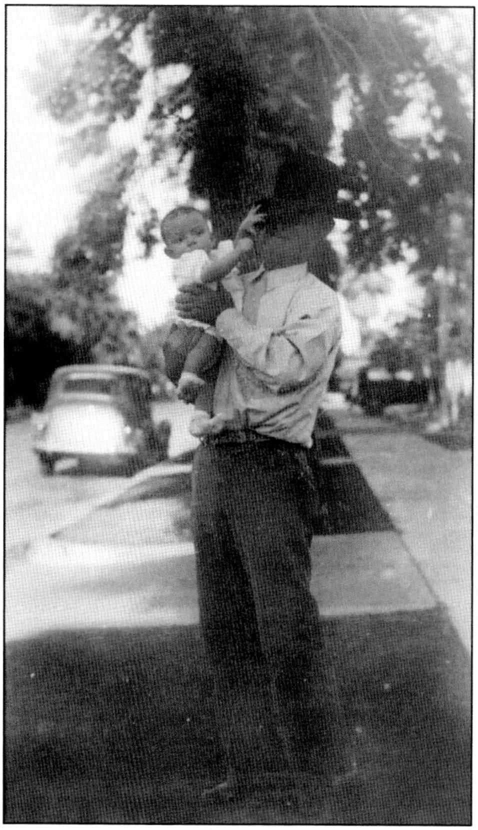

In 1926, George Hennessey sold his Holbrook home and other properties to A & B Schuster and moved to Washington Avenue. Upon selling his ranch in 1930, he and Frances moved to Phoenix, where daughter Evelyn married Clair Smith in 1934. Hennessey, pictured here with grandson George Wallace Smith, went to work as a cattle buyer.

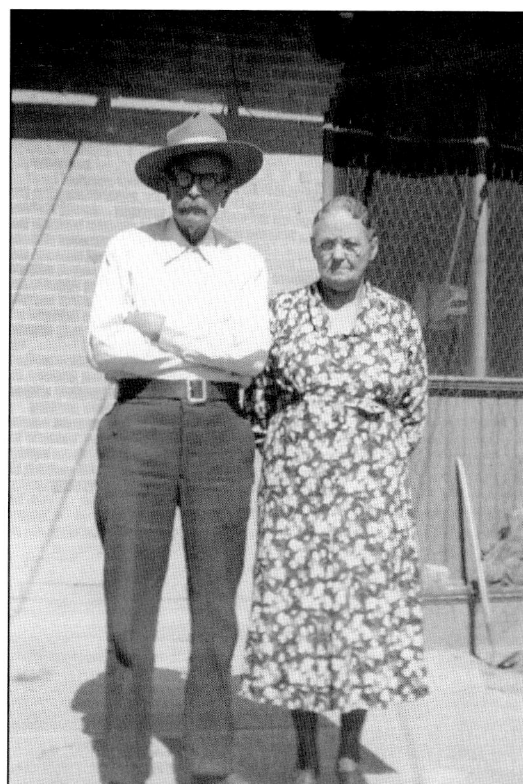

"I have not ridden in four years," Frank Wallace wrote in 1931. He and Cora were living with Ruth and Harold Moritz in Tucson, and celebrated their 50th wedding anniversary in 1938. Cora died the following year during a visit to Holbrook. Dick Grigsby, Fred Schuster, Johnny Paulsell, Boliver Lemmon, Bill Wyrick, Ed Bargman, and Dan Divelbess were among her pallbearers.

George Hennessey's mother, Matilda Jane Martin, divorced his father in 1902 after Tom Hennessey demolished her beloved organ with an axe. By 1910, she was living in New Mexico with her son John. Matilda sold the family land in Texas in 1922 and spent the rest of her life with daughter Rose. She died at Roswell, New Mexico, in 1940.

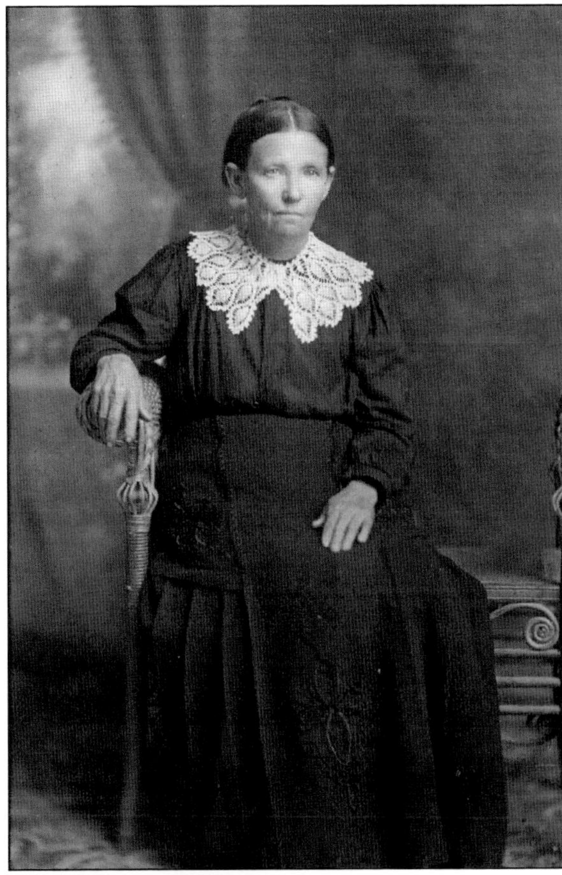

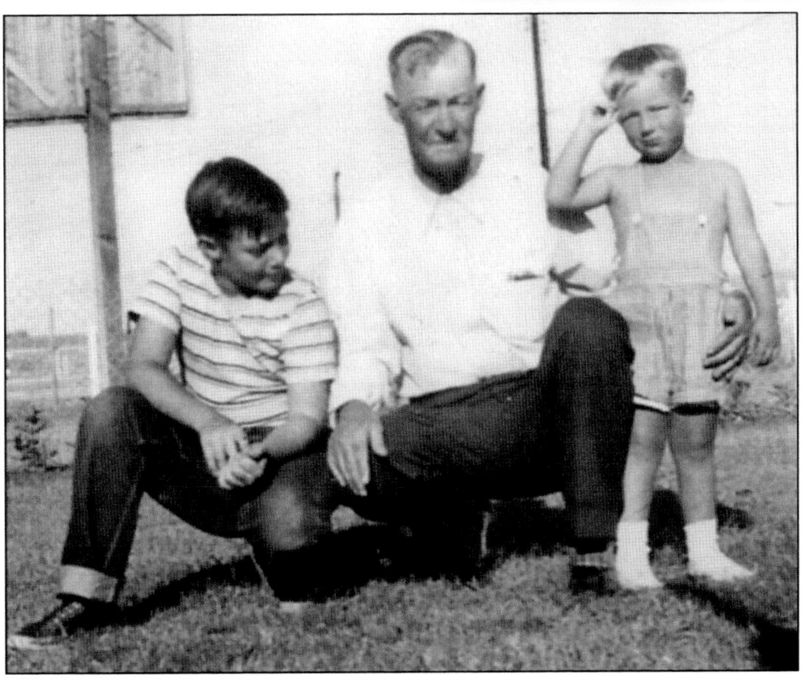

In 1945, Hennessey's second grandchild, George Arthur "Petie" Peterson, was born to his daughter Betty and her husband, Dale Peterson. This picture was taken in about 1949 with George Smith, Hennessey, and Petie. Tragically, Petie succumbed to the anesthetic during a tonsillectomy at Ganado. He is buried in Phoenix.

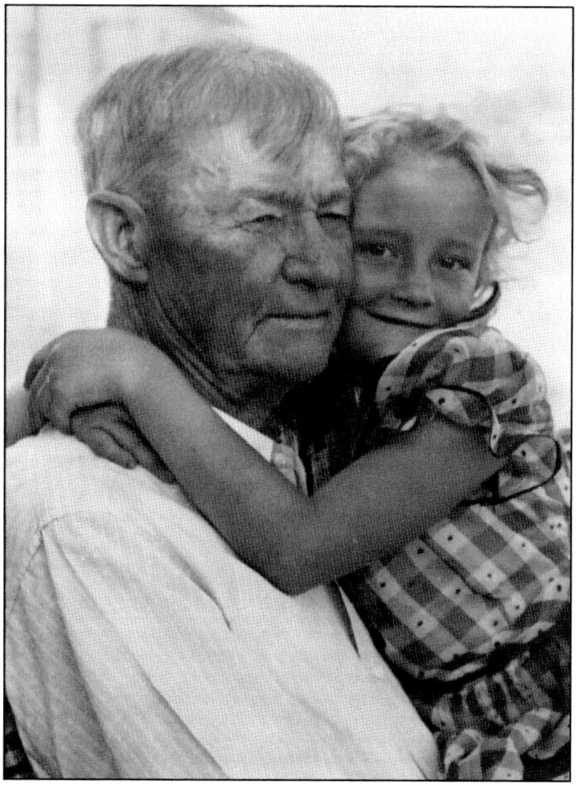

George Hennessey's granddaughter Suzanne Peterson remembered attending a dance at the Grand Canyon with her grandparents when she was about six. "A boy about my age came over and asked me to dance. I was way too shy and said no. After he left, my grandfather scolded me. He said 'Do you know how hard it was for that little boy to get the courage to ask you to dance?' "

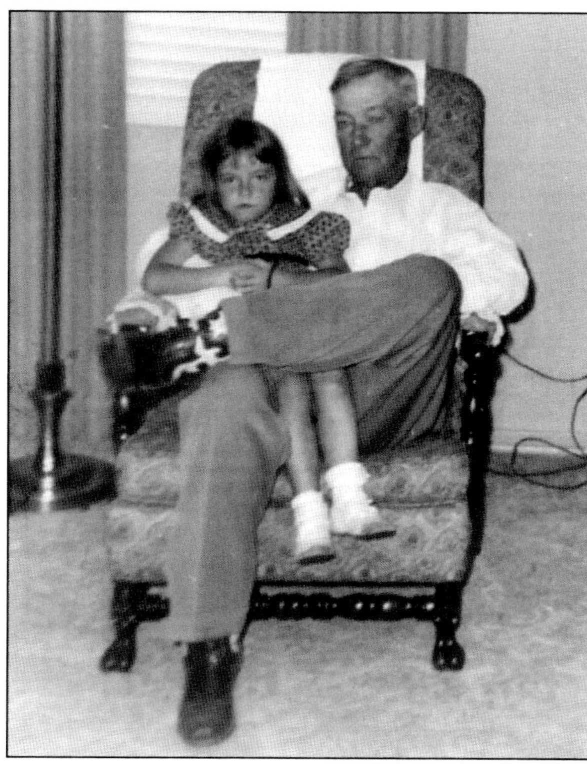

Hennessey, pictured here with his granddaughter Patricia Jane Peterson, doted on the children. Grandson George Smith occasionally accompanied Hennessey on his business trips for the First National Bank. Smith remembered a trip just the two of them took in about 1947, visiting ranches in Williams and Kingman, where they stayed at the Beale Hotel. "It was fun," Smith said. "We were riding horses and working cattle."

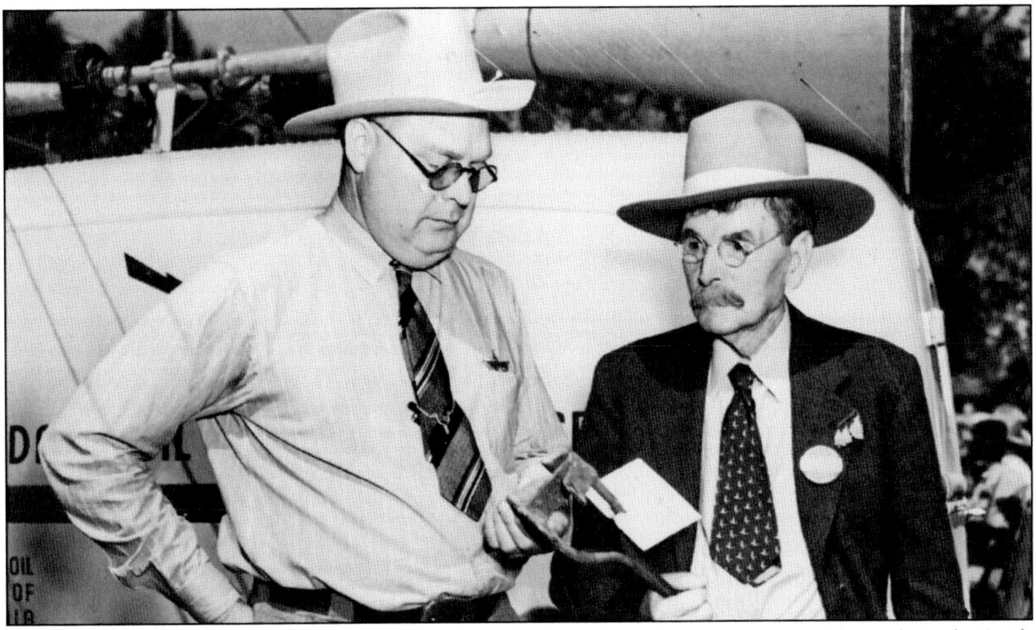

The occasion remains unknown when Frank Wallace (right) presented an original Hash Knife brand to an unidentified man. George Smith remembered visiting Wallace at the Holbrook Hotel as a young boy. In the spring of 1946, Wallace moved to Phoenix, passing away in July. His obituary commented, "It has been said many a time Frank Wallace probably 'turned' more cattle than any living man."

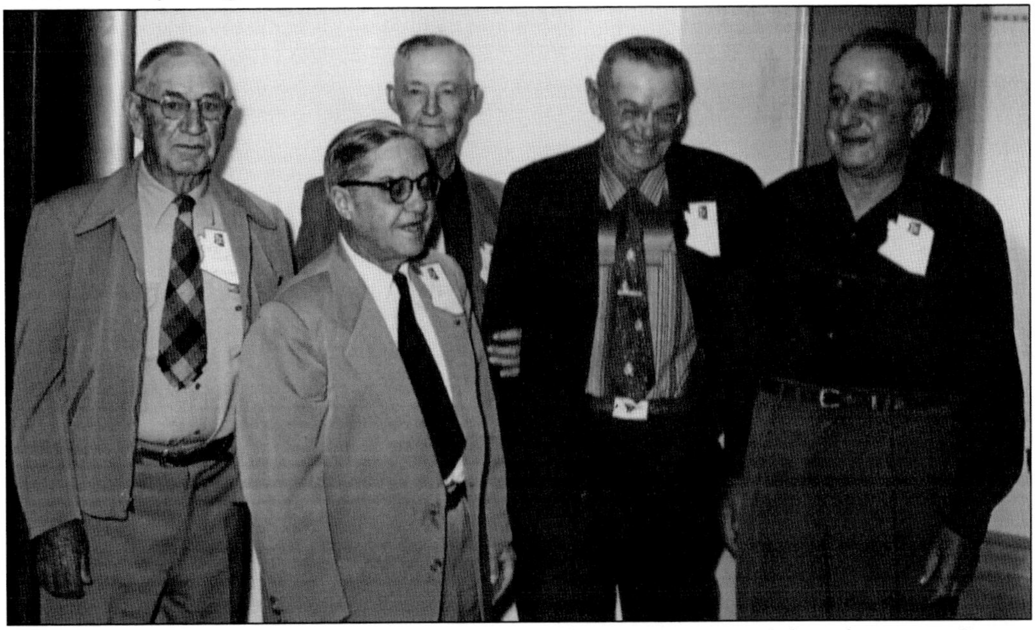

First National Bank in Phoenix held a number of banquets, many of them honoring George Hennessey's work in the cattle industry. Hennessey's scrapbooks are chock full of photographs, news articles, and other mementos from these events. Honored guests at this breakfast gathering in 1955 included, from left to right, Bob Crowder Sr., Shorty Davis, Hennessey, Dan Fain, and Wayne Thornburg.

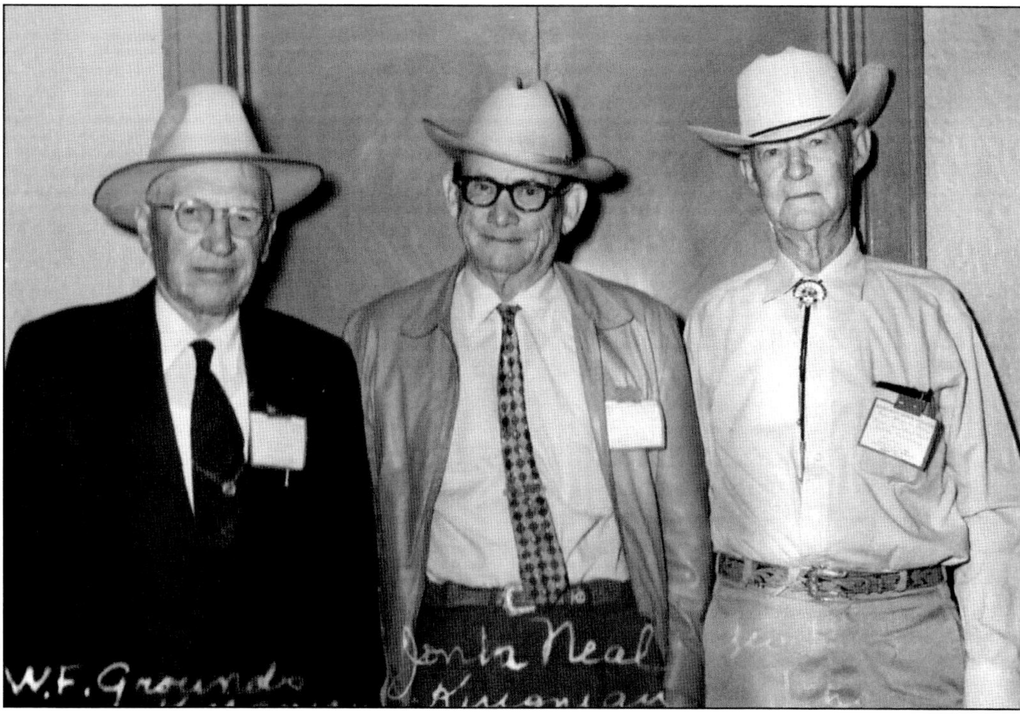

In 1956, the Arizona Ranch School at Flagstaff honored these three old-timers in the cattle business, applauded as representing "over two centuries of experience." The men, from left to right, are W.F. Grounds of Kingman's W.F. Cattle Company, John Neal [*sic*] of Kingman, and George Hennessey.

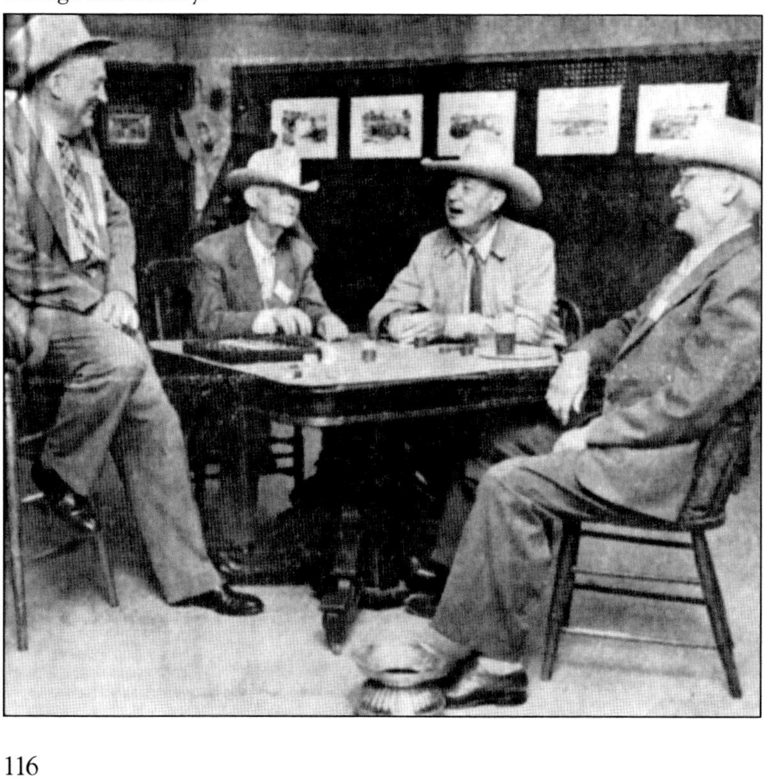

Charles Pickrell (left) was director of the agricultural extension at the University of Arizona. In 1956 he arranged for a cowboy from each Arizona county to attend the Arizona Cattle Grower's Association convention at the Arizona Pioneer Historical Society in Flagstaff. Seen here chatting over a game of old-time poker at the event are George Hennessey, Harry Knight, and Marion Lee.

In 1957, Hennessey was presented with an honorary Navajo County sheriff's badge. Hennessey (left) is seen here receiving the badge from Maricopa County sheriff Cal Boice. At the time, Hennessey was heralded as the last of the Hash Knife cowboys from the days before the brand was sold to Babbitt Brothers. The badge was notable since its design included the Hash Knife brand.

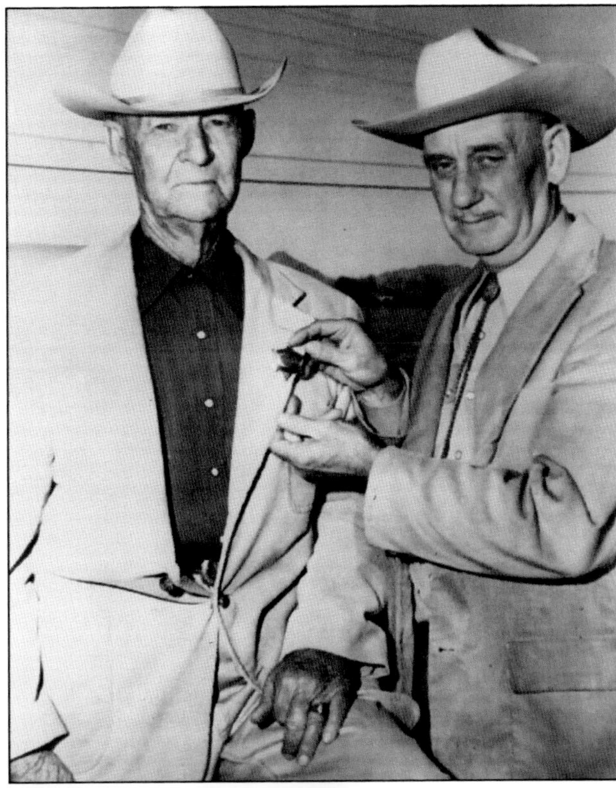

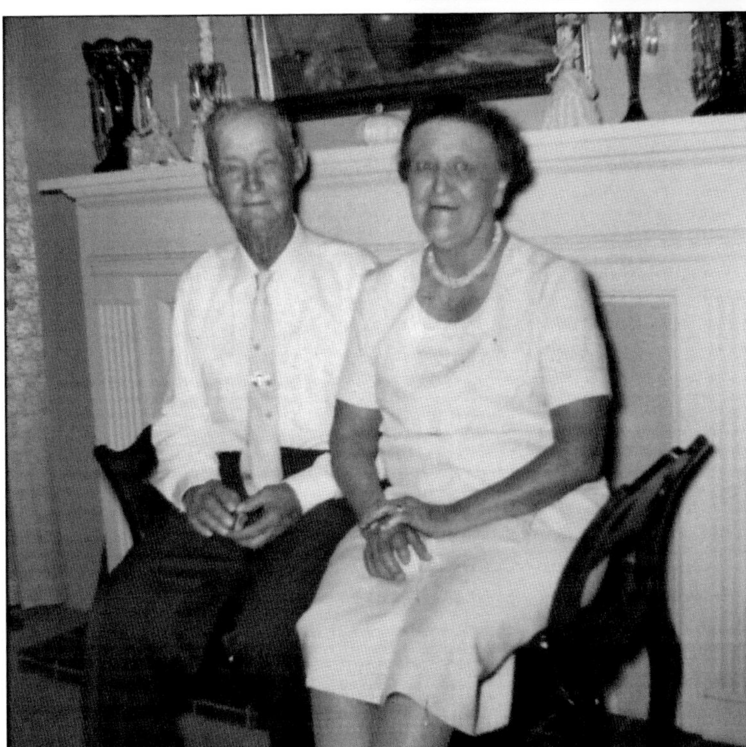

In 1961, George and Frances Hennessey celebrated their 50th wedding anniversary. Fellow cowboy "Mac" Schaefer wrote, "They have been fifty golden years for all of us who have known you and your great kindness and warmth."

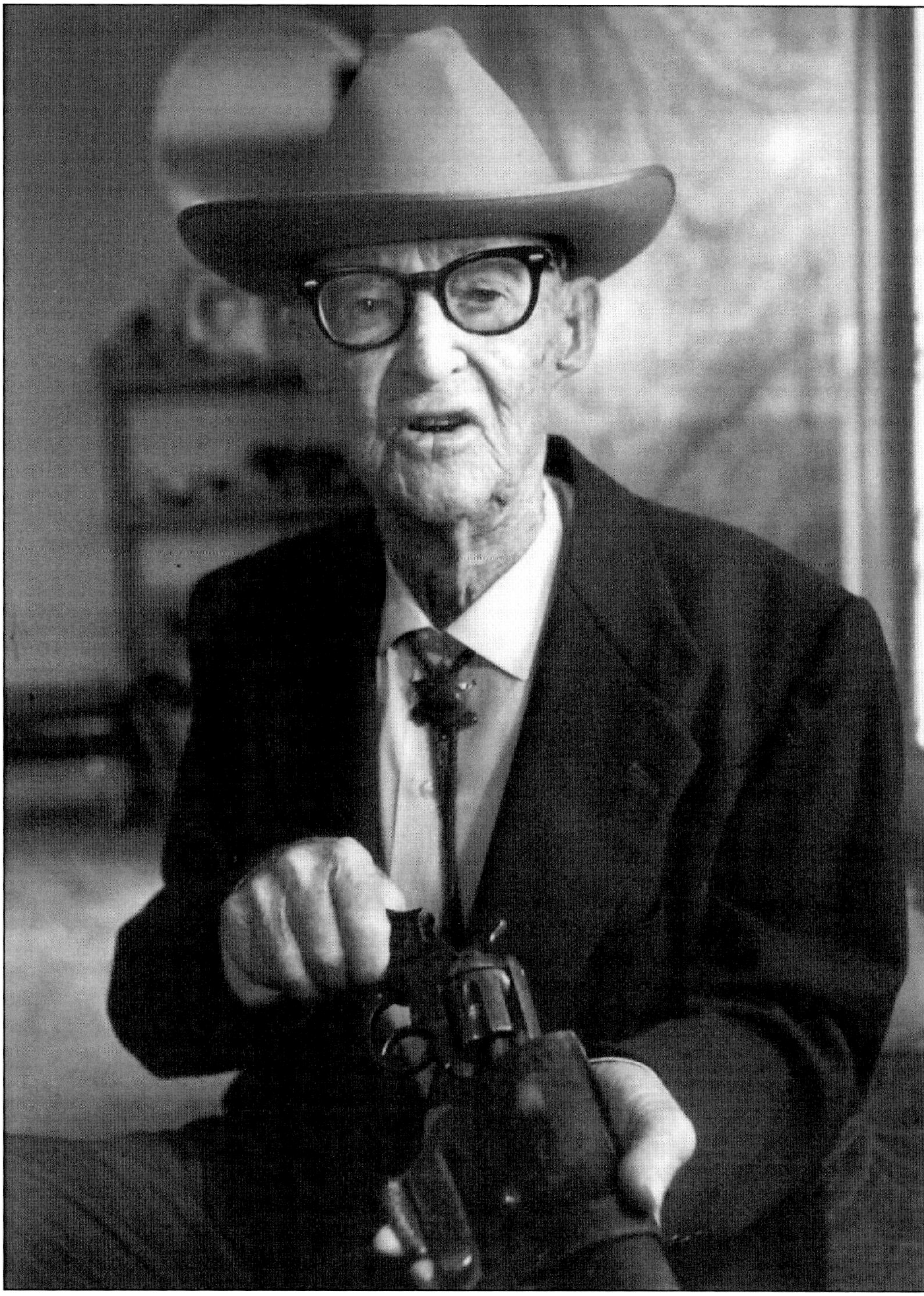

In 1963, Frank Wallace was inducted to the National Cowboy Hall of Fame in Oklahoma City, Oklahoma. Hennessey readily supplied a letter of support and remained much in the public eye. In 1970, the *Arizona Republic* featured a story and this image of Hennessey, who did not think much of retirement. "I think I'd enjoy myself a hell of a lot better if I was out on the range," he said.

Eight

The Brand Lives On

The Hash Knife brand has outright failed to fade into history. It is genuinely touching that so many historians, descendants, and others are still so proud of the outfit and everything it stood for. From Texas to Arizona and several places in between and even beyond, the Hash Knife name lives on.

In Texas, the Hashknife Bed and Breakfast in Abilene operates at the site of the first ranch headquarters. There is a Hashknife Cemetery in Baylor County, the Hashknife Farm and Ranch in Seymour, and a Hashknife Ranch at Rocksprings. There is also Hashknife on the Chisholm, a barbecue restaurant at Mineral Wells. Over the years, Hash Knife ranches in Wyoming, Montana, Kansas, New Mexico, and Oregon were all started by people who knew of or worked for the original Texas brand.

In Arizona, The Hashknife Outfit is a bluegrass band in Tempe. Roads named for the brand appear on maps in Phoenix, Heber, and Payson. There is also a Hashknife Ranch near Black Canyon City, and the Rock Art Ranch near Winslow preserves the only remaining cow camp from the Aztec Land and Cattle Company. Babbitt Ranches still promote their famed "Hashknife Horses" with an annual colt sale. Most notable is the Hashknife Pony Express, which honors the brand with an annual ride from Holbrook to Scottsdale.

Each tribute to the brand brings a sense of time and place to the cowboys from days gone by. They were not really so long ago. The respect for the brand and the men who worked for it still rings true today, bringing to memory the words of Amy Wallace: "I learned one thing, when a cowboy came riding through to ask him in and cook a meal for him. That was the way of the West."

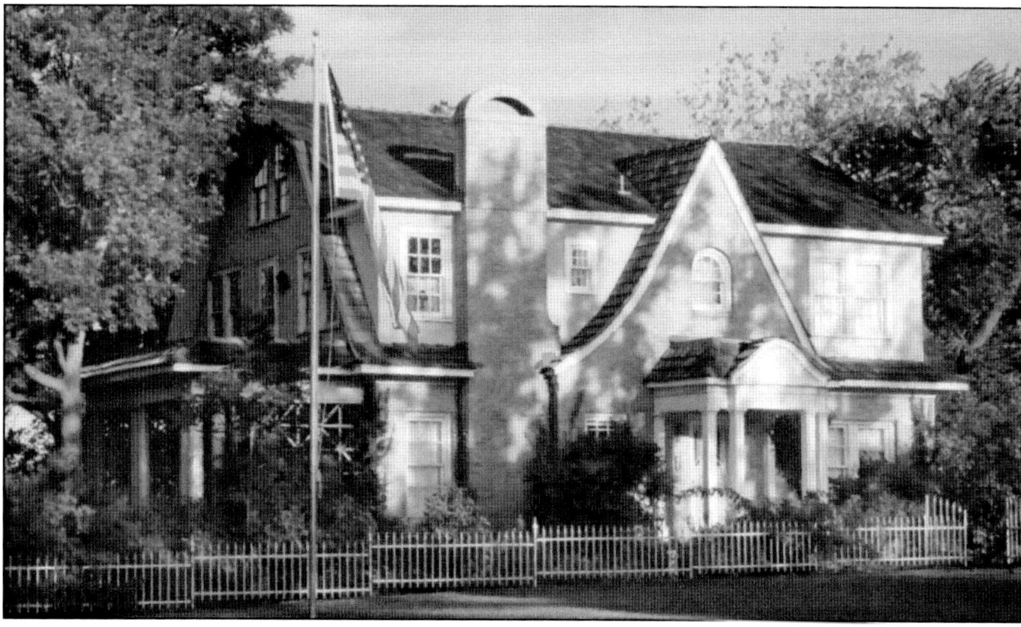

The Hashknife B&B is a luxurious hotel located at the historic site of the original Hash Knife ranch in Abilene, Texas. Built in 1929, the main house now offers queen-sized beds, a full breakfast, cable television, and Internet access. It's a far cry from the days when cowboys slept in a dugout by the river.

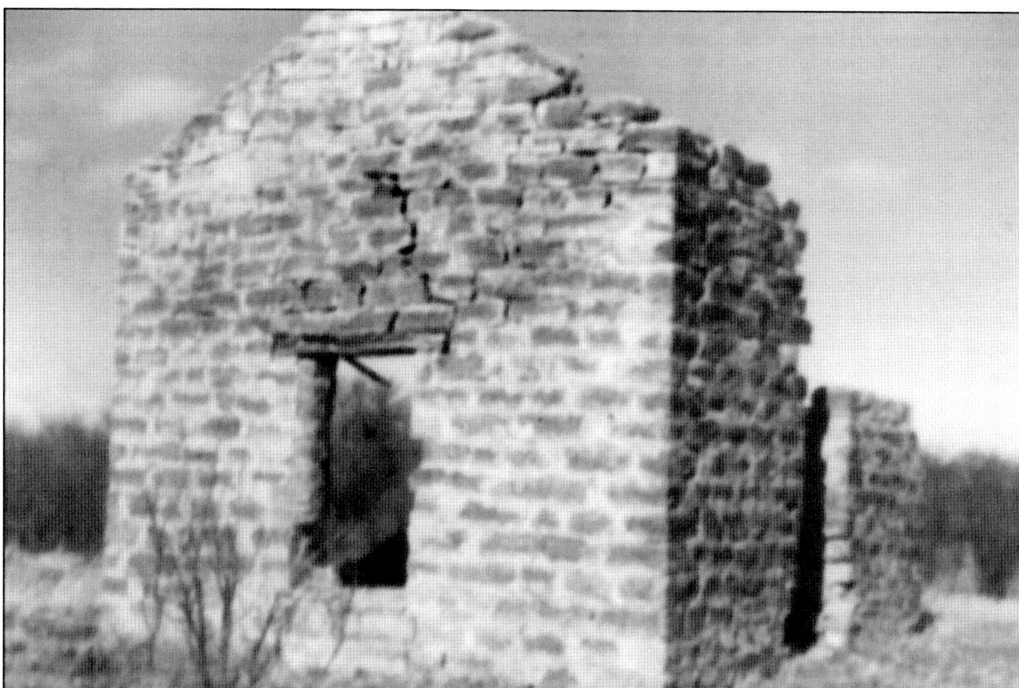

These ruins of the Millett house near Seymour, Texas, were still visible for many years. The Hashknife Farm and Ranch is nearby as well as the Hashknife Cemetery. The lone occupant, Ernest Hunt, inherited the Hashknife and ran it until his death in 1993. (Baylor County Free Library.)

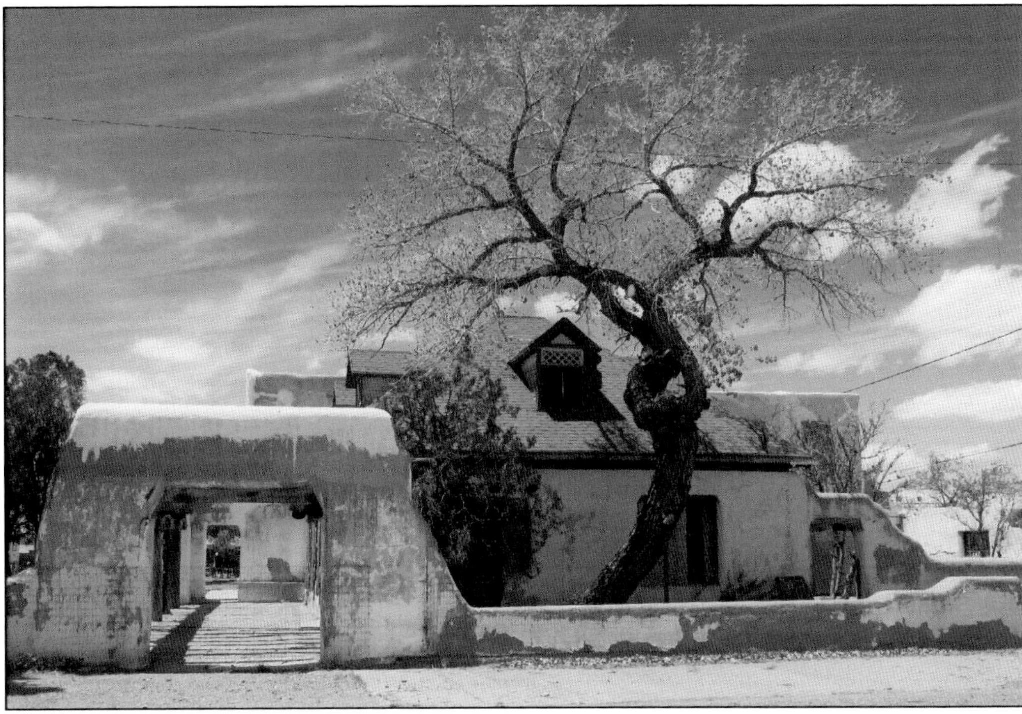

The Arizona Rancho in Holbrook, a remnant of the old Brunswick Hotel, still stands but has definitely seen better days. The property was listed in the National Register of Historic Places in 1997. In 2007, plans were being made to restore the old hotel as an essential step toward its survival as a historic landmark.

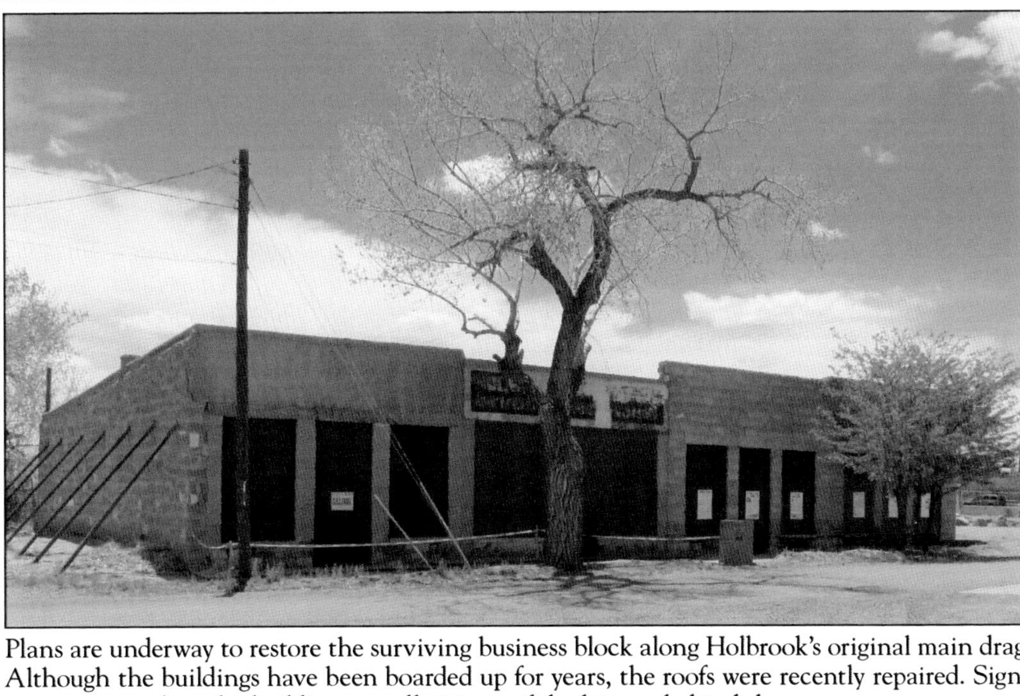

Plans are underway to restore the surviving business block along Holbrook's original main drag. Although the buildings have been boarded up for years, the roofs were recently repaired. Signs are now posted on the buildings to tell visitors of the history behind them.

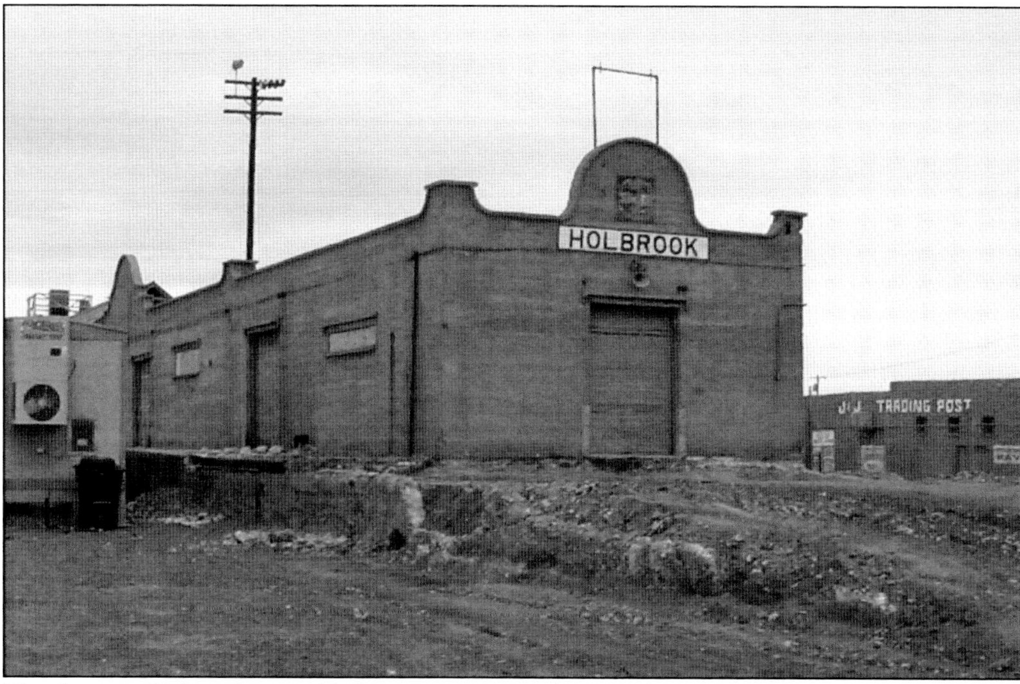

The depot at Holbrook was added on to in 1907 and 1912. The train still runs through town but no longer stops, and the building is now used for maintenance storage. Recent renovation efforts have included paving the area around the historic building.

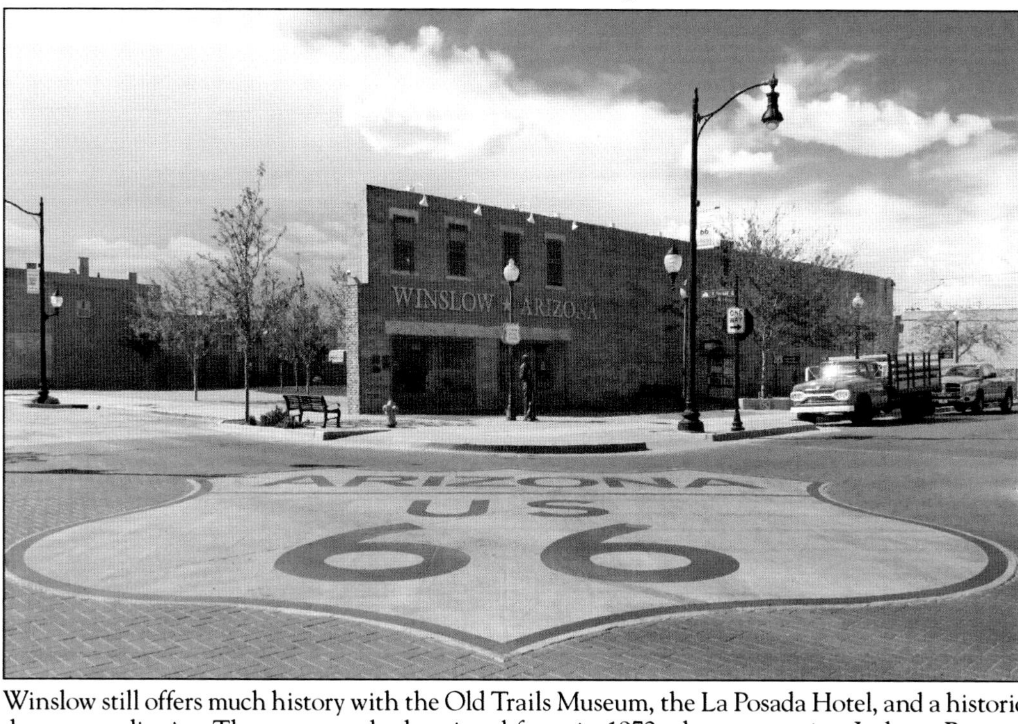

Winslow still offers much history with the Old Trails Museum, the La Posada Hotel, and a historic downtown district. The town reached national fame in 1972 when songwriter Jackson Browne penned "Take It Easy," which includes a line about "standin' on a corner in Winslow, Arizona."

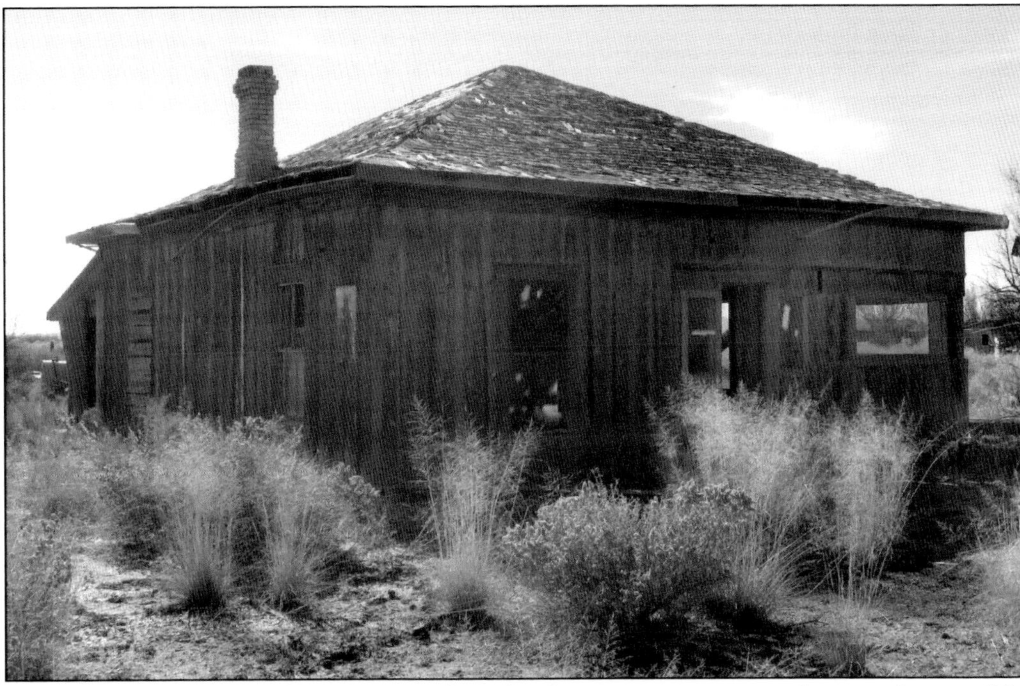

Not much remains at Adamana, save for a few historic structures and private homes. The Adamana Hotel burned in 1965, and the post office closed in 1969. Today, a natural gas plant all but obscures the town from view.

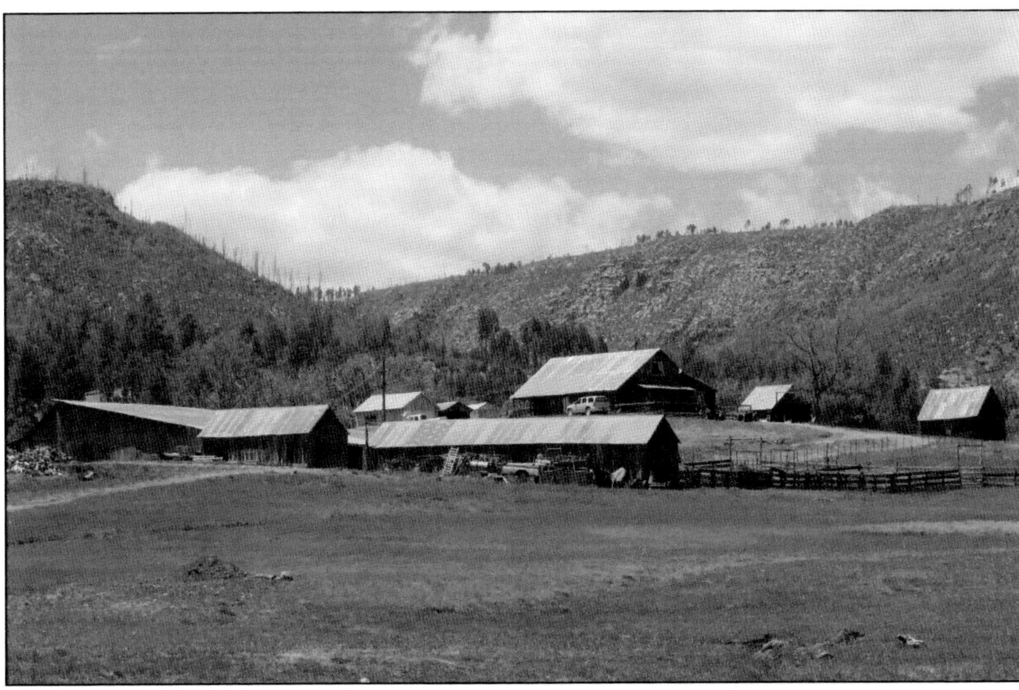

The OW Ranch remains virtually untouched by civilization. Resident caretakers still run about 400 head of cattle during the summer months. Of the Wallace family home, the only surviving structures are the root cellar and the fancy outhouse, which has been moved and restored.

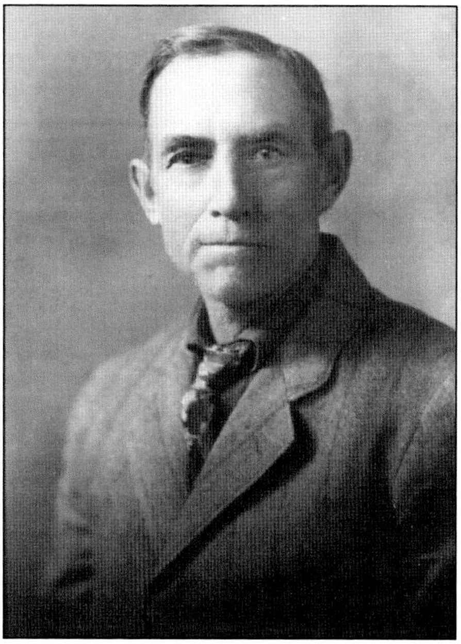

William Vandervert went to work for the Hash Knife in Texas and followed the herd to Arizona. He worked for the brand and built a corral at the Holbrook headquarters before moving to Oregon around 1889 and starting his own ranch. Vandervert used the Hash Knife brand in fond memory of his old outfit. (Grace McNellis.)

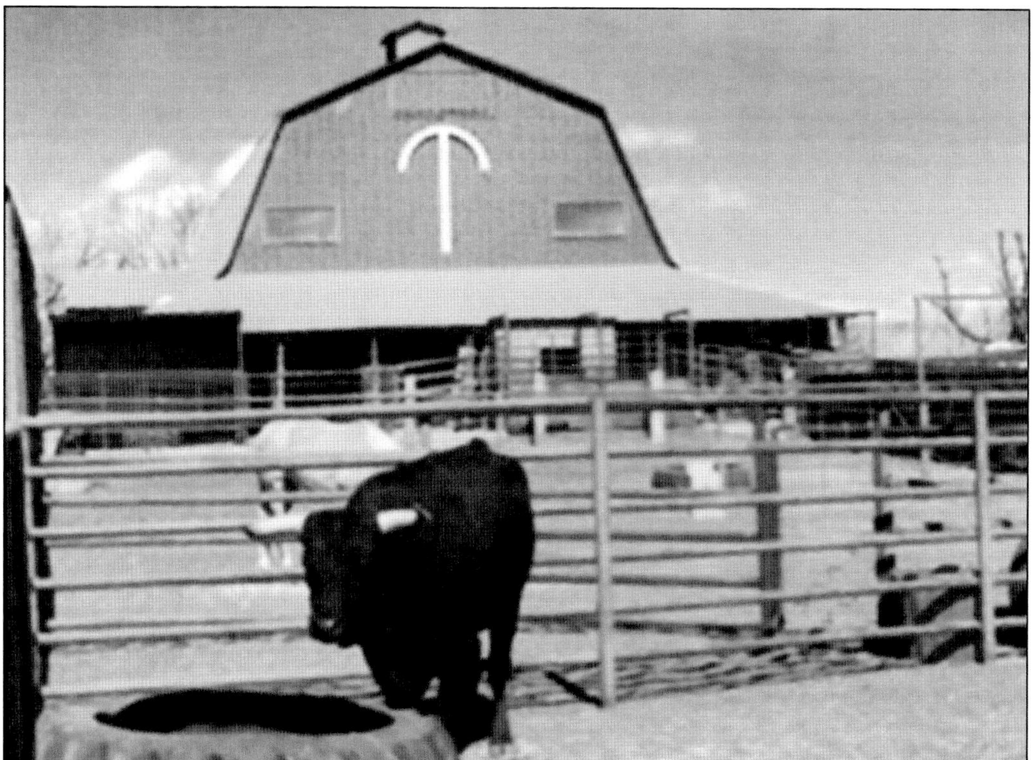

Frank Jones purchased cattle out of Arizona that bore the Hash Knife brand, taking them to his family ranch near Watrous, New Mexico. "Apparently, the Hash Knife brand was not recorded in the state of New Mexico," said Jones's grandson G.M. "Dogie" Jones, "therefore my grandfather took advantage and recorded the brand in his name." The barn, built in 1913 and bearing the brand, is visible from Interstate 25.

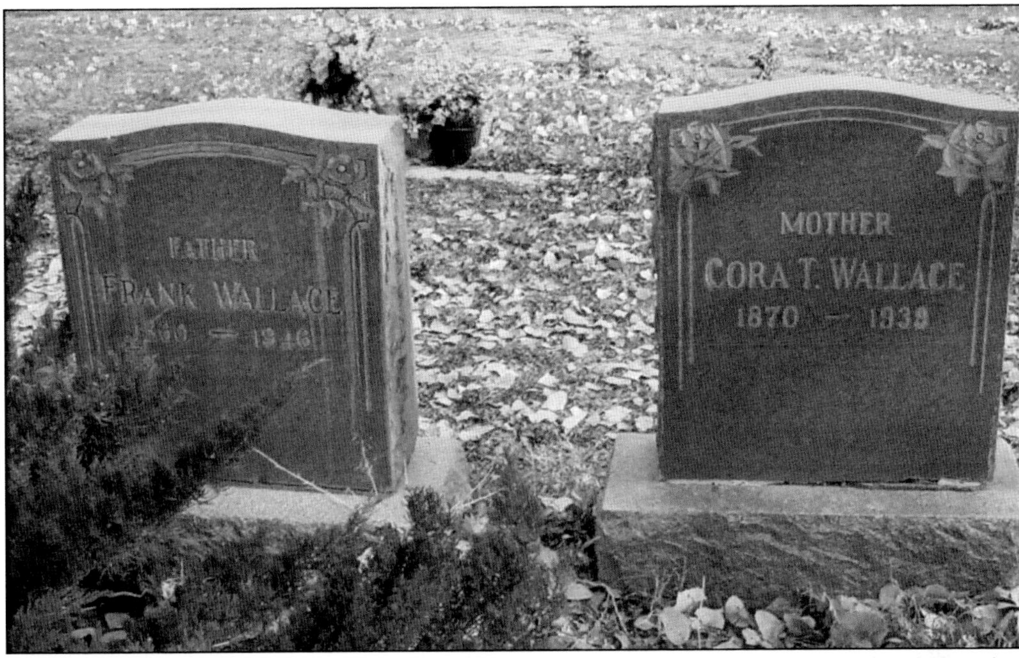

Frank and Cora Wallace are at rest in the Holbrook Cemetery along with several family members and friends. Other family, including George Hennessey, are buried in Phoenix. Wallace and Hennessey descendants today are most proud of their family history, collecting and sharing stories, photographs, and other memorabilia with each other.

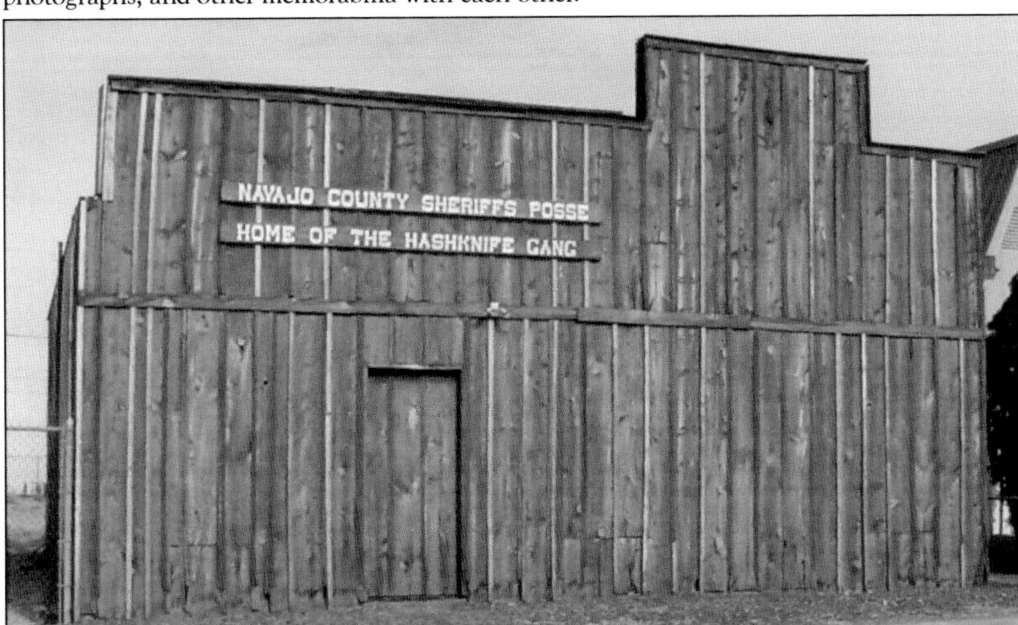

In 1958, members of the Navajo County sheriff's posse started an annual Hashknife Pony Express ride to carry specially postmarked letters from Holbrook to Phoenix, passing through parts of the old Aztec Land and Cattle Company spread. For several years, this building in Holbrook has served as the organization's clubhouse.

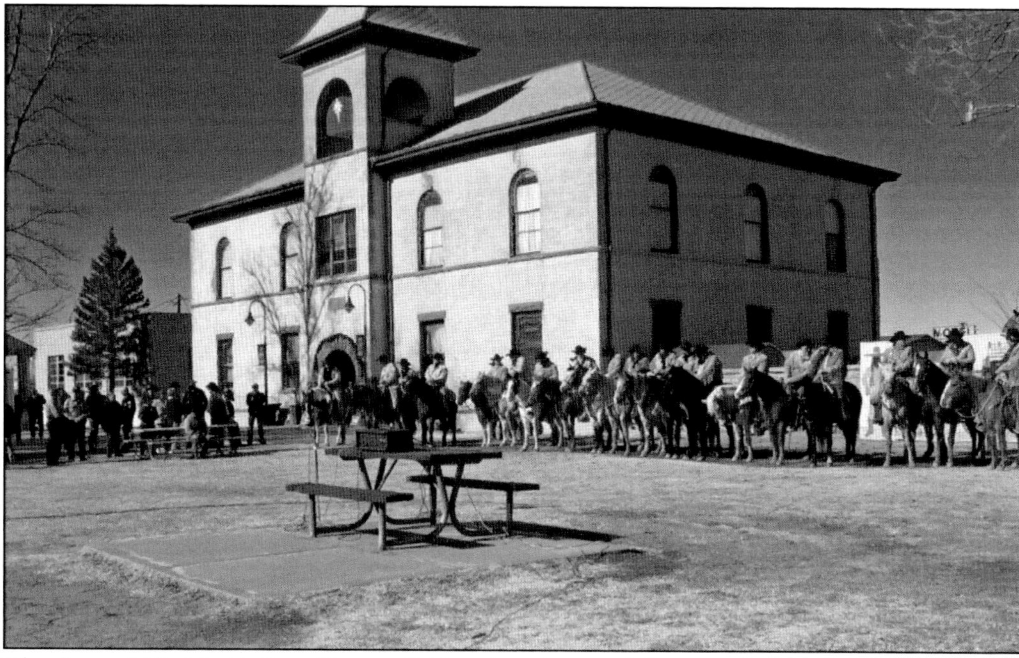

The Annual Hashknife Pony Express Ride takes place each January. Riders from a past year are shown here at the ride's starting point, the Navajo County Courthouse in Holbrook. Over time, the ride has been shortened to end in Scottsdale, with a stopover in Payson. The ride is the only Pony Express ride sanctioned by the US Postal Service. (Hashknife Pony Express.)

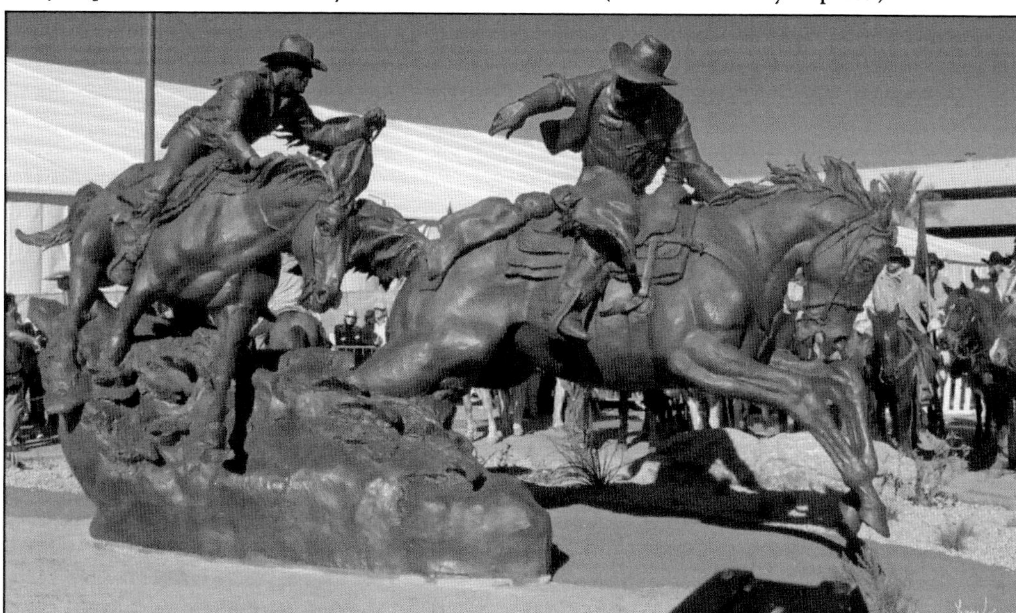

In 2008, a commemorative statue to the Hashknife Pony Express Ride, *Passing the Legacy*, was unveiled in downtown Scottsdale. Artist Herb Mignery was commissioned to cast the bronze sculpture. Around 500 people attended the ceremony as over two dozen Pony Express riders made their way to the statue. *Passing the Legacy* not only commemorates the historic Hash Knife brand but encourages others to do the same. (Hashknife Pony Express.)

Bibliography

Barnes, Will C. *Arizona Place Names*. Tucson, Arizona: University of Arizona Press, 1988.

Carlock, Robert H. *The Hashknife: The Early Days of the Aztec Land and Cattle Company, Limited*. Tucson, AZ: Westernlore Press, 1994.

Dedera, Don. *A Little War of Our Own: The Pleasant Valley Feud Revisited*. Flagstaff, AZ: Northland Press, 1988.

Ellis, Catherine H. *Holbrook and the Petrified Forest*. Charleston, SC: Arcadia Publishing, 2007.

Hanchett, Leland J. Jr., *The Crooked Trail to Holbrook*. Phoenix, AZ: Arrowhead Press, Inc., 1993.

Hughes, Stella. *Hashknife Cowboy: Recollections of Mack Hughes*. Tucson, AZ: University Press of Arizona, 1984.

Hunt, Frazier. *Cap Mossman, Last of the Great Cowmen*. New York, NY: Hastings House, 1951.

Lutzick, Ann-Mary, Winslow Historical Society and Old Trails Museum Archives. *Winslow*. Charleston, SC: Arcadia Publishing, 2013.

Malone, Michael P., Roeder, Richard B. and Long, William L. *Montana: a history of two centuries*. Seattle, WA: University of Washington Press, 1991.

Tinsley, Jim Bob. *The Hash Knife Brand*. Gainesville, FL: University Press of Florida, 1993.

Consistent with our mission to preserve history on a local level, this book was printed in South Carolina on American-made paper and manufactured entirely in the United States. Products carrying the accredited Forest Stewardship Council (FSC) label are printed on 100 percent FSC-certified paper.

MADE IN THE USA